Gleim® AVIATION

Fundamentals of Instructing

FAA KNOWLEDGE TEST PREP

2024 EDITION

by

Irvin N. Gleim, Ph.D., CFII, and Garrett W. Gleim, CFII

Gleim Publications, Inc.

PO Box 12848
Gainesville, Florida 32604

(352) 375-0772
(800) 874-5346

www.GleimAviation.com
aviationteam@gleim.com

> For updates to the first printing of the 2024 edition of
> ***Fundamentals of Instructing***
> ***FAA Knowledge Test Prep***
>
> **Go To:** www.GleimAviation.com/updates
>
> **Or:** Email update@gleim.com with **FOI 2024-1** in the subject line. You will receive our current update as a reply.
>
> Updates are available until the next edition is published.

ISSN 1553-6890

ISBN 978-1-61854-617-3

Let Us Know!

This 2024 edition is designed specifically for pilots who aspire to obtain the flight instructor certificate and/or ground instructor certificate. Feedback and suggestions for improvement will be received immediately through www.GleimAviation.com/questions.

A companion volume, ***Flight/Ground Instructor FAA Knowledge Test Prep***, is available, as is ***Flight Instructor Flight Maneuvers and Practical Test Prep***, which focuses on the FAA practical test, just as this book focuses on the FAA knowledge test. Save time, money, and frustration--order online at www.GleimAviation.com today! Please bring these books to the attention of flight instructors, fixed-base operators, and others with a potential interest in acquiring their flight instructor certificates. Wide distribution of these books and increased interest in flying depend on your assistance and good word. Thank you.

> Returns of books purchased from bookstores and other resellers should be made to the respective bookstore or reseller. For more information regarding the Gleim Return Policy, please contact our offices at (800) 874-5346 or visit www.GleimAviation.com/returnpolicy.

ABOUT THE AUTHORS

Irvin N. Gleim, who began publishing pilot training books over 40 years ago and received both the Excellence in Pilot Training Award and the Wright Brothers Master Pilot Award, earned his private pilot certificate in 1965 from the Institute of Aviation at the University of Illinois, where he subsequently received his Ph.D. He then became a commercial pilot and flight instructor (instrument) with multi-engine and seaplane ratings and was a member of the Aircraft Owners and Pilots Association, American Bonanza Society, Civil Air Patrol, Experimental Aircraft Association, National Association of Flight Instructors, and Seaplane Pilots Association. He authored flight maneuvers and practical test prep books for the sport, private, instrument, commercial, and flight instructor certificates/ratings and developed study guides for the remote, sport, private/recreational, instrument, commercial, flight/ground instructor, fundamentals of instructing, airline transport pilot, and flight engineer FAA knowledge tests. Three additional Gleim pilot training books are *Pilot Handbook*, *Aviation Weather and Weather Services*, and *FAR/AIM*.

The late Dr. Gleim also wrote articles for professional accounting and business law journals and authored widely used review manuals for the CIA (Certified Internal Auditor) exam, the CMA (Certified Management Accountant) exam, the CPA (Certified Public Accountant) Exam, and the EA (IRS Enrolled Agent) exam. He was Professor Emeritus at the Fisher School of Accounting, University of Florida, and a CFM, CIA, CMA, and CPA.

Garrett W. Gleim leads production of Gleim pilot training and resources. He earned his private pilot certificate in 1997 in a Piper Super Cub. He is a commercial pilot (single- and multi-engine), ground instructor (advanced and instrument), and flight instructor (instrument and multi-engine) and a member of the Aircraft Owners and Pilots Association, the National Association of Flight Instructors, and the Society of Aviation and Flight Educators. He is the author of study guides for the remote, sport, private/recreational, instrument, commercial, flight/ground instructor, fundamentals of instructing, and airline transport pilot FAA knowledge tests. He received a Bachelor of Science in Economics from The Wharton School, University of Pennsylvania. Mr. Gleim is also a CPA, CIA, and CGMA.

REVIEWERS AND CONTRIBUTORS

Sarah Cipolla, CFI/CFII, ATP, graduated from Lewis University with a bachelor's degree in Aviation Flight Management and is an ATP for a major airline. She researched questions, wrote and edited answer explanations, and incorporated revisions into the text.

Ryan Jeff, CFI, AGI, IGI, Remote Pilot, graduated summa cum laude from Embry-Riddle Aeronautical University with a degree in Aeronautics and a minor in Applied Meteorology. Mr. Jeff is our Part 141 Chief Ground Instructor and Flight Simulation Specialist. He researched questions, wrote and edited answer explanations, and incorporated revisions into the text.

Jim Ostrich, CFI, AGI, Glider, Remote Pilot, A&P, has over 40 years of aviation experience, including 23 years of teaching instructor-led private pilot, commercial pilot, and instrument rating ground schools using Gleim Aviation materials. Mr. Ostrich is a formation lead, check pilot, and avid warbird pilot. He researched questions, wrote and edited answer explanations, and incorporated revisions into the text.

The CFIs who have worked with us throughout the years to develop and improve our pilot training materials.

The many FAA employees who helped, in person or remotely, primarily in Gainesville; Orlando; Oklahoma City; and Washington, DC.

The many pilots and learners who have provided comments and suggestions about *Fundamentals of Instructing FAA Knowledge Test Prep* during the past several decades.

A PERSONAL THANKS

This manual would not have been possible without the extraordinary effort and dedication of Jacob Bennett, Julie Cutlip, Fernanda Martinez, Bobbie Stanley, Joanne Strong, Elmer Tucker, Ryan Van Tress, and Lau Wood, who typed the entire manuscript and all revisions and drafted and laid out the diagrams, illustrations, and cover for this book.

The authors also appreciate the production and editorial assistance of Brianna Barnett, Rayne Chance, Abigail Curtis, Doug Green, Jessica Hatker, Sonora Hospital-Medina, David Sox, and Alyssa Thomas.

The authors also appreciate the video production expertise of Gary Brook, Philip Brubaker, and Matthew Church, who helped produce and edit all Gleim Aviation videos.

Finally, we appreciate the encouragement, support, and tolerance of our families throughout this project.

TABLE OF CONTENTS

NOTE: The FAA does not release its complete database of test questions to the public. Instead, sample questions are released on the Airman Testing page of the FAA website. These questions are similar to the actual test questions, but they are not exact matches.

Gleim utilizes customer feedback and FAA publications to create additional sample questions that closely represent the topical coverage of each FAA knowledge test. In order to do well on the knowledge test, you must study the Gleim outlines in this book, answer all the questions under exam conditions (i.e., without looking at the answers first), and develop an understanding of the topics addressed. You should not simply memorize questions and answers. This will not prepare you for your FAA knowledge test, and it will not help you develop the knowledge you need to competently teach someone how to fly.

If you see topics covered on your FAA knowledge test that are not contained in this book, please contact us at www.GleimAviation.com/questions to report your experience and help us fine-tune our test preparation materials.

Thank you!

PREFACE

The primary purpose of this book is to provide you with the easiest, fastest, and least expensive means of passing the Fundamentals of Instructing (FOI) knowledge test. In addition, this book will help experienced and inexperienced aviation instructors improve instruction techniques and assist flight and/or ground instructors in organizing and presenting aviation ground schools that prepare individuals to pass the FAA pilot knowledge tests.

FOI Knowledge Test

Successful completion of the FOI knowledge test is required by the FAA for those seeking the flight instructor or ground instructor certificates. The introduction beginning on the next page contains a discussion of the requirements to obtain the flight instructor and ground instructor certificates and a description of the FOI knowledge test, how to prepare for it and take it, and how to maximize your score with minimum effort. Study Units 1 through 6 contain outlines of what you need to know to answer the FAA knowledge test questions, as well as all of the previously released FAA test questions and our own similar questions, each accompanied by a comprehensive explanation. Appendix A contains a practice test, consisting of 50 questions from this book, that reflects the subject matter composition of the FAA knowledge test.

Improving Instruction Methods

The FAA publishes an *Aviation Instructor's Handbook* (FAA-H-8083-9B), which explains the basic principles and processes of teaching and learning and is the subject matter of the FOI knowledge test. This material is more easily presented and studied in outline format, as it appears in Study Units 1 through 6 of this book. Both experienced and inexperienced aviation instructors will find the study of these outlines very useful in improving their instruction methods.

Appendix B of this book provides a link to the *Aviation Instructor's Handbook*. It is useful reading and a valuable periodic review for CFIs. The FAA text consists of 10 chapters and 4 appendixes, as well as a convenient glossary.

Ground School Course Suggestions

Many aviation instructors would like to increase the general public's interest in learning to fly. These instructors also enjoy teaching. Appendix C of this book consists of suggestions on how to find (or become) a sponsor for a ground school. It also contains suggestions on course organization, lecture outlines, and class presentation.

Enjoy Flying Safely!

Irvin N. Gleim
Garrett W. Gleim

INTRODUCTION: THE FAA PILOT KNOWLEDGE TEST

This introduction explains how to obtain a flight instructor certificate, including a sport pilot rating. The ground instructor certificate is also addressed. It explains the content and procedures of the relevant Federal Aviation Administration (FAA) knowledge tests, including how to take the test at a testing center.

Fundamentals of Instructing FAA Knowledge Test Prep is one of four related books for obtaining your flight and/or ground instructor certificate. The other three books are (1) **Flight/Ground Instructor FAA Knowledge Test Prep**, (2) **Flight Instructor Flight Maneuvers and Practical Test Prep**, and (3) **Pilot Handbook**.

Flight/Ground Instructor FAA Knowledge Test Prep prepares you to pass the FAA's flight and/or ground instructor knowledge test. If you are planning to obtain both the flight and ground instructor certificates, you only need to pass the Fundamentals of Instructing (FOI) test once.

Flight Instructor Flight Maneuvers and Practical Test Prep is a comprehensive, carefully organized presentation of everything you need to know to prepare for your flight training and for your flight instructor practical (flight) test. It integrates material from FAA publications and other sources.

Pilot Handbook is a complete pilot reference book that combines over 100 FAA books and documents, including *AIM*, Federal Aviation Regulations, ACs, and much more. Aerodynamics, airplane systems, airspace, and navigation are among the topics explained in **Pilot Handbook**.

While the following books are not included in the list above, you may want to purchase them if you do not already have them:

FAR/AIM is an essential part of every instructor's library. The Gleim **FAR/AIM** is an easy-to-read reference book containing all of the Federal Aviation Regulations applicable to general aviation flying, plus the full text of the FAA's *Aeronautical Information Manual (AIM)*.

The Gleim **Aviation Weather and Weather Services** book combines all of the information from the FAA's *Aviation Weather Handbook* (FAA-H-8083-28) and numerous other FAA publications into one easy-to-understand reference book.

WHAT IS A FLIGHT INSTRUCTOR CERTIFICATE?

A flight instructor certificate is similar in appearance to your commercial pilot certificate and will allow you to give flight and ground instruction. The certificate is sent to you by the FAA upon satisfactory completion of your training program, two knowledge tests, and a practical test. It expires at the end of the 24th month after issue. A new certificate is sent to you by the FAA upon renewal. The Gleim Flight Instructor Refresher Course (FIRC) aids you in renewing your flight instructor certificate. A sample flight instructor certificate is reproduced below.

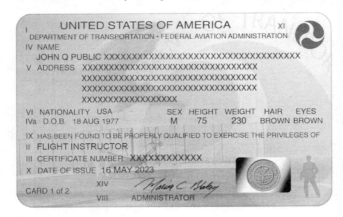 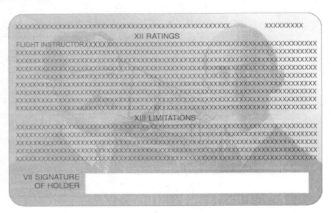

REQUIREMENTS TO OBTAIN A FLIGHT INSTRUCTOR CERTIFICATE

1. Be at least 18 years of age.
2. Be able to read, speak, write, and understand the English language (certificates with operating limitations may be available for medically related deficiencies).
3. Hold a commercial or airline transport pilot (ATP) certificate with an aircraft rating appropriate to the flight instructor rating sought (e.g., airplane, glider).
    a. You must also hold an instrument rating to be a flight instructor in an airplane.
4. Study this book, *Flight/Ground Instructor FAA Knowledge Test Prep*, *Flight Instructor Flight Maneuvers and Practical Test Prep*, *FAR/AIM*, *Aviation Weather and Weather Services*, and *Pilot Handbook* or use the Gleim Online Ground School to learn
    a. Fundamentals of instructing
    b. All other subject areas in which ground training is required for recreational, private, and commercial pilot certificates
5. Pass both the FOI and the flight instructor knowledge tests with scores of 70% or better.
    a. All FAA knowledge tests are administered at FAA-designated computer testing centers.
        1) Page 12 contains additional details.
    b. The FOI and flight instructor tests consist of 50 and 100 multiple-choice questions, respectively, selected from the airplane-related questions in the FAA's flight and ground instructor knowledge test bank.
    c. Questions similar to those you will see on the knowledge test are reproduced in this book with complete explanations.
    d. You are not required to take the FOI knowledge test if you
        1) Hold an FAA flight or ground instructor certificate,
        2) Hold a current teacher's certificate authorizing you to teach at an educational level of the 7th grade or higher, or
        3) Are employed as a teacher at an accredited college or university.

6. Demonstrate flight proficiency (14 CFR 61.187).

    a. You must receive and log flight and ground training and obtain a logbook endorsement from an authorized instructor on the following areas of operations for an airplane category rating with a single-engine or multi-engine class rating:

        1) Fundamentals of instructing
        2) Technical subject areas
        3) Preflight preparation
        4) Preflight lesson on a maneuver to be performed in flight
        5) Preflight procedures
        6) Airport and seaplane base operations
        7) Takeoffs, landings, and go-arounds
        8) Fundamentals of flight
        9) Performance maneuvers
        10) Ground reference maneuvers
        11) Slow flight, stalls, and spins (single-engine only)

            a) Slow flight and stalls (multi-engine only)

        12) Basic instrument maneuvers
        13) Emergency operations
        14) Multi-engine operations (multi-engine only)
        15) Postflight procedures

    b. A CFI who provides training to an initial applicant for a flight instructor certificate must have held a flight instructor certificate for at least 24 months and have given at least 200 hr. of flight training as a CFI.

    c. You must also obtain a logbook endorsement by an appropriately certificated and rated flight instructor who has provided you with spin entry, spins, and spin recovery training in an airplane that is certificated for spins and who has found you instructionally competent and proficient in those training areas, i.e., so you can teach spin recovery.

7. Alternatively, enroll in an FAA-certificated pilot school that has an approved flight instructor certification course (airplane).

    a. These are known as Part 141 schools or Part 142 training centers because they are authorized by Part 141 or Part 142 of the Federal Aviation Regulations.

        1) All other regulations concerning the certification of pilots are found in Part 61 of the Federal Aviation Regulations.

    b. The Part 141 course must consist of at least 40 hr. of ground instruction and 25 hr. of flight instructor training.

8. Successfully complete a practical (flight) test, which will be given as a final exam by an FAA inspector or Designated Pilot Examiner (DPE). The practical test will be conducted as specified in the FAA's Flight Instructor Practical Test Standards (FAA-S-8081-6).

    a. FAA inspectors are FAA employees and do not charge for their services.

    b. FAA-designated pilot examiners are proficient, experienced flight instructors and pilots who are authorized by the FAA to conduct flight tests. They do charge a fee.

The FAA's Flight Instructor Practical Test Standards are outlined and reprinted in the Gleim *Flight Instructor Flight Maneuvers and Practical Test Prep* book.

REQUIREMENTS TO OBTAIN A GROUND INSTRUCTOR CERTIFICATE

1.   To be eligible for a ground instructor certificate, you must

   a.   Be at least 18 years of age.

   b.   Be able to read, speak, write, and understand the English language (certificates with operating limitations may be available for medically related deficiencies).

   c.   Exhibit theoretical knowledge by passing the FOI and the appropriate ground instructor knowledge tests.

      1)   Item 5.d. on page 2 discusses when the FOI knowledge test is not required.

2.   Ground instructor certificates cover three levels of certification:

   a.   Basic ground instructor (BGI) may provide

      1)   Ground training in the aeronautical knowledge areas required for a sport, recreational, or private pilot certificate

      2)   Ground training required for a sport, recreational, or private pilot flight review

      3)   A recommendation for the sport, recreational, or private pilot knowledge test

   b.   Advanced ground instructor (AGI) may provide

      1)   Ground training in the aeronautical knowledge areas required for any certificate or rating (except for an instrument rating) issued under Part 61

      2)   Ground training required for any flight review, but not for an instrument proficiency check (IPC)

      3)   A recommendation for a knowledge test required for any certificate issued under Part 61 except for the instrument rating knowledge test

   c.   Instrument ground instructor (IGI) may provide

      1)   Ground training in the aeronautical knowledge areas required for an instrument rating to a pilot or instructor certificate

      2)   Ground training required for an instrument proficiency check

      3)   A recommendation for the instrument rating knowledge test for a pilot or instructor certificate

   NOTE: The Gleim *Instrument Pilot FAA Knowledge Test Prep* covers the IGI knowledge test, which consists of 50 questions with a 2.5 hr. time limit.

3.   If you are not a CFI, the Federal Aviation Regulations require you to have a ground instructor certificate to teach ground school or to sign off applicants for the appropriate pilot knowledge test.

> Recall that this book has its primary focus on flight instructor -- airplane. Your BGI or AGI knowledge test may have a few non-airplane questions. Use the knowledge you have acquired to answer these questions without worry.

REQUIREMENTS TO OBTAIN A FLIGHT INSTRUCTOR CERTIFICATE WITH A SPORT PILOT RATING

1. To obtain a flight instructor certificate with a sport pilot rating, you must pass both practical and knowledge tests.

   a. To take the knowledge tests for both the fundamentals of instructing and the aeronautical knowledge areas for a sport pilot certificate, you must receive a logbook endorsement from an authorized instructor who trained you or evaluated your home-study course on the materials. This certifies that you are prepared for the tests.

FAA PILOT KNOWLEDGE TEST AND TESTING SUPPLEMENT

1. This book is designed to help you prepare for and pass the FAA FOI knowledge test for the flight and/or ground instructor certificate, which consists of 50 questions and has a time limit of 1.5 hours.

   a. The remainder of this introduction explains the FAA test procedures.

2. The FAA has one FOI figure contained in a book titled *Airman Knowledge Testing Supplement for Flight Instructor, Ground Instructor, and Sport Pilot Instructor*, which you will be given to use at the time of your test.

   a. For the purpose of test preparation, we have reproduced the figure on page 141 in this book.

3. In an effort to develop better questions, the FAA frequently **pretests** questions on knowledge tests by adding up to five "pretest" questions. The pretest questions will not be graded.

   a. You will **not** know which questions are real and which are pretest, so you must attempt to answer all questions correctly.

   b. When you notice a question **not** covered by Gleim, it might be a pretest question.

      1) We want to know about each pretest question you see.

      2) Please contact us at www.GleimAviation.com/questions or call 800-874-5346 with your recollection of any possible pretest questions so we may improve our efforts to prepare future instructors.

KNOWLEDGE TESTS: CHEATING OR UNAUTHORIZED CONDUCT POLICY

The following is taken verbatim from an FAA knowledge test. It is reproduced here to remind all test takers about the FAA's policy against cheating and unauthorized conduct, a policy that Gleim consistently supports and upholds. Test takers must click "Yes" to proceed from this page into the actual knowledge test.

14 CFR part 61, section 61.37 Knowledge tests: Cheating or other unauthorized conduct

(a) An applicant for a knowledge test may not:
(1) Copy or intentionally remove any knowledge test;
(2) Give to another applicant or receive from another applicant any part or copy of a knowledge test;
(3) Give assistance on, or receive assistance on, a knowledge test during the period that test is being given;
(4) Take any part of a knowledge test on behalf of another person;
(5) Be represented by, or represent, another person for a knowledge test;
(6) Use any material or aid during the period that the test is being given, unless specifically authorized to do so by the Administrator; and
(7) Intentionally cause, assist, or participate in any act prohibited by this paragraph.

(b) An applicant who the Administrator finds has committed an act prohibited by paragraph (a) of this section is prohibited, for 1 year after the date of committing that act, from:
(1) Applying for any certificate, rating, or authorization issued under this chapter; and
(2) Applying for and taking any test under this chapter.

(c) Any certificate or rating held by an applicant may be suspended or revoked if the Administrator finds that person has committed an act prohibited by paragraph (a) of this section.

KNOWLEDGE TEST QUESTION BANK

In an effort to keep applicants from simply memorizing test questions, the FAA does not disclose all the questions you might see on your FAA knowledge test.

Using this book and other Gleim test preparation material to merely memorize the questions and answers is unwise and unproductive, and it will not ensure your success on your FAA knowledge test.

REORGANIZATION OF FAA QUESTIONS

1. Questions previously released by the FAA were **not** grouped together by topic; i.e., they appeared to be presented randomly.

    a. We have reorganized and renumbered the questions into study units and subunits.

2. The back of the book contains a list of all of the questions in FAA learning statement code order, with cross-references to their study units and question numbers.

    a. For example, question 3-19 is assigned the code PLT022, which means it is found in Study Unit 3 as question 19 in this book and is covered under the FAA learning statement, "Define Aeronautical Decision Making (ADM)."

HOW TO PREPARE FOR THE KNOWLEDGE TEST

1. Begin by carefully reading the rest of this introduction. You need to have a complete understanding of the examination process prior to initiating your study. This knowledge will make your studying more efficient.

2. After you have analyzed this introduction, set up a study schedule, including a target date for taking your knowledge test.

    a. Do not let the study process drag on and become discouraging; i.e., the quicker, the better.

    b. Consider enrolling in an organized ground school course, like the Gleim **Online Ground School**, or one held at your local FBO, community college, etc.

        1) Gleim Online Ground School is available 24/7. Demo Study Unit 1 for **free** at www.GleimAviation.com/free-demos.

    c. Determine where and when you are going to take your knowledge test.

        1) You can register for the test and see what testing locations are nearby at https://faa.psiexams.com/faa/login.

3. Work through Study Units 1 through 6.

    a. All previously released questions in the FAA's flight and ground instructor knowledge test question bank that are applicable to fundamentals of instructing have been grouped into the following six categories, which are the titles of Study Units 1 through 6:

        Study Unit 1 -- The Learning Process
        Study Unit 2 -- Barriers to Learning
        Study Unit 3 -- Factors Affecting Learning
        Study Unit 4 -- Teaching Methods
        Study Unit 5 -- Planning Instructional Activity
        Study Unit 6 -- Critique and Evaluation

    b. Within each of the study units listed, questions relating to the same subtopic are grouped together to facilitate your study program. Each subtopic is called a subunit.

    c. To the right of each question, we present

        1) The correct answer

        2) The appropriate source document for the answer explanation (e.g., *FAA-H-8083-9B Chap 1* means *Aviation Instructor's Handbook*, Chapter 1)

        3) A comprehensive answer explanation, including

            a) A discussion of the correct answer or concept
            b) An explanation of why the other two answer choices are incorrect

4. Each study unit begins with a list of its subunit titles. The number after each title is the number of questions that cover the information in that subunit. The two numbers following the number of questions are the page numbers on which the outline and the questions for that particular subunit begin, respectively.

5.   Begin by studying the outlines slowly and carefully. They are designed to help you pass the FAA knowledge test.

    a.   **CAUTION:** The **sole purpose** of this book is to expedite your passing the FAA knowledge test for the fundamentals of instructing certificate. Accordingly, extraneous material (i.e., topics not directly tested on the FAA knowledge test) is omitted, even though much more knowledge is necessary to be an instructor. This additional material is presented in three related Gleim books: *Flight/Ground Instructor FAA Knowledge Test Prep*, *Flight Instructor Flight Maneuvers and Practical Test Prep*, and *Pilot Handbook*.

6.   Answer the questions under exam conditions. Cover the answer explanations on the right side of each page with a piece of paper while you answer the questions.

 Remember, it is very important to the learning (and understanding) process that you honestly commit to an answer. If you are wrong, your memory will be reinforced by having discovered your error. Therefore, it is crucial to make an honest attempt to answer the question before reading the answer.

    a.   Study the answer explanation for each question that you answer incorrectly, do not understand, or have difficulty with.

    b.   Use our **Online Ground School** or **FAA Test Prep Online** to ensure you do not refer to answers before committing to one **and** to simulate actual testing center exam conditions.

7.   Note that this test book contains questions grouped by topic. Thus, some questions may appear repetitive, while others may be duplicates or near-duplicates.

8.   As you move through study units, you may need further explanation or clarification of certain topics. You may wish to obtain and use the following Gleim books described on page 1:

    a.   *Flight Instructor Flight Maneuvers and Practical Test Prep*
    b.   *Pilot Handbook*
    c.   *Aviation Weather and Weather Services*

9.   Keep track of your progress. As you complete a subunit, grade yourself with an A, B, C, or ? next to the subunit title at the front of the respective study unit.

    a.   The A, B, C, or ? is a self-evaluation of your comprehension of the material in that subunit and your ability to answer the questions.

        A   means a good understanding.
        B   means a fair understanding.
        C   means a shaky understanding.
        ?   means to ask your CFI or others about the material and/or questions, and read the pertinent sections in *Flight Instructor Flight Maneuvers and Practical Test Prep* and/or *Pilot Handbook*.

    b.   This procedure will provide you with the ability to quickly see (by looking at the first page of each study unit) how much studying you have done (and how much remains) and how well you have done.

    c.   This procedure will also facilitate review. You can spend more time on the subunits that were more difficult for you.

    d.   **FAA Test Prep Online** provides you with your historical performance data.

GLEIM FAA TEST PREP ONLINE

Gleim **FAA Test Prep Online** is an all-in-one program designed to help anyone with a device and an interest in flying pass the FAA knowledge tests. Order today at www.GleimAviation.com or (800) 874-5346, or demo Study Unit 1 for **free** at www.GleimAviation.com/free-demos.

Recommended Study Program

1. Start with Study Unit 1 and proceed through study units in chronological order. Follow the three-step process below.

    a. First, carefully study the Gleim Outline.
    b. Second, create a Study Session of all questions in the study unit. Answer and study all questions in the Study Session.
    c. Third, create a Test Session of all questions in the study unit. Answer all questions in the Test Session.

2. After each Study Session and Test Session, create a new Study Session from questions answered incorrectly. This is of critical importance to allow you to learn from your mistakes.

Practice Test

Take an exam in the actual testing environment of an FAA testing center. **FAA Test Prep Online** simulates the testing formats of these testing centers, making it easy for you to study questions under actual exam conditions. After studying with **FAA Test Prep Online**, you will know exactly what to expect when you go in to take your pilot knowledge test.

On-Screen Charts and Figures

One of the most convenient features of **FAA Test Prep Online** is the easily accessible on-screen charts and figures. Several of the questions refer to drawings, maps, charts, and other pictures that provide information to help answer the question. In **FAA Test Prep Online**, you can pull up any of these figures with the click of a button. You can increase or decrease the size of the images, and you may also use our drawing feature to calculate the true course between two given points (required only on the private pilot knowledge test).

KNOWLEDGE TEST QUESTION-ANSWERING TECHNIQUE

Because the FOI knowledge test has a set number of questions (50) and a set time limit (1.5 hours), you can plan your test-taking session to ensure that you leave yourself enough time to answer each question with relative certainty. The following steps will help you move through the knowledge test efficiently and produce better test results.

1. **Budget your time.** We make this point with emphasis.

    a. If you utilize the entire time limit for the test, you will have about 1.8 minutes per question.

    b. Time yourself when completing study sessions in this book to track your progress and adherence to the time limit and your own personal time allocation budget.

        1) Use any extra time you have to review questions that you are not sure about and similar questions in your exam that may help you answer other questions.

2. **Answer the questions in consecutive order.**

    a. Do **not** agonize over any one item. Stay within your time budget.

    b. Mark any questions you are unsure of and return to them later as time allows.

        1) Once you initiate test grading, you can no longer review/change any answers.

    c. Never leave a multiple-choice question unanswered. Make your best educated guess in the time allowed. Remember, your score is based on the number of correct responses.

3. **For each multiple-choice question,**

    a. **Try to ignore the answer choices.** Do not allow the answer choices to affect your reading of the question.

        1) With three answer choices present, two of them are incorrect. These choices are called **distractors** for good reason and often are written to appear correct at first glance until further analysis.

        2) In computational items, the distractors are carefully calculated such that they are the result of making common mistakes. Be careful, and double-check your computations if time permits.

    b. **Read the question carefully** to determine the precise requirement.

        1) Focusing on what is required enables you to ignore extraneous information, to focus on the relevant facts, and to proceed directly to determining the correct answer.

            a) Be especially careful to note when the requirement is an **exception**; e.g., "Which of the following is **not** a type of hypoxia?"

    c. **Determine the correct answer** before looking at the answer choices.

    d. **Read the answer choices carefully.**

        1) Even if the first answer appears to be the correct choice, do **not** skip the remaining answer choices. Questions often require the "best" answer of the choices provided. Thus, each choice requires your consideration.

        2) Treat each answer choice as a true/false question as you analyze it.

    e. **Click on the best answer.**

        1) For many multiple-choice questions, at least one answer choice can be eliminated with minimal effort, thereby increasing your educated guess to a 50-50 proposition.

4. After you have been through all the questions in the test, consult the question status list to determine which questions are unanswered and which are marked for review.

    a. Go back to the marked questions and finalize your answer choices.
    b. Verify that all questions have been answered.

EDUCATED GUESSING

 The FAA knowledge test sometimes includes questions that are poorly worded or confusing. Expect the unexpected and move forward. Do not let confusing questions affect your concentration or take up too much time; make your best guess and move on.

1. If you don't know the answer, make an educated guess as follows:

    a. Rule out answers that you think are incorrect.
    b. Select the best answer or guess between equally appealing answers. Your first guess is usually the most intuitive. If you cannot make an educated guess, re-read the stem and each answer choice and pick the most intuitive answer.

SIMULATED FAA PRACTICE TEST

Appendix A, "Fundamentals of Instructing Practice Test," beginning on page 173, allows you to practice without the answers next to the questions. This test has 50 questions with topical coverage similar to that of the FAA knowledge test.

It is important that you answer all 50 questions in one sitting. Do not consult the answers, especially when being referred to figures (charts, tables, etc.) where the questions are answered and explained. Analyze your performance based on the answer key that follows the practice test.

It is even better to practice with Test Sessions in the Gleim **FAA Test Prep Online**. These simulate actual testing conditions, including the screen layouts, instructions, etc.

AUTHORIZATION TO TAKE THE FAA PILOT KNOWLEDGE TEST

The FAA does not require an instructor endorsement for your initial attempt of the FOI. The flight instructor knowledge test also does not require an endorsement, except for sport pilot instructor applicants.

If you fail the knowledge test, you will need an instructor endorsement before you can retake the exam.

WHEN TO TAKE THE FAA PILOT KNOWLEDGE TEST

1. You must be at least 16 years of age to take the FOI knowledge test.

2. Take the FAA knowledge test within 30 days of beginning your study.

    a. Complete the knowledge test early in your training so you can focus your effort toward building your skills through aeronautical experience.

3. You must obtain your flight or ground instructor certificate within 24 months.

    a. Otherwise, you will have to retake your knowledge test.

KNOWLEDGE TESTING CENTERS AND PROCEDURES

PSI has testing centers throughout the country. More information can be found at www.GleimAviation.com/testingcenters.

Positive proof of identification and documentary evidence of your age is required. The identification must include your photograph, signature, date of birth, and actual residential address if different from the mailing address. This information may be presented in more than one form of identification.

Next, you will sign in on the testing center's daily log. Your signature on the logsheet certifies that, if this is a retest, you meet the applicable requirements (discussed in "Retaking the FAA Pilot Knowledge Test" on page 15) and that you have not passed this test in the past 2 years.

A person from the testing center will assist you in logging onto the system, and you will be asked to confirm your personal data (e.g., name, Social Security number, etc.). Then you will be given an online introduction to the testing system, and you will take a sample test. If you have used our **FAA Test Prep Online**, you will be conversant with the testing methodology and environment.

YOUR FAA KNOWLEDGE TEST REPORT

1. You will receive your FAA Knowledge Test Report (FAAKTR) upon completion of the test. An example test report is reproduced on the next page.

    a. The expiration date is the date by which you must take your FAA practical test.

    b. The report lists the FAA learning statement codes of the questions you missed so you can review the topics you missed prior to your practical test.

2. Reach out to us at Gleim with your test report at FAAKTR@gleim.com.

    a. We can provide feedback, resources, and guidance toward review and improvement in preparation for your FAA practical test.

U.S. DEPARTMENT OF TRANSPORTATION
Federal Aviation Administration
Airman Knowledge Test Report

NAME:

FAA TRACKING NUMBER (FTN):   **EXAM ID:**

EXAM: Fundamentals of Instructing (FOI)

EXAM DATE: 5/08/2023   **EXAM SITE:**

SCORE: 96   **GRADE:** Pass   **TAKE:** 1

Learning statement codes listed below represent incorrectly answered questions. Learning statement codes and their associated statements can be found at **www.faa.gov/training_testing/testing/airmen**.

Reference material associated with the learning statement codes can be found in the appropriate knowledge test guide at **www.faa.gov/training_testing/testing/airmen/test_guides**.

A single code may represent more than one incorrect response.
PLT229   PLT306

EXPIRATION DATE: 5/31/2025

DO NOT LOSE THIS REPORT

AUTHORIZED INSTRUCTOR'S STATEMENT: (if applicable)

On _____ (date) I gave the above named applicant _____ hours of additional instruction, covering each subject area shown to be deficient, and consider the applicant competent to pass the knowledge test.

Name _____

Cert. No. _____ *(print clearly)*

Type of instructor certificate _____

Signature _____

FRAUDULENT ALTERATION OF THIS FORM BY ANY PERSON IS A BASIS FOR SUSPENSION OR REVOCATION OF ANY CERTIFICATES OR RATINGS HELD BY THAT PERSON.
ISSUED BY: PSI Services LLC
FEDERAL AVIATION ADMINISTRATION

THIS INFORMATION IS PROTECTED BY THE PRIVACY ACT. FOR OFFICIAL USE ONLY.

3. Use the FAA Listing of Learning Statement Codes listed below to determine which topics you had difficulty with.

PLT022 Define Aeronautical Decision Making (ADM)

PLT103 Recall Aeronautical Decision Making (ADM) - hazardous attitudes

PLT104 Recall Aeronautical Decision Making (ADM) - human factors / CRM

PLT204 Recall effective communication - basic elements

PLT211 Recall evaluation testing characteristics

PLT227 Recall FOI techniques - integrated flight instruction

PLT228 Recall FOI techniques - lesson plans

PLT229 Recall FOI techniques - professionalism

PLT230 Recall FOI techniques - responsibilities

PLT231 Recall FOI techniques / human behavior - anxiety / fear / stress

PLT232 Recall FOI techniques / human behavior - dangerous tendencies

PLT233 Recall FOI techniques / human behavior - defense mechanisms

PLT270 Recall human behavior - personality / human needs / adult learning

PLT271 Recall human factors (ADM) - judgment

PLT272 Recall human factors - stress management

PLT295 Recall instructor techniques - obstacles / planning / activities / outcome

PLT306 Recall learning process - theory / definition / levels, style, transfer of learning / incidental learning / acquiring skill

PLT307 Recall learning process - memory / fact / recall

PLT308 Recall learning process - laws of learning elements

PLT481 Recall student evaluation - learning process

PLT482 Recall student evaluation - written tests / oral quiz / critiques

PLT487 Recall teaching methods - demonstration / performance

PLT488 Recall teaching methods - group / guided discussion / lecture

PLT489 Recall teaching methods - known to unknown

PLT490 Recall teaching methods - motivation / student feelings of insecurity

PLT491 Recall teaching methods - process / organize material / course of training

PLT504 Recall use of training aids - types / function / purpose

PLT505 Recall use of training aids - usefulness / simplicity / compatibility

PLT545 Recall teaching methods – problem-based

4. Keep your FAA Knowledge Test Report in a safe place. You must submit it to the FAA evaluator when you take your practical test.

APPLYING FOR YOUR GROUND INSTRUCTOR CERTIFICATE

Flight instructor applicants will take their FAA Airman Knowledge Test Reports to their FAA practical tests. A ground instructor applicant (BGI, AGI, or IGI) does not, however, have to take an FAA practical test.

You must take your FAA Airman Knowledge Test Report and a completed Airman Certificate and/or Rating Application (FAA Form 8710-1) to your local Flight Standards office or an FAA-designated examiner where you will be issued an appropriate temporary ground instructor certificate. Also, on FAA Form 8710-1, the Instructor's Recommendation block does not require an instructor's signature.

Your permanent ground instructor certificate will be mailed to you from the FAA in Oklahoma City.

RETAKING THE FAA PILOT KNOWLEDGE TEST

1. If you fail (score less than 70%) the knowledge test (which is virtually impossible if you follow the Gleim system), you may retake it after your instructor endorses the bottom of your FAA Knowledge Test Report certifying that you have received the necessary ground training to retake the test.

2. Upon retaking the test, you will find that the procedure is the same except that you must also submit your FAA Knowledge Test Report indicating the previous failure to the computer testing center. Your CFI must sign the FAAKTR to indicate that you have received additional instruction and are ready to retake the test.

3. Note that the pass rate on the FOI knowledge test is about 98%; i.e., fewer than 1 out of 10 fail the test initially. Reasons for failure include

    a. Failure to study the material tested and mere memorization of correct answers. (Relevant study material is contained in the outlines at the beginning of Study Units 1 through 6 of this book.)

    b. Failure to practice working through the questions under test conditions. (All of the previously released FAA questions appear in Study Units 1 through 6 of this book.)

    c. Poor examination technique, such as misreading questions and not understanding the requirements.

This Gleim Knowledge Test book will prepare you to pass the FAA knowledge test on your first attempt! In addition, the Gleim *Flight Instructor Flight Maneuvers and Practical Test Prep* book will save you time and frustration as you prepare for the FAA practical test.

Just as this book organizes and explains the knowledge needed to pass your FAA knowledge test, *Flight Instructor Flight Maneuvers and Practical Test Prep* will assist you in developing the competence and confidence to pass your FAA practical test.

Also, flight maneuvers are quickly perfected when you understand exactly what to expect before you get into an airplane to practice the flight maneuvers. You must be ahead of (not behind) your CFI and your airplane. Our flight maneuvers books explain and illustrate all flight maneuvers so the maneuvers and their execution are intuitively appealing to you. Visit www.GleimAviation.com or call (800) 874-5346 and order today!

STUDY UNIT ONE

THE LEARNING PROCESS

(14 pages of outline)

1.1 CHARACTERISTICS OF LEARNING

1. Learning can be defined as a change in behavior as a result of experience.

   a. The behavior change can be physical and overt (a better glide path, for instance), or intellectual and attitudinal (better motivation, more acute perceptions, insights).

2. Learning is purposeful.

   a. Learners learn from any activity that tends to further their goals.

   b. The individual needs and attitudes of learners may determine what they learn as much as what the instructor is trying to teach.

   c. In the process of learning, goals are of paramount significance. To be effective, aviation instructors need to find ways to relate new learning to learners' goals.

3. Learning is a result of experience.

   a. Learning is an individual process; the instructor cannot do it for the learner. The learner can learn only from personal experiences.

   b. If an experience challenges the learner and requires involvement with feelings, thoughts, memory of past experiences, and physical activity, it is a more effective learning tool than an experience involving rote memorization.

   c. Learning a physical skill requires actual experience in performing that skill.

   d. Mental habits are also learned through practice.

4. Learning is multifaceted.

   a. Individuals learn much more than expected if they fully exercise their minds and feelings.

   b. The learning process may include verbal, conceptual, perceptual, emotional, and problem-solving elements all taking place at once.

   c. While learning the subject at hand, the learner may be learning other useful things as well. This is called incidental learning and can have a significant impact on the learner's total development.

5.   Learning is an active process.

   a.   Learners do not soak up knowledge like a sponge absorbs water.

   b.   The instructor cannot assume that learners remember something just because they were in the classroom, shop, or aircraft when the instructor presented the material.

   c.   The instructor should not assume that learners can apply what they know simply because they can quote the correct answer verbatim.

   d.   For effective knowledge transfer, learners need to react and respond.

6.   Learning is the result of comparing new information with preexisting information and integrating it into meaningful connections.

7.   Learning occurs when there is a permanent change in cognition and behavior resulting from an experience.

8.   **Social learning** is learning by observation. There are four stages associated with social learning:

   a.   Attention – the learner's ability to pay attention to others around him or her in order to learn

   b.   Retention – the ability to remember an observed behavior and later repeat that behavior

   c.   Reproduction – the act of reproducing a previously observed behavior

   d.   Motivation – the reason the learner reproduces the observed behavior

1.2   THE LAWS OF LEARNING

1.   Educational psychology professor Edward L. Thorndike pioneered the "laws of learning" that apply to the learning process. They are referred to as principles, and although they are not absolute, they give important insight into effective teaching.

2.   The **principle of readiness** states that if a learner is ready to learn, and has a strong purpose, clear objective, and well-fixed reason for learning, (s)he will make more progress than if (s)he lacks motivation. Readiness implies single-mindedness.

   a.   Readiness to learn also involves what is called the "teachable moment," a moment of educational opportunity when a person is particularly responsive to being taught something.

3.   The **principle of exercise** states that those things most often repeated are best remembered or performed.

   a.   The basis of the principle is to provide opportunities for a learner to practice and then direct this process towards a goal.

   b.   Connections are strengthened with practice and weakened when practice is discontinued, reflecting the adage "use it or lose it."

4.   The **principle of effect** relates to the emotional reaction of the learner.

   a.   Learning is strengthened when accompanied by a pleasant or satisfying feeling.

   b.   Learning is weakened when associated with an unpleasant feeling.

   c.   Therefore, positive training experiences are more likely to lead to success and motivate the learner, while negative training experiences might stimulate forgetfulness or avoidance.

5. The **principle of primacy** states that those things learned first often create a strong, almost unshakable impression. This is the reason an instructor needs to teach correctly the first time.

    a. This principle means that bad habits learned early are hard to break. Instructors must thus insist on correct performance from the outset of maneuvers.

6. The **principle of intensity** states that a vivid, dramatic, or exciting experience teaches more than a routine or boring experience.

    a. The principle of intensity thus implies that a learner will learn more from the real thing than from a substitute.

7. The **principle of recency** states that the things most recently learned are best remembered.

    a. Instructors recognize the principle of recency when they determine the sequence of lectures within a course of instruction.

    b. Instructors may repeat, restate, or reemphasize important points at the end of a lesson to help learners remember them.

1.3 PERCEPTION AND INSIGHT

1. Perceiving involves more than the reception of stimuli from the five senses. Perceptions result when the person gives meaning to sensations being experienced.

    a. Thus, perceptions are the basis of all learning.

    b. New learners can be overwhelmed by stimuli and often focus on meaningless things, thus missing key information. The CFI's job is to direct new learners' perceptions so that key information is recognized, retained, and given meaning.

2. It takes time and opportunity to perceive.

    a. A properly planned training syllabus allows sufficient time and opportunity for key perceptions to occur.

3. A person's basic need is to maintain, enhance, preserve, and perpetuate the organized self.

    a. Thus, all perceptions are affected by this basic need.

4. Self-concept, or self-image, has a great influence on the total perceptual process.

5. Fear or the element of threat narrows the learner's perceptual field.

    a. The resulting anxiety may limit a person's ability to learn from perceptions.

6. Insight occurs when associated perceptions are grouped into meaningful wholes, i.e., when one "gets the whole picture."

    a. Evoking insights is the instructor's major responsibility.

    b. Instruction speeds the learning process by teaching the relationship of perceptions as they occur, thus promoting the development of insights by learners.

    c. An instructor can help develop learner insights by providing a secure and nonthreatening environment in which to learn.

1.4 MEMORY

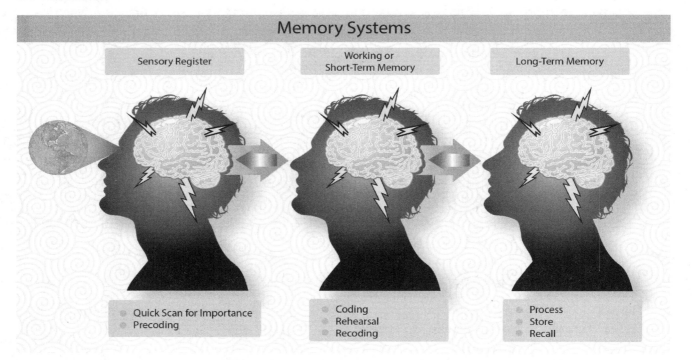

1.   Memory is an integral part of the learning process. It includes three parts: the sensory register, the short-term or working memory, and the long-term memory.

    a.   The **sensory register** receives input from the environment and quickly processes it according to the individual's preconceived concept of what is important. This occurs on a subconscious level.

        1)   **Precoding** is the selective process by which the sensory register recognizes certain stimuli and immediately transmits them to the working memory for action.

            a)   Irrelevant stimuli are discarded by the sensory register.

    b.   The **short-term memory** (STM), or working memory, is the receptacle of the information deemed important by the sensory register.

        1)   A key limitation of STM is that it takes 5-10 seconds to properly code information. If the coding process is interrupted, that information is easily lost because it is stored for only 30 seconds. The purpose of STM is to put information to immediate use.

        2)   The information may temporarily remain in the short-term memory, or it may rapidly fade.

            a)   Retention of information by the short-term memory is aided when the information is initially categorized into systematic chunks in a process known as **coding**.

            b)   Retention is also aided by repetition or rehearsal of the information (rote learning).

3) Information remains in the short-term memory for longer periods when it can be related to an individual's previous knowledge or experiences through a process known as recoding.

   a) **Recoding** may be described as a process of relating incoming information to concepts or knowledge already in memory.

   b) Methods of recoding vary with the subject matter, but they typically involve some type of association, such as mnemonics.

      i) Mnemonics include, but are not limited to, acronyms, acrostics, rhymes, and chaining.

      ii) A mnemonic uses a pattern of letters, ideas, images, or associations to assist in remembering information.

      iii) The use of associations such as rhymes and mnemonics is best suited to the short-term memory.

   c) Short-term memory is the part of the memory system where information is stored for roughly 30 seconds, after which it may rapidly fade or be consolidated into long-term memory, depending on the individual's priorities. Several common steps help retention in short-term memory. These include rehearsal or repetition of the information and sorting or categorization into systematic chunks.

      i) The short-term memory is not only time limited; it also has limited capacity, usually about seven bits or chunks of information at a time. A seven-digit telephone number is an example.

   d) The ability to retrieve knowledge or skills from memory is primarily related to two things: (1) how often that knowledge has been used in the past and (2) how recently the knowledge has been used.

      i) These two factors are called frequency and recency of use. Frequency and recency can be present individually or in combination.

c. The **long-term memory** (LTM) is where information is stored for future use.

   1) For the stored information to be useful, some special effort must have been expended during the recoding process.

   2) It should be noted that the long-term memory is a reconstruction, not a pure recall of information or events.

1.5 FORGETTING AND RETENTION

1.   The following are some basic theories of forgetting:

    a.   The **theory of retrieval failure** considers an individual's inability to retrieve information. Retrieval failure may be the byproduct of poor information encoding. The result is information not attaching to long-term memory.

        1)   An example of retrieval failure is the sensation of a word, phrase, or answer at the tip of one's tongue.

    b.   The **theory of fading** states that a person forgets information that is not used for an extended period of time. Learners are saddened by the small amount of actual data retained several years after graduation.

    c.   The **theory of interference** suggests that people forget something because a certain experience has overshadowed it or the learning of similar things has intervened.

        1)   This theory might explain how the range of experiences after graduation from school causes a person to forget or lose knowledge. In other words, new events displace many things that had been learned.

        2)   From experiments, at least two conclusions about interference may be drawn. First, similar material seems to interfere with memory more than dissimilar material; second, material not well learned suffers most from interference.

    d.   The **theory of repression or suppression** states that memories are pushed out of reach because the individual does not want to remember the feelings associated with them. Unpleasant or anxiety-producing material is forgotten by the individual.

        1)   **Repression** is an unconscious form of forgetting and is unintentional.
        2)   **Suppression** is conscious and intentional.

2.   Responses that produce a pleasurable return are called praise.

    a.   Praise stimulates remembering because responses that give a pleasurable return tend to be repeated.

1.6 TRANSFER OF LEARNING

1. The learner may be either aided or hindered by things learned previously. This process is called transfer of learning.

    a. Positive transfer occurs when the learning of one maneuver aids in learning another.

        1) EXAMPLE: Flying rectangular patterns to aid in flying traffic patterns.

    b. Negative transfer occurs when a performance of a maneuver interferes with the learning of another maneuver.

        1) EXAMPLE: Trying to steer a taxiing plane with the control yoke the way one drives a car.

        2) Negative transfer thus agrees with the interference theory of forgetting.

2. Habit Formation

    a. The formation of correct habit patterns from the beginning of any learning process is essential to further learning and for correct performance after the completion of training.

    b. Everything from intricate cognitive processes to simple motor skills depends on what the learner already knows and how that knowledge can be applied in the present.

    c. By making certain the learner understands that what is learned can be applied to other situations, the instructor helps facilitate a positive transfer of learning.

        1) This is the basic reason for the building-block technique of instruction in which each simple task is performed acceptably and correctly before the next learning task is introduced.

        2) The introduction of instruction in more advanced and complex operations before the initial instruction has been mastered leads to the development of poor habit patterns in the elements of performance.

3. Understanding Affects Memory

    a. The more deeply humans think about what they have learned, the more likely they are able to retrieve that knowledge later.

    b. The effects of depth of processing on memory are quite powerful and result from even the simplest attempts to elaborate on what has been learned.

1.7 LEVELS OF LEARNING

1.   Learning may be accomplished at any of four levels.

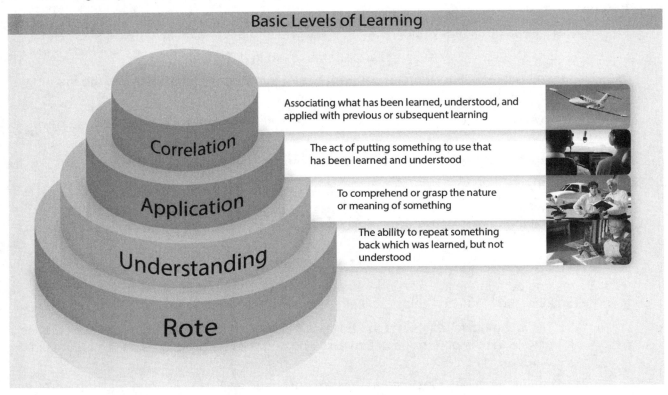

Basic Levels of Learning

Correlation — Associating what has been learned, understood, and applied with previous or subsequent learning

Application — The act of putting something to use that has been learned and understood

Understanding — To comprehend or grasp the nature or meaning of something

Rote — The ability to repeat something back which was learned, but not understood

a.   The lowest level, **rote learning**, is the ability to repeat back what one has been taught without necessarily understanding or being able to apply what has been learned.

   1)   EXAMPLE: Being able to cite the design maneuvering speed of an airplane.

   2)   Many learners use commercially-developed training material to memorize FAA testing concepts, which is another example of rote learning.

      a)   While test preparation materials may be effective in preparing learners for FAA tests, the danger is that learners may learn to pass a given test but fail to learn other critical information essential to safe piloting and maintenance practices.

      b)   FAA inspectors and designated examiners have found that learner applicants often exhibit a lack of knowledge during oral questioning, even though many have easily passed the FAA knowledge test.

      c)   Because test preparation materials emphasize rote learning, instructors should stress that these materials are not designed as stand-alone learning tools. They should be considered as a supplement to instructor-led training.

b.   At the **understanding** level, the learner not only can repeat what has been taught but also comprehends the principles and theory behind the knowledge.

   1)   EXAMPLE: Being able to explain how gross weight affects design maneuvering speed.

   2)   Being able to explain (not demonstrate) is the understanding level.

    c.   At the **application** level, the learner not only understands the theory but also can apply what has been learned and perform in accordance with that knowledge.

        1)   The learner understands the procedure, has had the procedure demonstrated, and has practiced the procedure to a point that it can be performed with consistency.

        2)   This is the level of learning at which most instructors stop teaching.

    d.   At the **correlation** level, the learner is able to associate various learned elements with other segments or blocks of learning or accomplishment.

        1)   EXAMPLE: Know what to do if, during the flight portion of the practical test, the examiner closes the throttle and announces "simulated engine failure."

1.8 DOMAINS OF LEARNING

1.   In addition to the four basic levels of learning discussed in Subunit 1.7, learning can be categorized in other ways.

2.   Three **domains of learning** have been identified based on what is learned:

    a.   The **cognitive domain (thinking)** deals with mental activity and knowledge (e.g., facts, concepts, or relationships).

    b.   The **affective domain (feeling)** relates to personal attitudes, beliefs, and values.

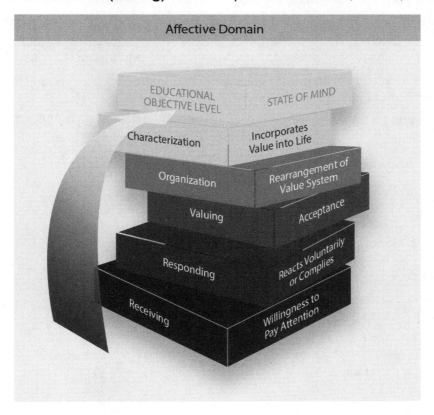

    c.   The **psychomotor domain (doing)** concerns physical skills. These skills involve physical movement, coordination, and the use of motor skills.

        1)   While various examples of the psychomotor domain exist, the practical instructional levels for aviation training purposes include the following:

            a)   Observation
            b)   Imitation
            c)   Practice
            d)   Habit

        2)   Skills involving the psychomotor domain include

            a)   Learning to fly a precision instrument approach procedure
            b)   Programming a global positioning system (GPS) receiver
            c)   Using sophisticated maintenance equipment

        3)   As physical tasks and equipment become more complex, the requirement for integration of cognitive and physical skills increases.

3.   Each of the domains of learning has a hierarchy of educational objectives.

    a.   A listing of the hierarchy of objectives is often referred to as a taxonomy.

        1)   A **taxonomy of educational objectives** is a systematic classification scheme for sorting possible learning outcomes into the three domains of learning and ranking them in a developmental hierarchy from least complex to most complex.

            a)   Each of the three domains of learning has several distinct learning outcomes. These outcomes are equivalent to the educational objective levels.

        2)   The hierarchical taxonomies for the three domains of learning are provided on the next page.

    b.   The educational objectives/learning outcomes become more complex from bottom to top.

Objective Level	Action Verbs for Each Level
COGNITIVE DOMAIN	
Evaluation	Assess, evaluate, interpret, judge, rate, score, or write
Synthesis	Compile, compose, design, reconstruct, or formulate
Analysis	Compare, discriminate, distinguish, or separate
Application	Compute, demonstrate, employ, operate, or solve
Comprehension	Convert, explain, locate, report, restate, or select
Knowledge	Describe, identify, name, point to, recognize, or recall
AFFECTIVE DOMAIN	
Characterization	Assess, delegate, practice, influence, revise, and maintain
Organization	Accept responsibility, adhere, defend, and formulate
Valuing	Appreciate, follow, join, justify, show concern, or share
Responding	Conform, greet, help, perform, recite, or write
Receiving	Ask, choose, give, locate, select, rely, or use
PSYCHOMOTOR DOMAIN	
Origination	Combine, compose, construct, design, or originate
Adaptation	Adapt, alter, change, rearrange, reorganize, or revise
Complex Overt Response	Same as guided response except more highly coordinated
Mechanism	Same as guided response except with greater proficiency
Guided Response	Assemble, build, calibrate, fix, grind, or mend
Set	Begin, move, react, respond, start, or select
Perception	Choose, detect, identify, isolate, or compare

1.9 LEARNING SKILLS AND THE LEARNING CURVE

1.   The best way to prepare a learner to perform a task is to provide a clear, step-by-step example. Learners need a clear picture of what they are to do and how they are to do it.

2.   Learning typically follows a pattern that, if shown on a graph, would be called the learning curve. The first part of the curve indicates rapid early improvement. Then the curve levels off. This leveling-off of an individual's learning rate is called a **learning plateau**.

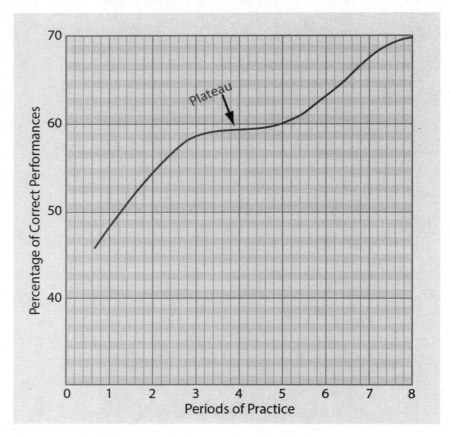

a.   Learning plateaus are a normal part of the learning process and tend to be temporary, but instructors and learners should be prepared for them.

    1)   Keep in mind that the apparent lack of increasing proficiency does not necessarily mean that learning has ceased.

b.   A learning plateau may signify any number of conditions. For example, the learner may

    1)   Have reached capability limits.
    2)   Be consolidating levels of skill.
    3)   Have lost interest.
    4)   Need a more efficient method for increasing progress.

c.   Instructors themselves can bring on a learning plateau by overpractice.

    1)   After repeating any task three or four times, give it a break to avoid causing a learning plateau.

d.   The instructor should prepare the learner for the likelihood of learning plateaus during training to avert discouragement.

e.   Instructors can help learners who fall into a learning plateau by moving them to a different place in the curriculum and giving the plateaued task a break.

3. The development of any skill acquisition has three characteristic stages: cognitive, associative, and automatic. An instructor must learn to recognize each stage in learner performance in order to assess learner progress.

    a. The **cognitive stage** of learning has a basis in factual knowledge. Since the learner has no prior knowledge of flying, the instructor first introduces him or her to a basic skill.

        1) The learner memorizes the steps required to perform the skill.

        2) As the learner carries out these memorized steps, (s)he is often unaware of progress or may fixate on one aspect of performance.

        3) Performing the skill at this stage typically requires all the learner's attention; distractions introduced by an instructor often cause performance to deteriorate or stop.

            a) A distraction is an unexpected event that causes the learner's attention to be momentarily diverted.

    b. The **associative stage** of learning involves the storage of a skill via practice.

        1) As practice continues, the learner learns to associate individual steps in performance with likely outcomes.

        2) The learner no longer performs a series of memorized steps but is able to assess his or her progress along the way and make adjustments in performance.

        3) Performing the skill still requires deliberate attention, but the learner is better able to deal with distractions.

    c. The **automatic response stage** of learning produces automaticity, which is one of the by-products of continued practice.

        1) As procedures become automatic, less attention is required to carry them out, so it is possible to do other things simultaneously, or at least do other things more comfortably.

        2) By this stage, learner performance of the skill is rapid and smooth. The learner devotes much less deliberate attention to performance and may be able to carry on a conversation or perform other tasks while performing the skill.

        3) The learner makes far fewer adjustments during his or her performance, and these adjustments tend to be small.

        4) The learner may no longer be able to remember the individual steps in the procedure or explain how to perform the skill.

        5) An example of a learner who has reached the automatic response stage is a learner who can fly an ILS approach while simultaneously handling the radio communications.

4.   There are three types of practice, each of which yields particular results in acquiring skills.

    a.   During **deliberate practice**, the learner practices specific areas for improvement and receives specific feedback after practice.

        1)   Studies of skill learning suggest a learner achieves better results if distractions are avoided during deliberate practice.

        2)   When feedback is needed to correct learner performance, it should be brief and explicit.

    b.   **Blocked practice** is practicing the same drill until the movement becomes automatic.

        1)   Doing the same task over and over leads to better short-term performance but poorer long-term learning.

        2)   It tends to fool not only the learner but also the instructor into thinking the skills have been well learned.

    c.   **Random practice** mixes the skills to be acquired throughout the practice session.

        1)   This type of practice leads to better retention because, by performing a series of separate skills in a random order, the learner starts to recognize the similarities and differences of each skill, which makes the practice more meaningful.

        2)   The learner also is able to store the skill more effectively in the long-term memory.

QUESTIONS AND ANSWER EXPLANATIONS: All of the Fundamentals of Instructing knowledge test questions chosen by the FAA for release as well as additional questions selected by Gleim relating to the material in the previous outlines are provided on the following pages. These questions have been organized into the same subunits as the outlines. To the immediate right of each question are the correct answer and answer explanations. You should cover these answers and answer explanations while responding to the questions. Refer to the general discussion in the Introduction on how to take the FAA knowledge test.

Remember that the questions from the FAA knowledge test bank have been reordered by topic and organized into a meaningful sequence. Also, the first line of the answer explanation gives the citation of the authoritative source for the answer.

QUESTIONS

1.1 Characteristics of Learning

1. A change in behavior as a result of experience can be defined as

    A. learning.

    B. knowledge.

    C. understanding.

Answer (A) is correct. (FAA-H-8083-9B Chap 3)
    DISCUSSION: Learning can be defined as a change in behavior as a result of experience.
    Answer (B) is incorrect. Knowledge is awareness as a result of experience but not necessarily a change in behavior. **Answer (C) is incorrect.** Understanding is only one of the four levels of learning.

2. The learning process may include some elements such as verbal, conceptual, and

    A. habitual.

    B. experiential.

    C. problem solving.

Answer (C) is correct. (FAA-H-8083-9B Chap 3)
    DISCUSSION: The learning process involves many elements. Verbal, conceptual, perceptual, motor skill, problem solving, and emotional elements may be used at the same time.
    Answer (A) is incorrect. Habits are the customary or usual way of doing things and can be changed by the learning process. **Answer (B) is incorrect.** All learning is by experience, but it takes place in different forms in different people.

3. While learning the material being taught, learners may be learning other things as well. This additional learning is called

    A. residual.

    B. conceptual.

    C. incidental.

Answer (C) is correct. (FAA-H-8083-9B Chap 3)
    DISCUSSION: While learning the subject at hand, learners may be learning other things as well. They may be developing attitudes (good or bad) about aviation depending on what they experience. This learning is called incidental, but it may have a great impact on the total development of the learner.
    Answer (A) is incorrect. Residual is not a term used to define any type of learning. **Answer (B) is incorrect.** Conceptual learning is an element of learning the subject at hand, not other incidental things.

1.2 The Laws of Learning

4. Individuals make more progress learning if they have a clear objective. This is one feature of the principle of

    A. primacy.

    B. readiness.

    C. willingness.

Answer (B) is correct. (FAA-H-8083-9B Chap 3)
    DISCUSSION: One feature of the principle of readiness is that when a learner has a strong purpose, a clear objective, and a well-fixed reason to learn something, (s)he will make more progress than if (s)he lacks motivation.
    Answer (A) is incorrect. The principle of primacy states that first experiences create a strong, almost unshakable impression. **Answer (C) is incorrect.** There is no principle of willingness.

5. Things most often repeated are best remembered because of which principle of learning?

    A. Principle of effect.

    B. Principle of recency.

    C. Principle of exercise.

Answer (C) is correct. (FAA-H-8083-9B Chap 3)
    DISCUSSION: The principle of exercise states that those things most often repeated are best remembered. This is the basis of practice and drill.
    Answer (A) is incorrect. The principle of effect relates to the learner's emotional reaction to the learning experience. **Answer (B) is incorrect.** The principle of recency states that things most recently learned are best remembered.

6. Providing opportunities for a learner to practice and then directing this process towards a goal is the basis of the principle of

    A. exercise.

    B. learning.

    C. readiness.

Answer (A) is correct. (FAA-H-8083-9B Chap 3)
    DISCUSSION: The principle of exercise states that those things most often repeated are best remembered. You must provide opportunities for your learner to practice and then direct this process towards a goal.
    Answer (B) is incorrect. Learning is a change in behavior as a result of experience. The principle of exercise is part of the learning process. **Answer (C) is incorrect.** The principle of readiness states that individuals learn best when they are ready to learn, not practicing a task.

7. Which law of learning is being employed when an instructor communicates a clear set of objectives to the learner and relates each new topic to those objectives?

    A. Primacy.

    B. Readiness.

    C. Intensity.

Answer (B) is correct. (FAA-H-8083-9B Chap 3)
    DISCUSSION: Keeping learners in a state of readiness to learn involves initially communicating a clear set of objectives and then relating each new topic to those objectives. The objectives should be introduced in a logical order that encourages a desire to learn the next topic.
    Answer (A) is incorrect. The principle of primacy in teaching and learning states that what is learned first often creates a strong and almost unshakable impression. **Answer (C) is incorrect.** Intensity can emphasize learning connections made with a learner through a real, immediate, and exciting situation as opposed to a routine or drab experience.

8. The principle that is based on the emotional reaction of the learner is the principle of

    A. effect.

    B. primacy.

    C. intensity.

Answer (A) is correct. (FAA-H-8083-9B Chap 3)
    DISCUSSION: The principle of effect is the one which directly relates to the learner's emotional reaction. Pleasant experiences strengthen the learning process, whereas unpleasant experiences tend to weaken it.
    Answer (B) is incorrect. The principle of primacy states that a strong, almost unshakable impression is created by first experiences. **Answer (C) is incorrect.** The principle of intensity states that dramatic or exciting experiences teach more than routine experiences.

9. Which principle of learning often creates a strong impression?

    A. Principle of primacy.

    B. Principle of intensity.

    C. Principle of readiness.

Answer (A) is correct. (FAA-H-8083-9B Chap 3)
    DISCUSSION: Primacy, the state of being first, often creates a strong, almost unshakable impression. For the instructor, this means that what is taught must be right the first time. The first experience should be positive and functional and should lay the foundation for all that is to follow.
    Answer (B) is incorrect. The principle of intensity means that a learner will learn more from the real thing than from a substitute. **Answer (C) is incorrect.** The principle of readiness means that a learner must be willing and eager to learn.

10. Which principle of learning implies that a learner will learn more from the real thing than from a substitute?

    A. Principle of effect.

    B. Principle of primacy.

    C. Principle of intensity.

Answer (C) is correct. (FAA-H-8083-9B Chap 3)
    DISCUSSION: The principle of intensity states that a vivid, dramatic, or exciting learning experience teaches more than a routine or boring experience. Thus, the principle of intensity implies that a learner will learn more from a real thing than from a substitute.
    Answer (A) is incorrect. The principle of effect is based on the emotional reaction of the learner. Thus, pleasant experiences strengthen the learning, while unpleasant experiences weaken the learning. These may be experienced by learning from either the real thing or a substitute. **Answer (B) is incorrect.** The principle of primacy states that a strong, almost unshakable impression is created by first experiences. These experiences may be from either a real thing or a substitute.

11. Which principle of learning often determines the sequence of lectures within a course of instruction?

    A. Principle of primacy.

    B. Principle of recency.

    C. Principle of intensity.

Answer (B) is correct. (FAA-H-8083-9B Chap 3)
    DISCUSSION: The principle of recency states that the things most recently learned are best remembered. The further a learner is removed time-wise from a new fact or understanding, the more difficult it is to remember it. The principle of recency often determines the sequence of lectures within a course of instruction.
    Answer (A) is incorrect. The principle of primacy means to the instructor that what is taught must be right the first time. **Answer (C) is incorrect.** The principle of intensity means that a learner will learn more from the real experience than a substitute.

1.3 Perception and Insight

12. What is the basis of all learning?

    A. Perception.

    B. Motivation.

    C. Positive self-concept.

Answer (A) is correct. (FAA-H-8083-9B Chap 3)
    DISCUSSION: Initially, all learning comes from perceptions that are directed to the brain by one or more of the five senses. Perceptions result when a person gives meaning to sensations.
    Answer (B) is incorrect. Motivation is the dominant force that governs a learner's progress and ability to learn, not the basis for all learning. **Answer (C) is incorrect.** Positive self-concept is a factor that affects an individual's ability to learn, not the basis of all learning.

13. Perceptions result when a person

    A. gives meaning to sensations being experienced.

    B. is able to discern items of useful information.

    C. responds to visual cues first, then aural cues, and relates these cues to ones previously learned.

Answer (A) is correct. (FAA-H-8083-9B Chap 3)
    DISCUSSION: Perceptions occur when a person gives meaning to sensations being experienced. This is the difference between just seeing something and understanding what is seen.
    Answer (B) is incorrect. A person who is able to discern items of useful information has learned, not just perceived. **Answer (C) is incorrect.** It describes the rote level of learning, i.e., memorization without concern for meaning.

14. Which factor affecting perception has a great influence on the total perceptual process?

    A. Self-concept.

    B. Goals and values.

    C. Time and opportunity.

Answer (A) is correct. (FAA-H-8083-9B Chap 3)
    DISCUSSION: A learner's self-concept (or self-image) has a great influence on the total perceptual process. Negative self-concepts inhibit the perceptual process by introducing psychological barriers, which tend to keep a learner from perceiving. Positive self-concepts allow the learner to be less defensive and more ready to digest experiences by assimilating all of the instructions and demonstrations offered.
    Answer (B) is incorrect. Perceptions depend on goals and values in that every experience is colored by the individual's own beliefs and value structures, but they do not have a great influence on the total perceptual process. **Answer (C) is incorrect.** It takes time and opportunity to perceive, but it is not a great influence on the total perceptual process.

15. Which factor affecting perceptions is based on the effectiveness of the use of a properly planned training syllabus?

    A. Basic need.

    B. Time and opportunity.

    C. Goals and values.

Answer (B) is correct. (FAA-H-8083-9B Chap 3)
    DISCUSSION: It takes time and opportunity to perceive. Learning some things depends on other perceptions that have preceded these learnings and on the availability of time to sense and relate these new things to the earlier perceptions. Thus, sequence and time are necessary to learn; a properly planned training syllabus facilitates sequencing and timing. The effectiveness of using a properly planned training syllabus is proportional to the consideration given by the instructor to the need for sufficient time and opportunity for perception to occur.
    Answer (A) is incorrect. A basic need is to maintain and enhance the organized self, which does not relate to a properly planned training syllabus. **Answer (C) is incorrect.** Goals and values are the basis for perceptions. Every experience and sensation that gets funneled into the central nervous system is colored by the individual's beliefs and value structures, which do not relate to a properly planned training syllabus.

16. Which is one of the ways in which anxiety will affect a learner?

    A. Anxiety may limit the learner's ability to learn from perceptions.

    B. Anxiety will speed up the learning process for the learner if properly controlled and directed by the instructor.

    C. Anxiety causes dispersal of the learner's attention over such a wide range of matters as to interfere with normal reactions.

Answer (A) is correct. (FAA-H-8083-9B Chap 2)
    DISCUSSION: Anxiety is a state of mental uneasiness arising from fear of anything, real or imagined, which threatens the person who experiences it. Anxiety may have a potent effect on actions and on the ability to learn from perceptions.
    Answer (B) is incorrect. Perceptions blocked by anxiety will tend to slow, not speed up, the learning process. **Answer (C) is incorrect.** Anxiety narrows, not disperses, a learner's attention.

17. In the learning process, fear or the element of threat will

    A. narrow the learner's perceptual field.

    B. decrease the rate of associative reactions.

    C. cause a learner to focus on several areas of perception.

Answer (A) is correct. (FAA-H-8083-9B Chap 3)
    DISCUSSION: Fear or the element of threat will impair the learner's perceptual field. This is because one tends to limit attention to the threatening object or condition rather than to what should be learned.
    Answer (B) is incorrect. The element of threat causes stress and anxiety; the mind tends to race, often irrationally, thereby increasing, not decreasing, the rate of associative reactions. **Answer (C) is incorrect.** Fear or the element of threat will cause a learner to focus only on the threatening object or condition, not on several areas of perception.

18. A basic need that affects all of a person's perceptions is the need to

    A. maintain and enhance the organized self.

    B. accomplish a higher level of satisfaction.

    C. avoid areas that pose a threat to success.

Answer (A) is correct. (FAA-H-8083-9B Chap 3)
    DISCUSSION: A person's basic need is to maintain and enhance the organized self. The self is a person's past, present, and future and is both physical and psychological. A person's most fundamental need is to preserve and perpetuate this self. Thus, all perceptions are affected by this need.
    Answer (B) is incorrect. Accomplishing a higher level of satisfaction is a goal, not a basic need. **Answer (C) is incorrect.** Avoiding areas that are a threat to success is a defense mechanism, not a basic need that affects perceptions.

19. The mental grouping of affiliated perceptions is called

    A. insights.

    B. association.

    C. conceptualization.

Answer (A) is correct. (FAA-H-8083-9B Chap 3)
    DISCUSSION: Many principles, theories, and learned tasks can be treated as pieces relating to other pieces in the overall pattern of the task to be learned. This mental relating or grouping of associated perceptions is called insight.
    Answer (B) is incorrect. Association is not the final, completed mental picture, although it is a necessary process to connect the affiliated perceptions. **Answer (C) is incorrect.** It refers only to the formation of individual ideas.

20. Insights, as applied to learning, involve a person's

    A. association of learning with change.

    B. grouping of associated perceptions into meaningful wholes.

    C. ability to recognize the reason for learning a procedure.

Answer (B) is correct. (FAA-H-8083-9B Chap 3)
    DISCUSSION: Insights, as applied to learning, involve a person's grouping of associated perceptions into meaningful wholes. As perceptions increase in number and are grouped to become insights by the learner, learning becomes more meaningful and permanent.
    Answer (A) is incorrect. Insights involve the grouping of perceptions into meaningful wholes, not the association of learning with change. **Answer (C) is incorrect.** The ability to recognize the reason for learning a procedure is a feature of the principle of readiness, not insight.

21. Instruction, as opposed to the trial and error method of learning, is desirable because competent instruction speeds the learning process by

    A. motivating the learner to a better performance.

    B. emphasizing only the important points of training.

    C. teaching the relationship of perceptions as they occur.

Answer (C) is correct. (FAA-H-8083-9B Chap 3)
    DISCUSSION: Competent instruction speeds the learning process by teaching the relationship of perceptions as they occur, thus promoting the development of insights by the learner.
    Answer (A) is incorrect. Motivating a learner to a better performance is just one element of instruction. **Answer (B) is incorrect.** Instructors must emphasize all points of training, not just the major, important points.

22. Name one way an instructor can help develop learner insights.

    A. Provide a secure and nonthreatening environment in which to learn.

    B. Point out various items to avoid during the learning process.

    C. Keep learning blocks small so they are easier to understand.

Answer (A) is correct. (FAA-H-8083-9B Chap 3)
    DISCUSSION: Pointing out the relationships of perceptions as they occur, providing a secure and nonthreatening environment in which to learn, and helping the learner acquire and maintain a favorable self-concept are most important in fostering the development of insights.
    Answer (B) is incorrect. The instructor should point out the relationships of perceptions as they occur, not point out various items to avoid during the learning process. **Answer (C) is incorrect.** Insights develop when a learner's perceptions increase in number and are assembled into larger, not smaller, blocks of learning.

1.4 Memory

23. The use or association of rhymes or word patterns to aid in remembering is called

    A. acronyms.

    B. mnemonics.

    C. coding.

Answer (B) is correct. (FAA-H-8083-9B Chap 3)
    DISCUSSION: A mnemonic uses a pattern of letters, ideas, images, or associations to assist in remembering information. It is a memory-enhancing strategy that involves teaching learners to link new information to information they already know.
    Answer (A) is incorrect. Mnemonics may include acronyms but are not necessarily acronyms themselves. **Answer (C) is incorrect.** Coding is a sorting process. It is not designed for remembering information.

24. Which memory system processes input from the environment?

    A. Working.

    B. Long-term.

    C. Sensory register.

Answer (C) is correct. (FAA-H-8083-9B Chap 3)
    DISCUSSION: The sensory register receives input from the environment and quickly processes it according to the individual's preconceived concept of what is important (i.e., it recognizes certain stimuli as significant). The sensory register processes inputs or stimuli from the environment within seconds, discards what is considered extraneous, and processes what is considered by the individual to be relevant.
    Answer (A) is incorrect. The working, or short-term, memory is the receptacle for the information determined to be relevant by the sensory register. Once in the short-term memory, the information may temporarily remain for immediate use, or it may fade rapidly. **Answer (B) is incorrect.** The long-term memory is where information is stored for future use.

25. While short-term memory is time-limited, it also has a capacity limit of

    A. usually 5 bits or chunks of information.

    B. usually 7 bits or chunks of information.

    C. usually 9 bits or chunks of information.

Answer (B) is correct. (FAA-H-8083-9B Chap 3)
    DISCUSSION: The short-term memory is not only time limited; it also has limited capacity, usually about seven bits or chunks of information at a time. A seven-digit telephone number is an example.
    Answer (A) is incorrect. The short-term memory is not only time limited; it also has limited capacity, usually about seven, not five, bits or chunks of information at a time. **Answer (C) is incorrect.** The short-term memory is not only time limited; it also has limited capacity, usually about seven, not nine, bits or chunks of information at a time.

26. The use of some type of association, such as rhymes or mnemonics is best suited to which memory system?

    A. Short-term.

    B. Sensory.

    C. Long-term.

Answer (A) is correct. (FAA-H-8083-9B Chap 3)
    DISCUSSION: For information to remain in the short-term memory for a significant amount of time, it must be categorized in some way. The information is initially grouped into systematic chunks in a process called coding. It must then be related to concepts or knowledge already in memory in a process called recoding. The use of some type of association, such as rhymes or mnemonic devices, is well suited to this task.
    Answer (B) is incorrect. The sensory register detects and processes stimuli on a subconscious level. They are then discarded or transferred to the short-term memory according the individual's preconceived concept of what is important. **Answer (C) is incorrect.** In order for information stored in long-term memory to be useful, some special effort must have been expended during the recoding process while the information was in short-term memory.

27. How can recoding be described?

    A. The relating of incoming information to concepts or knowledge already in memory.

    B. The initial storage of information in short-term memory.

    C. The selective process where the sensory register is set to recognize certain stimuli.

Answer (A) is correct. (FAA-H-8083-9B Chap 3)
    DISCUSSION: Recoding takes place in the short-term memory, when new information is adjusted to individual experiences. Recoding may be described as a process of relating incoming information to concepts or knowledge already in memory.
    Answer (B) is incorrect. The initial storage of information in short-term memory is coding, not recoding. **Answer (C) is incorrect.** The selective process where the sensory register is set to recognize certain stimuli is precoding, not recoding.

28. Which of the following memory systems would be enhanced with practice and repetition?

A. Long-term.

B. Short-term.

C. Perception.

Answer (B) is correct. (FAA-H-8083-9B Chap 3)
DISCUSSION: Short-term memory is the part of the memory system where information is stored for roughly 30 seconds, after which it may rapidly fade or be consolidated into long-term memory, depending on the individual's priorities. Several common steps help retention in short-term memory. These include rehearsal or repetition of the information and sorting or categorization into systematic chunks. The sorting process is usually called coding or chunking.
Answer (A) is incorrect. Practice and repetition enhance short-term memory, with the hope that these memories will become long-term memories. **Answer (C) is incorrect.** Learner perceptions are unrelated to short-term memory.

29. Which of the following statements about long-term memory is true?

A. Long-term memory is a reconstruction, not a pure recall of information or events.

B. Long-term memory is not subject to limitations such as time, biases, and, in many cases, personal inaccuracies.

C. Initial encoding is not related to long-term memory.

Answer (A) is correct. (FAA-H-8083-9B Chap 3)
DISCUSSION: Long-term memory is a reconstruction, not a pure recall of information or events.
Answer (B) is incorrect. Long-term memory is in fact subject to limitations, such as time, biases, and, in many cases, personal inaccuracies. **Answer (C) is incorrect.** If initial encoding is not properly accomplished, recall is distorted and may be impossible.

30. Where is information for future use stored?

A. Short-term memory.

B. Sensory register.

C. Long-term memory.

Answer (C) is correct. (FAA-H-8083-9B Chap 3)
DISCUSSION: Information for future use is stored in the long-term memory.
Answer (A) is incorrect. Short-term memory is where information is temporarily stored, not stored for future use, after the sensory register deems it to be significant. **Answer (B) is incorrect.** The sensory register processes stimuli from the environment according to the individual's preconception of what is important. Significant information is sent to the short-term memory for immediate, not future, use.

31. The selective process by which the sensory register discards and transmits certain stimuli to the working memory is called

A. recoding.

B. coding.

C. precoding.

Answer (C) is correct. (FAA-H-8083-9B Chap 3)
DISCUSSION: Precoding is the selective process by which the sensory register recognizes certain stimuli and immediately transmits them to the working memory for action.
Answer (A) is incorrect. Recoding is the process of relating incoming information to concepts already in memory. **Answer (B) is incorrect.** Coding is the initial sorting or categorization of information into systematic chunks in the short-term memory to aid in retention.

32. The ability to retrieve knowledge or skills from memory is primarily related to

A. absence of interference.

B. how often that knowledge has been used in the past.

C. the practice of "information chunking."

Answer (B) is correct. (FAA-H-8083-9B Chap 3)
DISCUSSION: The ability to retrieve knowledge or skills from memory is primarily related to how often and how recently the knowledge has been used in the past. These two factors are called frequency and recency of use. Frequency and recency can be present individually or in combination.
Answer (A) is incorrect. The absence of interference is not the primary factor in the ability to retrieve knowledge. **Answer (C) is incorrect.** Chunking is one of the steps that helps retention of short-term memory. After rehearsal or repetition of the information, it is sorted or categorized into systematic chunks. The sorting process is usually called coding or chunking.

1.5 Forgetting and Retention

33. The phenomenon of information not used for an extended period of time becoming harder to recall is termed

    A. fading.

    B. forgetting.

    C. retrieval failure.

Answer (A) is correct. (FAA-H-8083-9B Chap 3)
    DISCUSSION: The theory of fading, or decay, suggests that a person forgets information that is not used for an extended period of time. It has been suggested that humans are physiologically pre-programmed to eventually erase data that no longer appears pertinent.
    Answer (B) is incorrect. Forgetting typically involves a failure in memory retrieval. **Answer (C) is incorrect.** Retrieval failure is simply the inability to retrieve information, for example, the "tip-of-the-tongue" phenomenon when a person knows the meaning of a word or the answer to a question but cannot retrieve it.

34. When a person has difficulty recalling facts after several years, this is known as

    A. repression.

    B. fading.

    C. retrieval failure.

Answer (B) is correct. (FAA-H-8083-9B Chap 3)
    DISCUSSION: The theory of fading or decay suggests that a person forgets information that is not used for an extended period of time.
    Answer (A) is incorrect. Repression is the practice of submerging an unpleasant experience into the subconscious. **Answer (C) is incorrect.** Retrieval failure is simply the inability to retrieve information. Some would call it the "tip-of-the-tongue" phenomenon when a person knows the answer to a question but cannot retrieve it.

35. When the learning of similar things overshadows other learning experiences, it is called

    A. suppression.

    B. correlation.

    C. interference.

Answer (C) is correct. (FAA-H-8083-9B Chap 3)
    DISCUSSION: The theory of interference states that new or similar events can often replace previously learned facts. Most susceptible to this replacement by interference are closely similar materials and materials not well learned to begin with.
    Answer (A) is incorrect. Suppression is not a consideration (or theory) as to why a person forgets. **Answer (B) is incorrect.** Correlation is the highest level of learning, which means that it is resistant to forgetting.

36. According to one theory, some forgetting is due to the unconscious practice of submerging an unpleasant experience into the subconscious. This is called

    A. suppression.

    B. immersion.

    C. repression.

Answer (C) is correct. (FAA-H-8083-9B Chap 3)
    DISCUSSION: Repression is the unconscious form of forgetting where memories are pushed out of reach because the individual does not want to remember the feelings associated with them.
    Answer (A) is incorrect. Suppression is a conscious, not unconscious, form of forgetting. **Answer (B) is incorrect.** Immersion is not discussed in the *Aviation Instructor's Handbook* and is a nonsense answer in this context.

37. Responses that produce a pleasurable return are called

    A. reward.

    B. praise.

    C. positive feedback.

Answer (B) is correct. (FAA-H-8083-9B Chap 3)
    DISCUSSION: Responses that give a pleasurable return, called praise, tend to be repeated, thus stimulating and encouraging retention.
    Answer (A) is incorrect. Rewards are motivators and are not usually responses (e.g., praise); that is, they are normally financial, self-interest, or public recognition. **Answer (C) is incorrect.** Positive feedback (e.g., constructive criticism) is part of the learning, not retention, process. Positive feedback teaches a learner how to capitalize on things done well and to use them to compensate for lesser accomplishments.

38. The act of consciously pushing a memory out of reach due to feelings associated with remembering it is

- A. avoidance.
- B. suppression.
- C. repression.

Answer (B) is correct. (FAA-H-8083-9B Chap 3)
DISCUSSION: Suppression is a conscious form of forgetting where the learner intentionally forces memories that are unpleasant or anxiety-producing into the subconscious.
Answer (A) is incorrect. Avoidance is not a theory of forgetting and is not discussed in the *Aviation Instructor's Handbook*. **Answer (C) is incorrect.** Repression is an unconscious, not conscious, form of forgetting.

39. When a new experience displaces memories or information that had been previously learned, it is called

- A. fading.
- B. retrieval failure.
- C. interference.

Answer (C) is correct. (FAA-H-8083-9B Chap 3)
DISCUSSION: Interference theory suggests that people forget something because a certain experience has overshadowed it or the learning of similar things has intervened. In other words, new events displace many things that had been learned.
Answer (A) is incorrect. The theory of fading suggests that a person forgets information that is not used for an extended period of time. **Answer (B) is incorrect.** Retrieval failure is simply the inability to retrieve information, for example, the "tip-of-the-tongue" phenomenon when a person knows the meaning of a word or the answer to a question but cannot retrieve it.

1.6 Transfer of Learning

40. The performance of rectangular patterns helps a learner fly traffic patterns. What type transfer of learning is this?

- A. Lateral.
- B. Positive.
- C. Deliberate.

Answer (B) is correct. (FAA-H-8083-9B Chap 3)
DISCUSSION: Transfers of learning can be negative or positive. Since the learning of Task A (flying rectangular patterns) helps in the learning of Task B (flying traffic patterns), it is advantageous and therefore a positive transfer of learning.
Answer (A) is incorrect. There is no lateral transfer of learning, only positive or negative. **Answer (C) is incorrect.** There is no deliberate transfer of learning, only positive or negative.

41. Which transfer of learning occurs when the performance of a maneuver interferes with the learning of another maneuver?

- A. Adverse.
- B. Positive.
- C. Negative.

Answer (C) is correct. (FAA-H-8083-9B Chap 3)
DISCUSSION: Transfers of learning can be negative or positive. If the learning of Task A helps in the learning of Task B, the transfer of learning is deemed to be positive. If, on the other hand, Task A interferes with Task B, the transfer is a hindrance to learning and is thus negative.
Answer (A) is incorrect. There is no adverse transfer of learning, only positive or negative. **Answer (B) is incorrect.** The transfer of learning is a hindrance and is thus negative.

42. To ensure proper habits and correct techniques during training, an instructor should

- A. use the building block technique of instruction.
- B. repeat subject matter the learner has already learned.
- C. introduce challenging material to continually motivate the learner.

Answer (A) is correct. (FAA-H-8083-9B Chap 3)
DISCUSSION: The building-block technique of teaching insists that each simple task be performed correctly before the next is introduced. This technique fosters thorough and meaningful performance and good habits, which will be carried over into future learning.
Answer (B) is incorrect. Too much repetition can lead to boredom. The instructor must mix teaching methods to sustain interest and promote learning. **Answer (C) is incorrect.** Complex or difficult tasks introduced before simpler ones are mastered can be frustrating, not motivating, for the learner. This approach will not ensure proper habits; the learner will likely develop bad habits from trying to perform tasks not completely understood.

1.7 Levels of Learning

43. What level of knowledge is being tested if asked, "What is the maneuvering speed of the aircraft listed in the owner's manual?"

    A. Rote.

    B. Application.

    C. Understanding.

Answer (A) is correct. (FAA-H-8083-9B Chap 3)
    DISCUSSION: The lowest level, rote learning, is the ability to repeat something back that one has been taught without understanding or being able to apply what has been learned. An example of rote learning is to be able to cite the maneuvering speed of the aircraft listed in the owner's manual.
    Answer (B) is incorrect. Application is the ability of a learner to apply what has been taught. This is the third level of learning and is achieved after the learner understands, has practiced, and can consistently perform a task. **Answer (C) is incorrect.** The second level of learning is understanding, which has been achieved when a learner can put together a block of learning and develop an insight into the performance of a task.

44. Once a learner understands a procedure, has had the procedure demonstrated, and has practiced the procedure until it can be performed with consistency, the learner has demonstrated what level of learning?

    A. Application.

    B. Rote.

    C. Duplication.

Answer (A) is correct. (FAA-H-8083-9B Chap 3)
    DISCUSSION: Application is a basic level of learning at which the learner puts something to use that has been learned and understood.
    Answer (B) is incorrect. Rote learning is simple memorization without necessarily gaining an understanding of what has been memorized. **Answer (C) is incorrect.** Duplication is not a level of learning.

45. Learners who use test preparation materials in preparing for FAA tests may commit which of the following adverse actions?

    A. Focusing on test-taking skills rather than critical information essential for safe piloting.

    B. Excelling in the oral exam portion of practical tests.

    C. Focusing on correlation level learning.

Answer (A) is correct. (FAA-H-8083-9B Chap 5)
    DISCUSSION: By relying on test preparation materials as a source of learning, learners may learn to pass a given test but fail to learn other critical information essential to safe piloting and maintenance practices.
    Answer (B) is incorrect. FAA inspectors and designated examiners have found that learner applicants often exhibit a lack of knowledge during oral questioning, even though many have easily passed the FAA knowledge test. **Answer (C) is incorrect.** Test preparation materials often encourage rote-level learning, not correlation.

46. During the flight portion of a practical test, the examiner simulates complete loss of engine power by closing the throttle and announcing "simulated engine failure." What level of learning is being tested?

    A. Application.

    B. Correlation.

    C. Understanding.

Answer (B) is correct. (FAA-H-8083-9B Chap 3)
    DISCUSSION: When the examiner simulates complete loss of engine power by closing the throttle and announcing "simulated engine failure," the examiner is testing at the correlation level of learning. The applicant must be able to correlate (associate) the engine failure with the requirements to perform the elements of an emergency approach and landing; e.g., establish best-glide speed, select a field, perform restart checklist, plan a flight pattern to the selected field, complete all appropriate checklists, etc.
    Answer (A) is incorrect. The application level of learning is tested when the examiner closes the throttle and tells the applicant to perform an emergency approach and landing. **Answer (C) is incorrect.** The understanding level of learning is tested when the examiner asks the applicant to explain the elements of an emergency approach and landing.

47. At which level of learning do most instructors stop teaching?

    A. Application.

    B. Correlation.

    C. Understanding.

Answer (A) is correct. (FAA-H-8083-9B Chap 3)
    DISCUSSION: Most instructors stop teaching at the application level of learning. Discontinuing instruction on an element at this point and directing subsequent instruction exclusively to other elements is characteristic of piecemeal instruction, which is usually inefficient. It violates the building block concept of instruction by failing to apply what has been learned to future learning tasks.
    Answer (B) is incorrect. Correlation is the highest level of learning and should be the goal of each instructor. Instructors all too often stop at the application level. **Answer (C) is incorrect.** Understanding is the second level of learning, and at this point, a learner understands a task but may not be able to do it. Instructors usually teach to the next level, which is application.

48. Commercially-developed test preparation material

    A. teaches higher-order thinking skills.

    B. replaces instructor-led training.

    C. places emphasis on rote learning rather than more advanced learning levels.

Answer (C) is correct. *(FAA-H-8083-9B Chap 5)*
    DISCUSSION: While commercially-developed training material is a great study aid, it emphasizes rote learning rather than higher levels of learning that promote increased understanding. Commercially-developed training material should be used as a supplement to instructor-led, comprehensive training, not as a replacement for it. Gleim supports and encourages the view that learners should strive for a level of understanding beyond rote memorization. That is why all of our knowledge test preparation materials include both Knowledge Transfer Outlines and multiple-choice questions. The outlines and the detailed answer explanations help learners conceptualize why the correct answers are correct and the incorrect answers are incorrect. We also provide additional outline material for practical training in our Flight Maneuvers and Oral Exam Guide books. These texts prepare Gleim learners for the higher-level thinking demanded of future pilots.
    Answer (A) is incorrect. Higher-order thinking skills involve decision-making principles. Commercially-developed training material emphasizes rote learning rather than higher levels of learning that promote increased understanding. Thus, instructor-led training is essential for developing higher-order thinking skills. **Answer (B) is incorrect.** While commercially-developed training material is a great study aid, it cannot be used as a replacement to instructor-led training because it focuses on rote learning rather than higher levels of learning.

49. A disadvantage of using commercially-developed test preparation material is that

    A. the emphasis is on correlation learning.

    B. learners may learn to pass a given test.

    C. learners often exhibit a lack of knowledge during oral questioning.

Answer (C) is correct. *(FAA-H-8083-9B Chap 5)*
    DISCUSSION: FAA inspectors and designated examiners have found that learners often exhibit a lack of knowledge during oral questioning even though many have easily passed the FAA knowledge test. This is most often due to memorization rather than true concept understanding. Test preparation materials emphasize rote learning rather than higher levels of learning that promote increased understanding. Gleim supports and encourages the view that learners should strive for a level of understanding beyond rote memorization. That is why all of our knowledge test preparation materials include both Knowledge Transfer Outlines and multiple-choice questions. The outlines and the detailed answer explanations help learners conceptualize why the correct answers are correct and the incorrect answers are incorrect. We also provide additional outline material for practical training in our Flight Maneuvers and Oral Exam Guide books. These texts prepare Gleim learners for the higher-level thinking demanded of future pilots.
    Answer (A) is incorrect. While commercially-developed training material is a great study aid, it emphasizes rote learning rather than higher levels of learning, such as correlation, that promote increased understanding. **Answer (B) is incorrect.** Commercially-developed training material is incredibly useful at helping learners pass FAA tests. This is only a disadvantage if the learner memorizes the material and fails to develop understanding of the covered topics.

50. When asking a learner to explain how gross weight affects maneuvering speed, what level of learning is being tested?

    A. Application.

    B. Correlation.

    C. Understanding.

Answer (C) is correct. *(FAA-H-8083-9B Chap 3)*
    DISCUSSION: At the understanding level of learning, a learner will be able to explain how gross weight affects maneuvering speed (V_A). Understanding is the next level after rote memorization and the level before acquiring the skill to apply knowledge, which is application (correlation is the fourth and highest level of learning). Being able to explain (not demonstrate) is the understanding level of learning, not the application or correlation level.
    Answer (A) is incorrect. At the application level, a learner can apply the knowledge that gross weight affects maneuvering speed when determining the appropriate airspeed for entering turbulent air or maneuvers that require an airspeed at or below V_A. **Answer (B) is incorrect.** At the correlation level, a learner can correlate the elements of maneuvering speed with other concepts, such as gust loads, accelerated stalls, load factors, acceleration forces in the aircraft, etc.

1.8 Domains of Learning

51. Which domain of learning deals with knowledge?

- A. Affective.
- B. Cognitive.
- C. Psychomotor.

Answer (B) is correct. (FAA-H-8083-9B Chap 3)
DISCUSSION: Domains of learning are classified based on what is to be learned. The cognitive domain of learning deals with knowledge (e.g., facts, concepts, or relationships).
Answer (A) is incorrect. The affective domain deals with attitudes, beliefs, and values, not knowledge. **Answer (C) is incorrect.** The psychomotor domain deals with physical skills, not knowledge.

52. Affective domain relates to

- A. physical skills.
- B. knowledge.
- C. attitudes, beliefs, and values.

Answer (C) is correct. (FAA-H-8083-9B Chap 3)
DISCUSSION: Domains of learning are classified based on what is to be learned. The affective domain relates to attitudes, beliefs, and values.
Answer (A) is incorrect. The psychomotor domain, not the affective domain, relates to physical skills. **Answer (B) is incorrect.** The cognitive domain, not the affective domain, relates to knowledge.

53. The educational objective levels for the cognitive domain are

- A. receiving, responding, valuing, organization, and characterization.
- B. perception, set, guided response mechanism, complex overt response, adaptation, and origination.
- C. knowledge, comprehension, application, analysis, synthesis, and evaluation.

Answer (C) is correct. (FAA-H-8083-9B Chap 3)
DISCUSSION: Each domain of learning has multiple educational objective levels. The six educational objective levels of the cognitive domain are knowledge, comprehension, application, analysis, synthesis, and evaluation.
Answer (A) is incorrect. Receiving, responding, valuing, organization, and characterization are the five educational objective levels of the affective, not cognitive, domain. **Answer (B) is incorrect.** Perception, set, guided response mechanism, complex overt response, adaptation, and origination are the seven educational objective levels of the psychomotor, not cognitive, domain.

54. Which of the following domains is a grouping of levels of learning associated with personal attitudes?

- A. Cognitive.
- B. Affective.
- C. Psychomotor.

Answer (B) is correct. (FAA-H-8083-9B Chap 3)
DISCUSSION: The affective domain is a grouping of levels of learning associated with personal attitudes, beliefs, and values, which include objectives of receiving, responding, valuing, organization, and characterization.
Answer (A) is incorrect. The cognitive domain is a grouping of levels of learning associated with mental activity. In order of increasing complexity, the levels are knowledge, comprehension, application, analysis, synthesis, and evaluation. **Answer (C) is incorrect.** The psychomotor domain is a grouping of levels of learning associated with physical skill levels, which range from perception through set, guided response, mechanism, complex overt response, adaptation, and origination.

55. The most complex outcome in the affective domain is

- A. organization.
- B. characterization.
- C. valuing.

Answer (B) is correct. (FAA-H-8083-9B Chap 3)
DISCUSSION: A taxonomy of educational objectives is a systematic classification scheme for sorting learning outcomes into the three domains of learning (cognitive, affective, and psychomotor) and ranking the desired outcomes in a developmental hierarchy from least complex to most complex. The most complex learning outcome in the affective domain is characterization in which the learner incorporates a value or attitude into his or her life.
Answer (A) is incorrect. Organization (in which the learner rearranges his or her value system to accommodate a new value or attitude) is the second-most-complex, not the most complex, learning outcome in the affective domain. **Answer (C) is incorrect.** Valuing (in which the learner accepts a new value or attitude) is the third-most-complex, not the most complex, learning outcome in the affective domain.

56. The listing of the hierarchy of objectives is often referred to as a

    A. taxonomy.

    B. skill.

    C. domain.

Answer (A) is correct. (FAA-H-8083-9B Chap 3)
    DISCUSSION: Each of the domains of learning has a hierarchy of educational objectives. The listing of the hierarchy of objectives is often called a taxonomy.
    Answer (B) is incorrect. A skill is what is learned in the psychomotor domain of learning. It is not a hierarchy of educational objectives. **Answer (C) is incorrect.** Domains of learning contain, but are not, hierarchies of educational objectives.

57. Learning objectives can be sorted in a system known as a

    A. taxonomy.

    B. database.

    C. schema.

Answer (A) is correct. (FAA-H-8083-9B Chap 2)
    DISCUSSION: The hierarchy of learning objectives is known as a taxonomy. Taxonomy is the systematic classification of learning outcomes into one of the three broad categories or domains of learning (cognitive, affective, and psychomotor).
    Answer (B) is incorrect. A database is an interconnected group of data elements. **Answer (C) is incorrect.** "Schema" is a term used in information technology to refer to the layout of a database.

58. The least complex outcome in the psychomotor domain is

    A. adaptation.

    B. mechanism.

    C. perception.

Answer (C) is correct. (FAA-H-8083-9B Chap 3)
    DISCUSSION: A taxonomy of educational objectives is a systematic classification scheme for sorting learning outcomes into the three domains of learning (cognitive, affective, and psychomotor) and ranking the desired outcomes in a developmental hierarchy from least complex to most complex. The least complex learning outcome in the psychomotor domain is perception in which the learner has awareness of sensory stimuli.
    Answer (A) is incorrect. Adaptation (in which the learner modifies his or her performance of a skill for special problems) is the second-most-complex, not the least complex, learning outcome in the psychomotor domain. **Answer (B) is incorrect.** Mechanism (in which the learner performs simple acts well) is the fourth-least-complex, not the least complex, learning outcome in the psychomotor domain.

59. Which of the following domains relates a grouping of levels of learning associated with a person's attitudes?

    A. Affective.

    B. Cognitive.

    C. Psychomotor.

Answer (A) is correct. (FAA-H-8083-9B Chap 3)
    DISCUSSION: The affective domain is a grouping of levels of learning associated with a person's attitudes, personal beliefs, and values, which range from receiving through responding, valuing, and organization to characterization.
    Answer (B) is incorrect. The cognitive domain is a grouping of levels of learning associated with mental activity. In order of increasing complexity, the domains are knowledge, comprehension, application, analysis, synthesis, and evaluation. **Answer (C) is incorrect.** The psychomotor domain is a grouping of levels of learning associated with physical skill levels, which range from perception through set, guided response, mechanism, complex overt response, and adaptation to origination.

60. An example of a skill involving the cognitive domain would be

    A. Understanding how the flight controls should be positioned during a turn.

    B. A positive reception for learning new skills.

    C. Performing a short-field approach and landing to Practical Test Standards/Airman Certification.

Answer (A) is correct. (FAA-H-8083-9B Chap 3)
    DISCUSSION: The cognitive domain includes remembering specific facts (content knowledge) and concepts that help develop intellectual abilities and skills, such as understanding how and why the flight controls should be positioned in a certain way.
    Answer (B) is incorrect. This answer choice best describes the affective domain. The affective domain addresses a learner's emotions toward the learning experience. It includes feelings, values, enthusiasms, motivations, and attitudes. **Answer (C) is incorrect.** This answer choice best describes the psychomotor domain. The psychomotor domain is skill-based and includes physical movement, coordination, and use of the motor-skill areas.

61. An example of a skill involving the psychomotor domain would be

   A. Responsiveness to an instructor's demonstration of steep turns.

   B. Applying back pressure to maintain altitude during a steep turn.

   C. Correlating pitch control inputs during a medium-bank with those of a steep turn.

Answer (B) is correct. (FAA-H-8083-9B Chap 3)
DISCUSSION: The psychomotor domain is skill-based and includes physical movement, coordination, and use of the motor-skill areas, such as physically manipulating the flight controls during a steep turn.
Answer (A) is incorrect. This answer choice best describes the affective domain. The affective domain addresses a learner's emotions toward the learning experience. It includes feelings, values, enthusiasms, motivations, and attitudes.
Answer (C) is incorrect. This answer choice best describes the cognitive domain. The cognitive domain includes remembering specific facts (content knowledge) and concepts that help develop intellectual abilities and skills.

62. Which of the following would be an example of a skill involving the psychomotor domain?

   A. Memorizing aircraft V-speeds.

   B. Computing takeoff distance over a 50 foot obstacle.

   C. Programming a Global Positioning System (GPS) receiver.

Answer (C) is correct. (FAA-H-8083-9B Chap 3)
DISCUSSION: The psychomotor domain is skill-based and includes physical movement, coordination, and use of the motor-skill areas. Development of these skills requires repetitive practice and is measured in terms of speed, precision, distance, and techniques. Skills involving the psychomotor domain include learning to fly a precision instrument approach procedure, programming a global positioning system (GPS) receiver, or using sophisticated maintenance equipment.

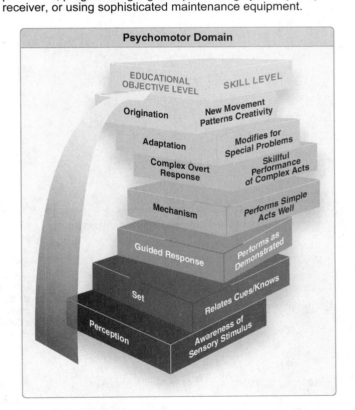

Answer (A) is incorrect. Skills in the psychomotor domain involve physical movement, coordination, and use of the motor-skill areas. Memorization is only the cognitive domain and does not encompass all seven educational objective levels.
Answer (B) is incorrect. Skills in the psychomotor domain involve physical movement, coordination, and use of the motor-skill areas. Computing a takeoff distance does not require physical movement or coordination and, therefore, does not require all seven education objective levels.

63. An example of a skill involving the affective domain would be

   A. Responding to an instructor's question.

   B. Recalling the information needed to answer an instructor's question.

   C. Practicing the conditions of an instructor's question to determine an answer.

Answer (A) is correct. (FAA-H-8083-9B Chap 3)
   DISCUSSION: The affective domain addresses a learner's emotions toward the learning experience. It includes feelings, values, enthusiasms, motivations, and attitudes, including responsiveness to instructor inquiries.
   Answer (B) is incorrect. This answer choice best describes the cognitive domain. The cognitive domain includes remembering specific facts (content knowledge) and concepts that help develop intellectual abilities and skills. **Answer (C) is incorrect.** This answer choice best describes the psychomotor domain. The psychomotor domain is skill-based and includes physical movement, coordination, and use of the motor-skill areas.

64. Which domain of learning includes physical movement and coordination?

   A. Affective.

   B. Cognitive.

   C. Psychomotor.

Answer (C) is correct. (FAA-H-8083-9B Chap 3)
   DISCUSSION: Domains of learning are classified based on what is to be learned. The psychomotor domain concerns physical skills (e.g., movement and coordination).
   Answer (A) is incorrect. The affective domain relates to attitudes, beliefs, and values, not physical skills. **Answer (B) is incorrect.** The cognitive domain deals with knowledge (e.g., facts, concepts, or relationships), not physical skills.

65. The educational objective levels; receiving, responding, valuing, organization, and characterization; are a part of which domain of learning?

   A. Psychomotor.

   B. Affective.

   C. Cognitive.

Answer (B) is correct. (FAA-H-8083-9B Chap 3)
   DISCUSSION: Each domain of learning has multiple educational objective levels that start with the least complex and end with the most complex. Receiving, responding, valuing, organization, and characterization are the five educational objective levels of the affective domain.
   Answer (A) is incorrect. The educational objective levels of the psychomotor domain are perception, set, guided response, mechanism, complex overt response, adaptation, and origination. **Answer (C) is incorrect.** The educational objective levels of the cognitive domain are knowledge, comprehension, application, analysis, synthesis, and evaluation.

66. The educational objective level of the psychomotor domain at which a learner's skill demonstrates new movement patterns and creativity is

   A. origination.

   B. complex overt response.

   C. adaptation.

Answer (A) is correct. (FAA-H-8083-9B Chap 3)
   DISCUSSION: Each educational objective level of the domains of learning has a distinct learning outcome. The learning outcome where a learner's skill demonstrates new movement patterns and creativity is equivalent to the origination educational objective level of the psychomotor domain.
   Answer (B) is incorrect. At the complex overt response educational objective level, the learner would demonstrate skillful performance of complex acts, not new movement patterns and creativity. **Answer (C) is incorrect.** At the adaptation educational objective level, the learner would demonstrate modifiers for special problems, not new movement patterns and creativity.

67. The least complex outcome in the cognitive domain is

   A. synthesis.

   B. knowledge.

   C. comprehension.

Answer (B) is correct. (FAA-H-8083-9B Chap 3)
   DISCUSSION: A taxonomy of educational objectives is a systematic classification scheme for sorting learning outcomes into three domains of learning (cognitive, affective, and psychomotor) and ranking the desired outcomes in a developmental hierarchy from least complex to most complex. The least complex learning outcome in the cognitive domain is knowledge where the learner has the capacity to recall and recognize facts, concepts, or relationships.
   Answer (A) is incorrect. Synthesis (in which the learner has the capacity to create new relationships) is the fifth most complex, not the least complex, learning outcome in the cognitive domain. **Answer (C) is incorrect.** Comprehension (in which the learner has the capacity to translate, interpret, and extrapolate) is the second most complex, not the least complex, learning outcome in the cognitive domain.

1.9 Learning Skills and the Learning Curve

68. The best way to prepare a learner to perform a task is to

- A. explain the purpose of the task.
- B. provide a clear, step-by-step example.
- C. give the learner an outline of the task.

Answer (B) is correct. (FAA-H-8083-9B Chap 3)
DISCUSSION: The best way to prepare a learner to perform a task is to provide a clear, step-by-step example. Having a model to follow permits a learner to get a clear picture of each step in the sequence (e.g., what it is, how to do it).
Answer (A) is incorrect. While a learner should know the purpose of a task, (s)he must be provided with a clear, step-by-step example showing how to perform the task. **Answer (C) is incorrect.** An outline is not as useful as a clear, step-by-step example.

69. During learning, a leveling-off process or plateau is

- A. normal and should be expected after an initial period of rapid improvement.
- B. normal and can be overcome with more practice.
- C. not normal and requires that the instructor reteach the lesson in a different format to ensure learner learning and retention.

Answer (A) is correct. (FAA-H-8083-9B Chap 3)
DISCUSSION: Learning plateaus are normal and should be expected after an initial period of rapid improvement.
Answer (B) is incorrect. Instructors should also be aware that they can bring on a learning plateau by over-practice. After repeating any task three or four times, give it a break to avoid causing a learning plateau. **Answer (C) is incorrect.** Learning plateaus are normal and can sometimes be alleviated by the instructor better explaining the lesson, the reason for the lesson, and how it applies to the learner. Reteaching lesson content is not necessary in the event of a learning plateau.

70. Which is true concerning "learning plateaus"?

- A. Learning plateaus are the direct result of poor instruction.
- B. Learning plateaus are a normal part of the learning process and tend to be temporary.
- C. Learning plateaus are caused by under-practice.

Answer (B) is correct. (FAA-H-8083-9B Chap 3)
DISCUSSION: Learning plateaus are a normal part of the learning process and tend to be temporary, but instructors and learners should be prepared for them to avoid discouragement.
Answer (A) is incorrect. Learning plateaus are normal, even in quality instruction. They often occur after a period of rapid improvement on the part of the learner. **Answer (C) is incorrect.** Learning plateaus can be caused by over-practice, not under-practice. After repeating any task three or four times, give it a break to avoid causing a learning plateau. Keep in mind that the apparent lack of increasing proficiency does not necessarily mean that learning has ceased.

71. Which stage of skill acquisition is characterized by the ability to perform a procedure rapidly and smoothly while devoting little deliberate attention to performance and simultaneously performing other tasks?

- A. Cognitive stage.
- B. Associative stage.
- C. Automatic response stage.

Answer (C) is correct. (FAA-H-8083-9B Chap 3)
DISCUSSION: By the automatic response stage, learner performance of the skill is rapid and smooth. The learner devotes much less deliberate attention to performance and may be able to carry on a conversation or perform other tasks while performing the skill.
Answer (A) is incorrect. There is a lack of understanding of the skill in the cognitive stage; thus, there can be no automatic performance of the skill by the learner. **Answer (B) is incorrect.** At the associative stage, the learner no longer performs a series of memorized steps but is able to assess his or her progress along the way and make adjustments in performance. There is, however, no smooth or rapid skill performance associated with this stage.

72. Studies of skill learning suggest that a learner achieves better results if distractions are avoided during what type of practice?

- A. Deliberate practice.
- B. Blocked practice.
- C. Random practice.

Answer (A) is correct. (FAA-H-8083-9B Chap 3)
DISCUSSION: During deliberate practice, the learner practices specific areas for improvement and receives specific feedback after practice. Studies of skill learning suggest a learner achieves better results if distractions are avoided during deliberate practice. When feedback is needed to correct learner performance, it should be brief and explicit.
Answer (B) is incorrect. Using distractions during blocked practice can actually be helpful in preventing learner and instructor from falsely determining that repeated skills have been well learned. **Answer (C) is incorrect.** Random practice relies heavily on the incorporation of distractions to mix up the skills to be acquired throughout the practice session. This type of practice leads to better retention because performing a series of separate skills in a random order helps the learner recognize the similarities and differences of each skill.

73. A learning plateau may be defined as the

    A. leveling-off in learning at the point which a learner has reached the highest competence of a particular subject.

    B. gradual decrease in learning almost to the point where it appears to have ceased before it resumes and proficiency increases.

    C. point in the learning curve at which skill proficiency retrogresses.

Answer (B) is correct. (FAA-H-8083-9B Chap 3)
    DISCUSSION: A learning plateau may be defined as the gradual decrease in learning rate. This is normal and should be expected by the instructor and learner after an initial period of rapid improvement. Note that the apparent lack of increasing proficiency does not necessarily mean that learning has ceased.
    Answer (A) is incorrect. A learning plateau is the leveling-off of an individual's rate of learning, usually after a period of rapid improvement, not after reaching the highest competence of a particular subject. **Answer (C) is incorrect.** A learning plateau is a gradual decrease in learning rate almost to the point where it appears to have ceased before it resumes and proficiency increases, not retrogresses.

74. Instructors can help learners who arrive at a learning plateau by

    A. Continuing practice to help the learner move past it.

    B. Assuming that the plateau represents the learner's maximum skill achievement.

    C. Moving the learner to a different place in the curriculum.

Answer (C) is correct. (FAA-H-8083-9B Chap 3)
    DISCUSSION: Instructors can help learners who fall into a learning plateau by moving them to a different place in the curriculum and giving the current task a break. Learning plateau problems can sometimes also be alleviated by the instructor better explaining the lesson, the reason for the lesson, and how it applies to the learner.
    Answer (A) is incorrect. Rather than treating a learning plateau, overpractice can actually create one. After repeating any task three or four times, give it a break to avoid causing a learning plateau. **Answer (B) is incorrect.** Keep in mind that the apparent lack of increasing proficiency does not necessarily mean that learning has ceased. The point is that, in learning motor skills, a leveling-off process, or plateau, is normal and should be expected after an initial period of rapid improvement.

75. Which stage of skill acquisition may be characterized by performing memorized steps unaware of progress?

    A. Cognitive stage.

    B. Associative stage.

    C. Automatic response stage.

Answer (A) is correct. (FAA-H-8083-9B Chap 3)
    DISCUSSION: In the cognitive stage, learning has a basis in factual knowledge. Since the learner has no prior knowledge of flying, the instructor first introduces him or her to a basic skill. The learner then memorizes the steps required to perform the skill. As the learner carries out these memorized steps, (s)he is often unaware of progress or may fixate on one aspect of performance. Performance is deliberate and often characterized by the learner making many abrupt control inputs.
    Answer (B) is incorrect. At the associative stage, the learner no longer performs a series of memorized steps but is able to assess his or her progress along the way and make adjustments in performance. **Answer (C) is incorrect.** By the automatic response stage, learner performance of the skill is rapid and smooth. The learner devotes much less deliberate attention to performance and may be able to carry on a conversation or perform other tasks while performing a skill.

76. If a learner can fly an ILS while communicating with ATC at the same time, (s)he has reached which stage of skill acquisition?

    A. Associative stage.

    B. Automatic response stage.

    C. Psychomotor stage.

Answer (B) is correct. (FAA-H-8083-9B Chap 3)
    DISCUSSION: As procedures become automatic, less attention is required to carry them out, so it is possible to do other things simultaneously, or at least do other things more comfortably. By the automatic response stage, learner performance of the skill is rapid and smooth.
    Answer (A) is incorrect. Even demonstrating how to do something does not result in the learner learning the skill. Practice is necessary in order to learn how to coordinate muscles with visual and tactile senses. Learning to perform various aircraft maintenance skills or flight maneuvers requires practice. Another benefit of practice is that as the learner gains proficiency in a skill, verbal instructions become more meaningful. A long, detailed explanation is confusing before the learner begins performing, whereas specific comments are more meaningful and useful after the skill has been partially mastered. **Answer (C) is incorrect.** As the storage of a skill via practice continues, the learner associates individual steps in performance with likely outcomes. The learner no longer performs a series of memorized steps but is able to assess his or her progress along the way and make adjustments in performance. Performing the skill still requires deliberate attention, but the learner is better able to deal with distractions.

77. The three stages of skill acquisition are

    A. cognitive, associative, and automatic.

    B. cognitive, understanding, and automatic.

    C. cognitive, additional, and automatic.

Answer (A) is correct. (FAA-H-8083-9B Chap 3)
    DISCUSSION: The three stages of skill acquisition are cognitive, associative, and automatic.
    Answer (B) is incorrect. Understanding is not one of the three stages of skill acquisition. **Answer (C) is incorrect.** The three stages of skill acquisition are cognitive, associative, and automatic.

78. Which stage of skill acquisition may be characterized by learner ability to assess personal progress and make adjustments in performance?

    A. Cognitive stage.

    B. Associative stage.

    C. Automatic response stage.

Answer (B) is correct. (FAA-H-8083-9B Chap 3)
    DISCUSSION: As the storage of a skill continues due to practice, the learner associates individual steps in performance with likely outcomes. The learner no longer performs a series of memorized steps but is able to assess his or her progress along the way and make adjustments in performance.
    Answer (A) is incorrect. Cognitive learning has a basis in factual knowledge. Since the learner has no prior knowledge of flying, the instructor first introduces him or her to a basic skill. The learner then memorizes the steps required to perform the skill. As the learner carries out these memorized steps, (s)he is often unaware of progress or may fixate on one aspect of performance. **Answer (C) is incorrect.** While learner performance assessment exists in the automatic response stage, it is not the characterizing trait. The characterizing trait of the automatic response stage is that a learner performs automatically, even instinctively, to flight tasks. The learner devotes far less deliberate attention to performing the task.

79. Distractions can be used as a valuable learning tool, but they should be avoided during

    A. deliberate practice.

    B. blocked practice.

    C. random practice.

Answer (A) is correct. (FAA-H-8083-9B Chap 3)
    DISCUSSION: In order for a learner to gain skill knowledge and learn how to perform the skill on the automatic level, (s)he must engage in deliberate practice. Studies of skill learning suggest a learner achieves better results if distractions are avoided during deliberate practice. When feedback is needed to correct learner performance, it should be brief and explicit.
    Answer (B) is incorrect. Blocked practice is practicing the same drill until the movement becomes automatic. The *Aviation Instructor's Handbook* does not specifically state distractions should be avoided during blocked practice. **Answer (C) is incorrect.** Random practice mixes up the skills to be acquired throughout the practice session. The *Aviation Instructor's Handbook* does not specifically state distractions should be avoided during random practice.

80. Distractions interjected by instructors during training may help

    A. learners learn to ignore distractions.

    B. learners determine whether or not a distraction warrants further attention or action on their part.

    C. learners learn more effective multitasking techniques.

Answer (B) is correct. (FAA-H-8083-9B Chap 3)
    DISCUSSION: A distraction is an unexpected event that causes the learner's attention to be momentarily diverted. Learners must learn to decide whether or not a distraction warrants further attention or action on their part. Once this has been decided, the learners must either turn their attention back to what they were doing or act on the distraction.
    Answer (A) is incorrect. Not all in-flight distractions should be ignored. Some require immediate action on the part of the pilot. **Answer (C) is incorrect.** Multitasking is not a strategy for identifying and prioritizing distractions during flight.

81. What type of practice is repeating the same drill or doing the same task again and again until the movement becomes automatic?

    A. Deliberate.

    B. Blocked.

    C. Random.

Answer (B) is correct. (FAA-H-8083-9B Chap 3)
    DISCUSSION: Blocked practice is practicing the same drill until the movement becomes automatic. Doing the same task over and over leads to better short-term performance but poorer long-term learning.
    Answer (A) is incorrect. In order for a learner to gain skill knowledge and learn how to perform the skill on the automatic level, a learner must engage in deliberate practice. However, this type of practice in and of itself does not produce the ability to perform skills automatically. **Answer (C) is incorrect.** Random practice mixes up the skills to be acquired throughout the practice session to increase long-term skill retention. This practice type is not effective at producing automatic responses, but rather more meaningful ones.

Gleim Basic Aviation Training Device (BATD)

Powerful, FAA-Approved Flight Simulation

An affordable, turn-key flight training device designed by pilots for pilots. Log time toward your pilot certificate, instrument rating, or instrument currency in the comfort of your own home or office. Switch the fully functional touchscreen instrument panel to your panel of choice with a click of a button.

✈ Comfortable and adjustable racing style seat

✈ Standard triple-monitor, 180° panoramic view

✈ Includes the Gleim X-Plane Flight Training Course

✈ Independent Instructor Operating Station (IOS)

✈ Heavy-duty steel frame construction

STUDY UNIT TWO

BARRIERS TO LEARNING

(6 pages of outline)

2.1 SELF-CONCEPT

1.   Self-concept is how one pictures oneself.

   a.   Self-concept or self-image can be described in terms such as "confident" or "insecure."

      1)   "Confident" denotes a favorable view of self, or positive self-concept.
      2)   "Insecure" denotes an unfavorable view of self, or negative self-concept.

   b.   This is a powerful determinant in learning.

   c.   Self-concept has a great influence on the total perceptual process.

2.   If a learner's experiences tend to support a favorable self-image, the learner tends to remain receptive to subsequent experiences. These learners are less defensive and more receptive to new experiences, instructions, and demonstrations.

3.   Negative self-concept contributes most to a learner's failure to remain receptive to new experiences and creates a tendency to reject additional training.

4.   Instructors must be able to detect negative self-image in their learners and strive to prevent these feelings from undermining the instructional process.

   a.   An instructor can foster the development of insights by helping the learner acquire and maintain a favorable self-concept.

      1)   The way instructors conduct themselves, their own positive attitudes, and the manner in which they instruct can help their learners achieve this positive view.

         a)   EXAMPLE: During an introductory flight with a potential flight learner, the instructor does not focus on emergency procedures or potential hazards to flight, but instead emphasizes how smooth, efficient, and enjoyable the flight was.

2.2 DEFENSE MECHANISMS

1. Certain behavior patterns are called defense mechanisms because they are subconscious defenses against the reality of unpleasant situations.

    a. People use these defenses to soften feelings of failure, alleviate feelings of guilt, and protect feelings of personal worth and adequacy.

2. Although defense mechanisms can serve a useful purpose, they can involve some degree of self-deception and distortion of reality.

    a. They alleviate symptoms, not causes.

3. Common defense mechanisms:

    a. **Repression** – A person places uncomfortable thoughts into inaccessible areas of the unconscious mind. For example, a learner pilot may have a repressed fear of flying that inhibits his or her ability to learn how to fly.

        1) Things a person is unable to cope with at present are pushed away to be dealt with at another time, or hopefully never to be dealt with because they faded away on their own accord.

        2) The level of repression can vary from temporarily forgetting an uncomfortable thought to amnesia, where the events that triggered the anxiety are deeply buried.

        3) Repressed memories do not disappear and may reappear in dreams or slips of the tongue ("Freudian slips").

    b. **Denial** – Refusal to accept external reality because it is too threatening. It is the refusal to acknowledge what has happened, is happening, or will happen.

        1) Denial is a form of repression through which stressful thoughts are banned from memory.

        2) Related to denial is minimization. When a person minimizes something, (s)he accepts what happened, but in a diluted form, usually justifying the event because "nothing bad happened."

    c. **Compensation** – Process of psychologically counterbalancing perceived weaknesses by emphasizing strength in other areas.

        1) Learners often attempt to disguise the presence of a weak or undesirable quality by emphasizing a more positive one.

        2) Compensation involves substituting success in a realm of life other than the realm in which the person suffers a weakness.

    d.   **Projection** – An individual places his or her own unacceptable impulses onto someone else. A person relegates the blame for personal shortcomings, mistakes, and transgressions to others.

        1)   A learner pilot who fails a flight exam and says, "I failed because I had a poor examiner" believes the failure was not due to his or her lack of personal skill or knowledge.

        2)   This learner projects blame onto an "unfair" examiner or inadequate instruction by their CFI.

    e.   **Rationalization** – When a person cannot accept the real reasons for his or her own behavior, this device permits the substitution of excuses for reasons. Rationalization is a subconscious technique for justifying actions that otherwise would be unacceptable.

    f.   **Reaction formation** – A person fakes a belief opposite to his or her true belief because the true belief causes anxiety. The person feels an urge to do or say something and then actually does or says something that is the opposite of what (s)he really wants.

    g.   **Fantasy** – Occurs when a learner engages in daydreams about how things should be rather than doing anything about how things are. The learner uses his or her imagination to escape from reality into a fictitious world–a world of success or pleasure.

        1)   Fantasy provides a simple and satisfying escape from problems, but if a learner gets sufficient satisfaction from daydreaming, (s)he may stop trying to achieve goals altogether.

        2)   Lost in the fantasy, the learner spends more time dreaming about being a successful pilot than working toward the goal.

        3)   When carried to extremes, the worlds of fantasy and reality can become so confused that the dreamer cannot distinguish one from the other.

    h.   **Displacement** – Results in an unconscious shift of emotion, affect, or desire from the original object to a more acceptable, less threatening substitute.

        1)   Displacement avoids the risk associated with feeling unpleasant emotions and puts them somewhere other than where they belong, similar to repression.

2.3 STRESS, ANXIETY, AND FATIGUE

1. Normal individuals react to stress by responding rapidly and exactly, often automatically, within their experience and training.

    a. This underlines the need for proper training prior to emergency situations.

    b. The effective individual thinks rapidly, acts rapidly, and is extremely sensitive to his or her surroundings.

2. Abnormal reactions to stress may result in inadequate, illogical, or random responses. These may include

    a. Inappropriate reactions, such as extreme overcooperation, painstaking self-control, inappropriate laughter or singing, and very rapid changes in emotion

    b. Marked changes in mood (e.g., high spirits followed by deep depression)

    c. Severe, unreasonable anger toward the flight instructor, service personnel, or others

3. Anxiety is a feeling of worry, nervousness, or unease, often about something that is going to happen, typically something with an uncertain outcome. It results from the fear of anything, real or imagined, which threatens the person who experiences it, and may have a potent effect on actions and the ability to learn from perceptions.

    a. Anxiety is probably the most significant psychological barrier affecting flight instruction. It is the extreme worry brought on by stressful situations (e.g., an emergency, an exam, etc.). Anxiety can be countered by

        1) Treating fears as a normal reaction rather than ignoring them,
        2) Reinforcing the learner's enjoyment of flying, and
        3) Teaching learners to cope with fears.

4. Fatigue is one of the most treacherous hazards to flight safety as it may not be apparent to a pilot until serious errors are made. Fatigue can be either acute (short-term) or chronic (long-term).

    a. **Acute fatigue**, a normal occurrence of everyday living, is the tiredness felt after long periods of physical and mental strain, including strenuous muscular effort, immobility, heavy mental workload, strong emotional pressure, monotony, and lack of sleep.

        1) A CFI who is familiar with the signs indicative of acute fatigue will be more aware if the learner is experiencing them, as the signs of acute fatigue are often apparent to others before the individual notices any signs of fatigue.

        2) Acute fatigue is characterized by

            a) Inattention
            b) Distractibility
            c) Errors in timing
            d) Neglect of secondary tasks
            e) Loss of accuracy and control
            f) Lack of awareness of error accumulation
            g) Irritability

b. **Chronic fatigue** is a combination of both physiological problems and psychological issues and occurs when there is not enough time for a full recovery from repeated episodes of acute fatigue.

    1) Without resolution, human performance continues to fall off, judgment becomes impaired, and unwarranted risks may be taken.

    2) Recovery from chronic fatigue requires a prolonged and deliberate solution.

        a) Chronic fatigue's underlying cause is generally not "rest-related" and may have deeper points of origin. Therefore, rest alone may not resolve chronic fatigue.

            i) Psychological problems such as financial, home life, or job-related stresses cause a lack of quality rest that is only solved by mitigating the underlying problems before the fatigue is solved.

2.4 THE OVERCONFIDENT OR IMPATIENT LEARNER

1. Because they make few mistakes, those who are fast learners may assume that the correction of errors is unimportant.

    a. This overconfidence soon results in faulty performance.

    b. For apt learners, a good instructor will constantly raise the standard of performance for each lesson, demanding greater effort.

2. Impatience is a greater deterrent to learning pilot skills than is generally recognized. For example, a learner may have a strong desire to make an early solo flight or to start on cross-country flights before the basics of flight, navigation, and communications have been learned.

    a. The impatient learner fails to understand the need for preliminary training. (S)he seeks only the final objective without considering the means necessary to reach it.

    b. Instructors can correct impatience by presenting the necessary preliminary training one step at a time, with clearly stated goals for each step.

        1) Instructors should emphasize that it is necessary to master the basics if the entire task is to be performed competently and safely.

    c. Impatience can result from instruction set at the pace of a slow learner when it is applied to a motivated, fast learner.

        1) It is important that an instructor analyze each learner's ability and adapt lessons accordingly to counteract this trait.

3. Adult learners have a wealth of life experience that can be tapped by an effective instructor. They often are self-directed and autonomous and may exhibit the need to be independent and exercise control.

    a. Instructors should

        1) Help learners integrate new ideas with what they already know to ensure they keep and use the new information and

        2) Recognize learners' need to control pace and start/stop time.

2.5 ERRORS

1.   Instructors and learners are vulnerable to occasional errors that naturally occur as a byproduct of human performance. An understanding of errors provides insight into how errors can be minimized.

2.   There are two main types of error:

   a.   **Mistakes** occur when an individual plans to do the incorrect thing and is successful.

     1)   Mistakes are errors of thought and are sometimes the result of gaps or misconceptions in the learner's understanding.

   b.   **Slips** occur when an individual plans to do one thing but inadvertently does something else.

3.   Ways to reduce errors:

   a.   **Learning and practice** are the best tools against errors, and higher skill and knowledge levels are associated with lower error occurrence.

   b.   **Taking time** to work deliberately at a comfortable pace can mitigate errors.

   c.   **Checking for errors**, to catch potential errors, is critical.

   d.   **Using reminders** such as checklists can reduce the potential for errors.

   e.   **Developing routines** or standardized procedures can significantly reduce error occurrence.

   f.   **Raising awareness** of the environment can reduce susceptibility to error.

QUESTIONS AND ANSWER EXPLANATIONS: All of the Fundamentals of Instructing knowledge test questions chosen by the FAA for release as well as additional questions selected by Gleim relating to the material in the previous outlines are provided on the following pages. These questions have been organized into the same subunits as the outlines. To the immediate right of each question are the correct answer and answer explanations. You should cover these answers and answer explanations while responding to the questions. Refer to the general discussion in the Introduction on how to take the FAA knowledge test.

Remember that the questions from the FAA knowledge test bank have been reordered by topic and organized into a meaningful sequence. Also, the first line of the answer explanation gives the citation of the authoritative source for the answer.

QUESTIONS

2.1 Self-Concept

1. The factor which contributes most to a learner's failure to remain receptive to new experiences and which creates a tendency to reject additional training is

    A. basic needs.

    B. element of threat.

    C. negative self-concept.

Answer (C) is correct. (FAA-H-8083-9B Chap 3)
    DISCUSSION: A learner with a negative self-concept is resistant to new experiences and may reject additional training. People tend to avoid experiences that contradict their self-concept.
    Answer (A) is incorrect. A learner's basic needs can be used by the instructor to promote learning. For instance, personal safety is one of the most important basic needs, and aviation training heavily emphasizes this need. **Answer (B) is incorrect.** An element of threat will cause a learner to limit his or her attention to the threatening object or condition. Once this is removed, the learner will be able to learn.

2. An instructor may foster the development of insights by

    A. helping the learner acquire and maintain a favorable self-concept.

    B. pointing out the attractive features of the activity to be learned.

    C. keeping the rate of learning consistent so that it is predictable.

Answer (A) is correct. (FAA-H-8083-9B Chap 3)
    DISCUSSION: Especially in a field such as aviation training, the instructor can foster the development of insights by helping the learner acquire and maintain a favorable self-concept. The learner who feels sure of his or her knowledge, skills, and judgments learned in class will also feel better about actual performance and his or her own ability to fly.
    Answer (B) is incorrect. The attractive features in a learning situation tend to increase motivation rather than insight. **Answer (C) is incorrect.** Learning rates will vary, not stay constant, with each training lesson.

3. What is an outcome of a learner showing a favorable self-concept?

    A. A more receptive attitude to experiences.

    B. Failure to remain open to new learning experiences.

    C. A positive attitude on the part of the flight instructor.

Answer (A) is correct. (FAA-H-8083-9B Chap 3)
    DISCUSSION: Learners with a favorable self-concept will be more receptive to subsequent experiences. Learners who show favorable self-concept are less defensive and more receptive to new experiences, instructions, and demonstrations.
    Answer (B) is incorrect. Failure to remain open to new learning experiences is a result of an unfavorable view of self, or negative self-concept. **Answer (C) is incorrect.** An outcome of a learner's favorable self-concept will not guarantee that a positive attitude will be shown by the instructor. However, the way in which instructors conduct themselves, and their own positive attitudes, can help their learners achieve this same positive view.

4. Which term denotes a favorable view of self?

    A. Insecure.

    B. Unassured.

    C. Confident.

Answer (C) is correct. (FAA-H-8083-9B Chap 3)
    DISCUSSION: Being confident denotes a favorable view of self, or positive self-concept.
    Answer (A) is incorrect. The term "insecure" denotes an unfavorable view of self, or negative self-concept. **Answer (B) is incorrect.** The term "unassured" is similar to the term "insecure" and portrays a negative view of self.

2.2 Defense Mechanisms

5. Defense mechanisms

- A. are subject to the learner's normal behavioral processes.
- B. are related to the conscious domain.
- C. involve some degree of self-deception and distortion of reality.

Answer (C) is correct. (FAA-H-8083-9B Chap 2)
DISCUSSION: Defense mechanisms involve some degree of self-deception and distortion of reality. They alleviate the symptoms but not the causes. Defense mechanisms do not solve problems. Moreover, because defense mechanisms operate on an unconscious level, they are not subject to normal conscious checks and balances.
Answer (A) is incorrect. Defense mechanisms occur on a subconscious level and are thus not subject to the learner's normal behavioral processes. **Answer (B) is incorrect.** Defense mechanisms are not related to the conscious domain.

6. Although defense mechanisms can serve a useful purpose, they can

- A. provide feelings of adequacy.
- B. alleviate the cause of problems.
- C. involve some degree of self-deception and distortion of reality.

Answer (C) is correct. (FAA-H-8083-9B Chap 2)
DISCUSSION: Although defense mechanisms can serve a useful purpose, they can also be hindrances. Because they involve some self-deception and distortion of reality, defense mechanisms do not solve problems.
Answer (A) is incorrect. Defense mechanisms mask and protect feelings of adequacy rather than provide them. **Answer (B) is incorrect.** Defense mechanisms alleviate symptoms, not causes, of problems.

7. If an instructor has a learner with a hidden fear of flying that inhibits learning, the learner is most likely displaying which defense mechanism?

- A. Reaction formation.
- B. Repression.
- C. Projection.

Answer (B) is correct. (FAA-H-8083-9B Chap 2)
DISCUSSION: Repression is the defense mechanism whereby a person places uncomfortable thoughts into inaccessible areas of the unconscious mind.
Answer (A) is incorrect. In reaction formation, a person fakes a belief opposite to the true belief because the true belief causes anxiety. **Answer (C) is incorrect.** Through projection, an individual places his or her own unacceptable impulses onto someone else.

8. When a learner uses excuses to justify inadequate performance, it is an indication of the defense mechanism known as

- A. fantasy.
- B. displacement.
- C. rationalization.

Answer (C) is correct. (FAA-H-8083-9B Chap 2)
DISCUSSION: Rationalization is a subconscious technique for justifying unacceptable actions or performance. This allows a learner to substitute excuses for reasons and make those excuses plausible and acceptable to themselves.
Answer (A) is incorrect. Fantasy is the defense mechanism in which the learner escapes (either physically or mentally) from a frustrating experience. **Answer (B) is incorrect.** Displacement is the defense mechanism in which the learner shifts emotion, affect, or desire from the original object to a more acceptable, less threatening substitute.

9. Fantasy is a defense mechanism learners use when they

- A. want to escape from frustrating situations.
- B. cannot accept the real reasons for their behavior.
- C. place blame on someone or something other than themselves.

Answer (A) is correct. (FAA-H-8083-9B Chap 2)
DISCUSSION: The defense mechanism of flight allows a learner to escape from a frustrating situation. This escape can be physical flight (absenteeism, illness, etc.) or mental flight (daydreaming).
Answer (B) is incorrect. If a learner cannot accept the real reasons for his or her behavior, (s)he may rationalize, not take flight. **Answer (C) is incorrect.** Learners who place blame on someone or something other than themselves are displaying the defense mechanism of projection.

10. Learners may display the defense mechanism called denial, which is revealed by the learner's

- A. hostility.
- B. attempts to minimize the situation.
- C. attempts at rationalization.

Answer (B) is correct. (FAA-H-8083-9B Chap 2)
DISCUSSION: Minimization is related to denial. When a person minimizes something, (s)he accepts what happened but in a diluted form.
Answer (A) is incorrect. Aggression is not associated with the defense mechanism of denial. **Answer (C) is incorrect.** Rationalization is the process of justifying a course of action, not denying it.

11. When learners subconsciously use the defense mechanism called rationalization, they

A. use excuses to justify acceptable behavior.

B. cannot accept the real reasons for their behavior.

C. fake a belief opposite to their true belief because the true belief causes anxiety.

Answer (B) is correct. *(FAA-H-8083-9B Chap 2)*
DISCUSSION: Rationalization is a subconscious technique for justifying unacceptable actions or performance. This allows learners to substitute excuses for reasons and make those excuses plausible and acceptable to themselves.
Answer (A) is incorrect. In rationalization, excuses are used to justify unacceptable, not acceptable, behavior.
Answer (C) is incorrect. When learners fake a belief opposite to their true belief, they are displaying the defense mechanism of reaction formation. This is done because their true belief causes them anxiety.

12. When a learner engages in daydreaming, it is the defense mechanism of

A. compensation.

B. fantasy.

C. denial.

Answer (B) is correct. *(FAA-H-8083-9B Chap 2)*
DISCUSSION: A learner engaging in daydreaming is an example of fantasy or mental escape.
Answer (A) is incorrect. Through compensation, learners often attempt to disguise the presence of a weak or undesirable quality by emphasizing a more positive one. **Answer (C) is incorrect.** Denial is a refusal to accept external reality because it is too threatening. It is the refusal to acknowledge what has happened, is happening, or will happen.

13. When learners display the defense mechanism called repression, they

A. refuse to accept reality.

B. place uncomfortable thoughts into inaccessible areas of the unconscious mind.

C. attempt to justify actions by asking numerous questions.

Answer (B) is correct. *(FAA-H-8083-9B Chap 2)*
DISCUSSION: In repression, things a person is unable to cope with in the present are pushed away to be dealt with at another time, or hopefully never to be dealt with at all because they faded away on their own accord.
Answer (A) is incorrect. When learners refuse to accept reality, they are exhibiting the defense mechanism of denial.
Answer (C) is incorrect. Attempting to justify actions is an example of rationalization.

14. Which term is used to describe why a person pushes a memory out of reach because that person does not want to remember the feelings associated with it?

A. Compensation.

B. Regression.

C. Repression.

Answer (C) is correct. *(FAA-H-8083-9B Chap 2)*
DISCUSSION: Repression is the defense mechanism describing an individual placing uncomfortable thoughts out of reach and into inaccessible areas of the unconscious mind.
Answer (A) is incorrect. Compensation best describes an individual's tendency to attempt to disguise the presence of a weak or undesirable quality by emphasizing a more positive one. **Answer (B) is incorrect.** Regression, as it pertains to defense mechanisms, describes an individual inadequately coping with stressors by demonstrating immature, and often inappropriate, responses through helplessness and dependency.

15. When a learner presents a belief opposite to what (s)he truly believes, it usually is an indication of the defense mechanism known as

A. fantasy.

B. reaction formation.

C. displacement.

Answer (B) is correct. *(FAA-H-8083-9B Chap 2)*
DISCUSSION: In reaction formation, a person fakes a belief opposite to his or her true belief because the true belief causes anxiety.
Answer (A) is incorrect. Fantasy is the defense mechanism when a person mentally removes himself or herself from a frustrating situation. **Answer (C) is incorrect.** Displacement is the defense mechanism in which the learner shifts emotion, affect, or desire from the original object to a more acceptable, less threatening substitute.

16. When a learner attempts to disguise the presence of a weak or undesirable quality by emphasizing a more positive one, the defense mechanism is usually in the form of

A. projection.

B. compensation.

C. rationalization.

Answer (B) is correct. *(FAA-H-8083-9B Chap 2)*
DISCUSSION: Compensation is a process of psychologically counterbalancing perceived weaknesses by emphasizing strength in other areas.
Answer (A) is incorrect. Through projection, an individual places blame for his or her own unacceptable impulses onto someone else. **Answer (C) is incorrect.** Rationalization is a process of making excuses for unacceptable behavior.

17. Which defense mechanism is displayed when a learner performs poorly on a test and justifies the poor grade by claiming there was not enough time to learn the required information but did not take advantage of a computerized pre-test offered by the instructor?

    A. Displacement.

    B. Reaction formation.

    C. Rationalization.

Answer (C) is correct. (FAA-H-8083-9B Chap 2)
    DISCUSSION: The subconscious technique of rationalization is the defense mechanism displayed when a learner justifies a poor grade in this manner. Learners are often sincere in this rationalization and fail to recognize that the pre-test is provided as an assistance to success.
    Answer (A) is incorrect. Displacement refers to avoiding the risks associated with unpleasant emotional feelings and putting them somewhere other than where they belong. **Answer (B) is incorrect.** Reaction formation is a defense mechanism whereby the learner fakes a belief opposite to a true belief because acknowledgment of the true belief is a source of anxiety.

18. A learner pilot who fails a practical test and attributes the failure to an "unfair" evaluation by the examiner may be demonstrating a defense mechanism known as

    A. Rationalization.

    B. Projection.

    C. Denial.

Answer (B) is correct. (FAA-H-8083-9B Chap 2)
    DISCUSSION: Through projection, an individual places his or her own unacceptable impulses onto someone else. A person relegates the blame for personal shortcomings, mistakes, and transgressions to others.
    Answer (A) is incorrect. Rationalization is a subconscious technique for justifying actions that otherwise would be unacceptable. It does not involve the placement of blame on any other party. **Answer (C) is incorrect.** Denial is a refusal to accept external reality because it is too threatening. It does not involve the placement of blame on any other party.

2.3 Stress, Anxiety, and Fatigue

19. When under stress, normal individuals usually react

    A. by showing excellent morale followed by deep depression.

    B. by responding rapidly and exactly, often automatically, within the limits of their experience and training.

    C. inappropriately such as extreme overcooperation, painstaking self-control, and inappropriate laughing or singing.

Answer (B) is correct. (FAA-H-8083-9B Chap 2)
    DISCUSSION: When under stress, normal individuals begin to respond rapidly and exactly, within the limits of their experience and training. Many responses are automatic, which indicates the need for proper training in emergency operations prior to an actual emergency.
    Answer (A) is incorrect. Marked changes in mood, e.g., excellent morale followed by deep depression is an abnormal, not a normal, reaction to stress. **Answer (C) is incorrect.** Inappropriate reactions, such as extreme overcooperation, painstaking self-control, and inappropriate laughter or singing, are abnormal, not normal, reactions to stress.

20. A learner reacting abnormally to stress is most likely to display which of the following indications?

    A. The learner is using automatic responses.

    B. The learner has a rapid and exacting response.

    C. The learner is using inadequate, illogical, random responses or no response at all.

Answer (C) is correct. (FAA-H-8083-9B Chap 2)
    DISCUSSION: The following learner reactions are indicative of abnormal reactions to stress. None of them provides an absolute indication, but the presence of any of them under conditions of stress is reason for careful instructor evaluation. Instructors should look for inappropriate reactions, such as extreme over-cooperation, painstaking self-control, inappropriate laughter or singing, and very rapid changes in emotions. Marked changes in mood on different lessons, such as excellent morale followed by deep depression and severe anger directed toward the flight instructor, service personnel, and others are warning signs of unusual reactions to stress.
    Answer (A) is incorrect. A learner using automatic responses is a normal reaction to stress. **Answer (B) is incorrect.** A rapid and exacting response is a normal reaction to stress.

21. Which would most likely be an indication that a learner is reacting abnormally to stress?

    A. Slow learning.

    B. Inappropriate laughter or singing.

    C. Automatic response to a given situation.

Answer (B) is correct. (FAA-H-8083-9B Chap 2)
    DISCUSSION: Inappropriate laughter or singing is an abnormal reaction to stress. The instructor should be alert for other inappropriate (and possibly dangerous) reactions.
    Answer (A) is incorrect. Slow learning is a normal, not an abnormal, reaction to stress. **Answer (C) is incorrect.** Automatic response to a given situation is a normal, not an abnormal, reaction to stress.

22. One possible indication of a learner's abnormal reaction to stress would be

   A. a hesitancy to act.

   B. extreme overcooperation.

   C. a noticeable lack of self-control.

Answer (B) is correct. (FAA-H-8083-9B Chap 2)
   DISCUSSION: Extreme overcooperation is an indication that a learner is reacting abnormally to stress. The abnormally tense or anxious learner may be noticeably over-agreeable.
   Answer (A) is incorrect. A hesitancy to act is an indication of anxiety, not an abnormal reaction to stress. **Answer (C) is incorrect.** Painstaking self-control, not a lack thereof, is an indication of an abnormal reaction to stress.

23. The instructor can counteract anxiety in a learner by

   A. treating the learner's fears as a normal reaction.

   B. discontinuing instruction in tasks that cause anxiety.

   C. allowing the learner to decide when he or she is ready for a new maneuver to be introduced.

Answer (A) is correct. (FAA-H-8083-9B Chap 2)
   DISCUSSION: Psychologists tell us that a learner's fear is a normal reaction and should be treated as such by an instructor. Treating fear as normal will help in counteracting anxiety.
   Answer (B) is incorrect. Discontinuing instruction in stressful tasks will not help the learner to overcome the anxiety. Perhaps a different approach to the task is necessary. **Answer (C) is incorrect.** It describes an example of negative motivation, which would tend to contribute to the learner's anxiety.

24. Which of the following is required to recover from chronic fatigue?

   A. Mitigating the underlying physiological and psychological causes.

   B. A break in instruction and practice.

   C. Proper rest and time to "clear your thoughts."

Answer (A) is correct. (FAA-H-8083-9B Chap 2)
   DISCUSSION: The underlying cause of chronic fatigue is generally not rest-related and may have deeper points of origin. Psychological problems such as financial, home life, or job-related stresses are some examples. Mitigating the underlying problems is essential before the fatigue issue can be solved.
   Answer (B) is incorrect. Chronic fatigue is only solved by mitigating the underlying problems that are causing the fatigue. **Answer (C) is incorrect.** Chronic fatigue is only solved by mitigating the underlying problems that are causing the fatigue.

25. The principal reason why fatigue is one of the most treacherous hazards to flight safety is that

   A. fatigue can overtake even a physically robust person.

   B. it is usually impossible for a CFI to detect learner fatigue early in a lesson.

   C. it may not be apparent to a pilot until serious errors are made.

Answer (C) is correct. (FAA-H-8083-9B Chap 2)
   DISCUSSION: Fatigue is one of the most treacherous hazards to flight safety because it may not be apparent to a pilot until serious errors are made.
   Answer (A) is incorrect. Although it is true that fatigue can overtake even a physically robust person, this is not the principal reason why it is such a treacherous hazard. **Answer (B) is incorrect.** It is important for a CFI to be able to detect fatigue, both in assessing a learner's substandard performance early in a lesson and in recognizing the deterioration of performance.

26. Chronic fatigue

   A. Occurs when there is not enough time for a full recovery from repeated episodes of acute fatigue.

   B. Is the tiredness felt after long periods of physical and mental strain and lack of sleep.

   C. Impairs personal performance and ability but not pilot judgment.

Answer (A) is correct. (FAA-H-8083-9B Chap 2)
   DISCUSSION: Prolonged exposure to acute fatigue without adequate time for recovery can result in chronic fatigue.
   Answer (B) is incorrect. This describes acute, not chronic, fatigue. Chronic fatigue's underlying cause is generally not "rest-related" and may have deeper points of origin. **Answer (C) is incorrect.** Unless preventive measures are taken, chronic fatigue will certainly impact both personal performance and pilot judgment.

27. Chronic fatigue may best be described as a

   A. combination of both physiological problems and psychological issues.

   B. cluster of specific symptoms such as errors in timing and neglect of secondary tasks.

   C. result of over-application of a learning task.

Answer (A) is correct. (FAA-H-8083-9B Chap 2)
   DISCUSSION: Chronic fatigue is a combination of both physiological problems and psychological issues.
   Answer (B) is incorrect. Errors in timing and neglect of secondary tasks are symptoms of acute, not chronic, fatigue. **Answer (C) is incorrect.** Acute fatigue occurs as a result of the over-application of a learning task. To prevent this, the learner should be given a break in instruction and practice.

28. Chronic fatigue as a result of physiological problems and/or psychological issues may be evidenced by a learner pilot's apparent

    A. Increase in knowledge and skill retention.

    B. Need for sleep.

    C. Acceptance of unwarranted risks.

Answer (C) is correct. (FAA-H-8083-9B Chap 2)
    DISCUSSION: Without resolving the underlying causes of chronic fatigue, human performance gradually falls off, judgment becomes impaired, and unwarranted risks may be taken.
    Answer (A) is incorrect. Chronic fatigue brings about a decrease, not an increase, in a learner's knowledge and skill retention. **Answer (B) is incorrect.** Chronic fatigue's underlying cause is generally not "rest-related" and may have deeper points of origin. Therefore, rest alone may not resolve chronic fatigue.

29. Acute fatigue symptoms may include

    A. error accumulation, inattention, and distractibility.

    B. dizziness, weakness, nausea, tingling of hands and feet, abdominal cramps, and extreme thirst.

    C. unwarranted risk taking.

Answer (A) is correct. (FAA-H-8083-9B Chap 2)
    DISCUSSION: Acute fatigue is characterized by, among other things, inattention, distractibility, and errors in timing.
    Answer (B) is incorrect. Dizziness, weakness, nausea, tingling of hands and feet, abdominal cramps, and extreme thirst are symptoms of dehydration, not acute fatigue. **Answer (C) is incorrect.** Unwarranted risk taking is a symptom of chronic fatigue, not acute fatigue.

30. A sign that a learner may be experiencing acute fatigue is

    A. Acceptance of unwarranted risks.

    B. Neglect of secondary tasks.

    C. Increased attention to detail.

Answer (B) is correct. (FAA-H-8083-9B Chap 2)
    DISCUSSION: A CFI who is familiar with the signs indicative of acute fatigue will be more aware if the learner is experiencing them. One common sign of acute fatigue is the neglect of secondary tasks. Because the mind's resources are limited, secondary or non-essential tasks are often overlooked.
    Answer (A) is incorrect. Acceptance of unwarranted risks is a common indicator of chronic, not acute, fatigue. Pilot judgment as it relates to safety decisions is not typically compromised in acute fatigue, but this would be a common deficiency in someone suffering from chronic fatigue. **Answer (C) is incorrect.** Inattention, not increased attention, to detail is a common sign of acute fatigue.

31. Acute fatigue is

    A. a function of physical robustness or mental acuity.

    B. a combination of both physiological problems and psychological issues.

    C. observable by performance deficiencies that are apparent to others before the individual notices any physical signs of fatigue.

Answer (C) is correct. (FAA-H-8083-9B Chap 2)
    DISCUSSION: Acute fatigue may be observed by performance deficiencies that are apparent to others before the individual notices any physical signs of fatigue. One of the main characteristics of acute fatigue is lack of awareness of error accumulation. Third parties can, therefore, notice errors before you.
    Answer (A) is incorrect. Acute fatigue is not necessarily a function of physical robustness or mental acuity. **Answer (B) is incorrect.** Chronic fatigue, not acute fatigue, is a combination of both physiological problems and psychological issues.

32. Which of the following is a sign of acute fatigue?

    A. Error accumulation.

    B. Nausea.

    C. Acuteness of vision.

Answer (A) is correct. (FAA-H-8083-9B Chap 2)
    DISCUSSION: Acute fatigue is characterized by such symptoms as inattention, distractibility, errors in timing, and neglect of secondary tasks. Error accumulation is a result of these types of symptoms.
    Answer (B) is incorrect. Nausea is a symptom of dehydration, not acute fatigue. **Answer (C) is incorrect.** Acuteness of vision is a possible symptom of a minor illness, such as a cold, not acute fatigue.

33. Acute fatigue may be evident by a learner's apparent

    A. desire to take unwarranted risks.

    B. dizziness, weakness, and nausea.

    C. errors in timing.

Answer (C) is correct. (FAA-H-8083-9B Chap 2)
    DISCUSSION: Acute fatigue is characterized by such symptoms as inattention, distractibility, and errors in timing.
    Answer (A) is incorrect. The desire to take unwarranted risks is a symptom of chronic, not acute, fatigue. **Answer (B) is incorrect.** Dizziness, weakness, and nausea are symptoms of dehydration and heat stroke.

34. What is the difference between acute and chronic fatigue?

    A. Chronic fatigue results from apathy, but acute fatigue does not.

    B. Chronic fatigue results from repeated episodes of acute fatigue when there is not enough recovery time between episodes.

    C. Acute fatigue results from repeated episodes of chronic fatigue when there is not enough recovery time between episodes.

Answer (B) is correct. (FAA-H-8083-9B Chap 2)
    DISCUSSION: Chronic fatigue occurs when there is not enough time for a full recovery from repeated episodes of acute fatigue. The underlying cause is generally not "rest-related" and often has deeper points of origin. Once a person is in a condition of chronic fatigue, rest alone may not resolve the fatigue.
    Answer (A) is incorrect. Apathy in a learner often results from inadequate instruction. Chronic fatigue is a combination of both physiological problems and psychological issues. **Answer (C) is incorrect.** Acute fatigue resulting from training operations is often mental or physical or, occasionally, both. When recognized in time, it may be resolved with a break in the training regimen.

35. Which would most likely be an indication that a learner is reacting normally to stress?

    A. Slow learning.

    B. Inappropriate laughter or singing.

    C. Automatic response to a given situation.

Answer (C) is correct. (FAA-H-8083-9B Chap 2)
    DISCUSSION: When under stress, normal individuals begin to respond rapidly and exactly, within the limits of their experience and training. Many responses are automatic, which indicates the need for proper training in emergency operations prior to an actual emergency.
    Answer (A) is incorrect. While slow learning can be a normal reaction to stress, it could also be the result of a learning plateau. This choice is not the best answer to the question because it could just as likely be the result of something else as the result of an abnormal reaction to stress. **Answer (B) is incorrect.** Inappropriate laughter or singing is an abnormal, not a normal, reaction to stress.

2.4 The Overconfident or Impatient Learner

36. Learners who grow impatient when learning the basic elements of a task are those who

    A. are less easily discouraged than the unaggressive learners.

    B. should have the preliminary training presented one step at a time with clearly stated goals for each step.

    C. should be advanced to the next higher level of learning and not held back by insisting that the immediate goal be reached before they proceed to the next level.

Answer (B) is correct. (FAA-H-8083-9B Chap 2)
    DISCUSSION: Impatient learners fail to see why they must learn one step thoroughly before they move to the next. Presenting the preliminary training with clearly stated goals for each step will minimize learner impatience.
    Answer (A) is incorrect. Impatient learners are often aggressive and more easily discouraged than unaggressive learners. **Answer (C) is incorrect.** It is necessary to hold a learner until (s)he masters the basics if the whole task is to be performed competently and safely. This is the basis of the building block technique of instruction.

37. Which obstacle to learning is a greater deterrent to learning pilot skills than is generally recognized?

    A. Anxiety.

    B. Impatience.

    C. Physical discomfort.

Answer (B) is correct. (FAA-H-8083-9B Chap 2)
    DISCUSSION: Failing to understand the need for preliminary training, the impatient learner can only see the ultimate objective of flying an airplane. This impatience can be detrimental to the usual, careful acquisition of pilot skills.
    Answer (A) is incorrect. Although anxiety may be detrimental to the learning process, it is generally recognized as such, whereas impatience has an equal effect and is not widely recognized. **Answer (C) is incorrect.** Although physical discomfort may be detrimental to the learning process, it is generally recognized as such, whereas impatience has an equal effect and is not widely recognized.

38. Should an instructor be concerned about an apt learner who makes very few mistakes?

    A. No. Some learners have an innate, natural aptitude for flight.

    B. Yes. The learner may assume that the correction of errors is unimportant.

    C. Yes. The learner will lose confidence in the instructor if the instructor does not invent deficiencies in the learner's performance.

Answer (B) is correct. (FAA-H-8083-9B Chap 8)
    DISCUSSION: Because apt learners make few mistakes, they may assume that the correction of errors is not important. Such overconfidence soon results in faulty performance. For such learners, a good instructor will constantly raise the standard of performance for each lesson, demanding greater effort.
    Answer (A) is incorrect. Regardless of natural gift, apt learners may assume that the correction of errors is not important. Such overconfidence soon results in faulty performance. **Answer (C) is incorrect.** The instructor should not invent deficiencies in order to diminish a learner's confidence. On the contrary, a good instructor will constantly raise the standard of performance for each lesson, demanding greater effort.

39. What should an instructor do with a learner who assumes that correction of errors is not important?

    A. Divide complex flight maneuvers into elements.

    B. Try to reduce the learner's overconfidence to reduce the chance of an accident.

    C. Raise the standard of performance for each lesson, demanding greater effort.

Answer (C) is correct. (FAA-H-8083-9B Chap 8)
    DISCUSSION: Because apt learners make few mistakes, they may assume that the correction of errors is not important. Such overconfidence soon results in faulty performance. For such learners, a good instructor will constantly raise the standard of performance for each lesson, demanding greater effort.
    Answer (A) is incorrect. Dividing complex tasks into simpler elements should be done with learners whose slow progress is due to a lack of confidence, not apt learners. **Answer (B) is incorrect.** Reducing learners' overconfidence would be inefficient for properly motivating the apt learner. After realizing the impatience of such learners comes only from improperly paced instruction, instructors should give them challenges fitting their abilities.

40. The overconfidence of fast learners should be corrected by

    A. high praise when no errors are made.

    B. raising the standard of performance for each lesson.

    C. providing strong, negative evaluation at the end of each lesson.

Answer (B) is correct. (FAA-H-8083-9B Chap 8)
    DISCUSSION: Because apt learners make few mistakes, they may assume that the correction of errors is not important. Such overconfidence soon results in faulty performance. For such learners, a good instructor will constantly raise the standard of performance for each lesson, demanding greater effort.
    Answer (A) is incorrect. High praise will only lead the learner to become more overconfident. **Answer (C) is incorrect.** A strong, negative evaluation should not be used to diminish a learner's confidence. On the contrary, a good instructor will constantly raise the standard of performance for each lesson, demanding greater effort.

41. Faulty performance due to learner overconfidence should be corrected by

    A. increasing the standard of performance for each lesson.

    B. praising the learner only when the performance is perfect.

    C. providing strong, negative evaluation at the end of each lesson.

Answer (A) is correct. (FAA-H-8083-9B Chap 8)
    DISCUSSION: Because apt learners make few mistakes, they may assume that the correction of errors is not important. Such overconfidence soon results in faulty performance. For such learners, a good instructor will constantly raise the standard of performance for each lesson, demanding greater effort.
    Answer (B) is incorrect. Learners need consistent, fair critique of every performance, perfect or not. Overly high standards also frustrate learners by making them work too hard without reward (and for an unrealistic goal). **Answer (C) is incorrect.** The principle of effect states that learning is weakened when associated with an unpleasant feeling. Aside from being unfair, the continual negative evaluations will also increasingly frustrate learners.

42. A method for correcting learner impatience is for the instructor to

    A. Present the necessary preliminary training one step at a time, with clearly stated goals for each step.

    B. Key the instruction to utilize the interests and enthusiasm learners bring with them.

    C. Avoid assigning impossible or unreasonable goals for the learner to accomplish.

Answer (A) is correct. (FAA-H-8083-9B Chap 2)
    DISCUSSION: With every complex human endeavor, it is necessary to master the basics if the whole task is to be performed competently and safely. The instructor can correct learner impatience by presenting the necessary preliminary training one step at a time, with clearly stated goals for each step.
    Answer (B) is incorrect. This solution is appropriate for combating worry or lack of interest on the part of the learner, not impatience. **Answer (C) is incorrect.** This solution is appropriate for combating a learner's feelings of unfair treatment during flight instruction, not impatience.

43. What is an example of a learner showing impatience?

    A. A learner not wanting to fly without an instructor on board.

    B. A learner desiring to conduct a cross-country flight before the basic elements of flight have been learned.

    C. A learner wishing to solo an aircraft.

Answer (B) is correct. (FAA-H-8083-9B Chap 2)
    DISCUSSION: An impatient learner wants to undertake tasks before (s)he is ready or competent. An impatient learner seeks only the final objective without considering the means necessary to reach it.
    Answer (A) is incorrect. An example of a learner not wanting to fly solo would show worry, not impatience. **Answer (C) is incorrect.** There is nothing wrong with a learner desiring to accomplish a task such as flying an aircraft solo. An impatient learner, however, would want to solo before (s)he is properly prepared and competent.

44. When teaching adult learners, instructors should

    A. recognize the adult learner's need to control pace and start/stop time.

    B. provide a uniform, specific, and predictable pace for all instructional activities.

    C. ensure that new ideas are separate from an already established body of knowledge.

Answer (A) is correct. (FAA-H-8083-9B Chap 2)
    DISCUSSION: Adult learners benefit from a cooperative learning climate wherein the instructor should recognize learners' need to control pace and start/stop time.
    Answer (B) is incorrect. Adult learners may crave the flexibility of a cooperative learning environment and will often exhibit a need to control pace and start/stop time. **Answer (C) is incorrect.** Instructors should help learners integrate new ideas with what they already know to ensure they keep and use the new information.

2.5 Errors

45. How can errors be reduced?

    A. Through learning and practice.

    B. Hurrying to achieve faster results.

    C. Waiting for the learner to detect them.

Answer (A) is correct. (FAA-H-8083-9B Chap 3)
    DISCUSSION: Learning and practice is the first line of defense against errors. Through practice and learning, higher levels of knowledge and skill are attained, which are associated with lower frequency and magnitude of errors.
    Answer (B) is incorrect. Hurrying to achieve faster results is not a means to reduce errors and, in the course of learning, may amplify the potential for errors. Errors can be reduced by working deliberately and at a comfortable pace. **Answer (C) is incorrect.** Waiting for learners to detect errors is not a proactive way to reduce errors. Learners should be encouraged to actively seek evidence of potential errors and look for new ways to check their work.

STUDY UNIT THREE

FACTORS AFFECTING LEARNING

(17 pages of outline)

Study Units 1 and 2 cover the learning process and barriers to learning, respectively. This study unit discusses human behavior, communication skills, and instructor professionalism. Understanding all three of these topics will help you become an exemplary instructor.

1) You need to understand human behavior and how to guide your learners to be safe and responsible pilots.

   a) The subunit on Aeronautical Decision Making and Risk Management will help you correct the negative behaviors your learners may have.

   b) Understanding a learner's motivation will encourage positive behaviors and hard work and propel the learner to the top.

2) Possessing knowledge of what it takes to be a safe and proficient pilot is but one important element of being a competent instructor.

   a) You must also have effective communication skills so you can pass this knowledge to your learners.

3) Being an instructor is a significant responsibility. Pilots and others in the aviation community hold Flight Instructors and Ground Instructors in the highest esteem, and your daily actions must reflect professionalism.

   a) It is imperative that you model your behavior as a standard-setter and always be professional.

3.1 HUMAN NEEDS

1. Human needs can be organized into a series of levels. The "pyramid of human needs" has been suggested by Abraham Maslow.

    a. For instance, physical needs must be satisfied before so-called "higher" needs can be used as motivators.

    b. Maslow suggests that needs must be satisfied in an ascending order.

2. However, multiple psychological studies have since shown that humans can experience higher levels of motivation before their lower basic needs are met.

    a. These studies show that lower needs do not have to be completely fulfilled before people are able to achieve higher needs.

    b. What matters is that parts of each level have been met, which allows the learner to focus on the instructions given.

    c. The order in which needs are met does not matter. Instructors should verify that most of the learner's needs have been met (law of readiness) and then focus the learner's perception on the lesson.

3. **Physiological needs** are biological needs.

    a. They consist of the need for air, food, water, and maintenance of the human body.

    b. Unless the biological needs are met, a person cannot concentrate fully on learning, self-expression, or any other tasks.

    c. Instructors should monitor their learners to make sure that their basic physical needs have been met. A hungry or tired learner may not be able to perform as expected.

4. **Safety and security needs** become essential after the basic biological needs are met.

    a. Security needs are about keeping oneself from harm.

    b. The aviation instructor who stresses flight safety during training mitigates feelings of insecurity.

5. **Love and belonging needs** are social needs that people pursue to overcome feelings of loneliness and alienation.

    a. Aviation learners are usually out of their normal surroundings during training, and their need for association and belonging is more pronounced.

    b. Instructors should make every effort to help new learners feel at ease and to reinforce their decision to pursue a career or hobby in aviation.

6. **Esteem needs** are about feeling good about oneself.

   a. Humans have a need for a stable, firmly based, high level of self-respect and respect from others.

   b. Humans get esteem in two ways: internally or externally.

      1) Internally, a person judges himself or herself worthy by personally defined standards.

         a) High self-esteem results in self-confidence, independence, achievement, competence, and knowledge.

      2) Most people, however, seek external esteem through social approval and esteem from other people, judging themselves by what others think of them.

         a) External self-esteem relates to one's reputation, such as status, recognition, appreciation, and respect of associates.

   c. When esteem needs are satisfied, a person feels self-confident and valuable as a person in the world.

      1) When these needs are frustrated, the person feels inferior, weak, helpless, and worthless.

      2) Esteem needs not only have a strong influence on the learner-instructor relationship but also may be the main reason for a learner's interest in aviation training.

7. **Cognitive and aesthetic needs** include the need to know and understand and the emotional results of achievement.

   a. Humans have a deep need to understand what is going on around them. If a person understands what is going on, (s)he can either control the situation or make informed choices about what steps might be taken next.

   b. The brain even reinforces this need by giving humans a rush of dopamine whenever something is learned, which accounts for that satisfying "eureka!" moment, such as when a learner completes his or her first solo flight.

   c. Aesthetic needs (e.g., how well something is liked) can factor into the learner-instructor relationship. If an instructor does not "like" a learner, this subtle feeling may affect the instructor's ability to teach that learner, and vice versa.

8. **Self-actualization needs** include a person's need to be and do what the person was "born to do."

   a. These needs are only triggered when all underlying needs are met.

   b. Self-actualized people realize their potential, seek to develop themselves further, and think creatively.

   c. Self-actualized people are characterized by

      1) Being problem-focused
      2) Incorporating an ongoing freshness of appreciation of life
      3) A concern about personal growth
      4) The ability to have peak experiences

   d. Helping a learner achieve his or her individual potential in aviation training offers the greatest challenge as well as the greatest reward to the instructor.

3.2 MOTIVATION

1. Motivation is the reason one acts or behaves in a certain way and lies at the heart of goals.

    a. Motivation is likely the dominant force governing the learner's progress and ability to learn.
    b. Slumps in learning are often due to declining motivation.

2. Motivations may be

    a. Positive or negative
    b. Tangible or intangible
    c. Obvious or subtle and difficult to identify

3. **Positive motivation** is essential to true learning, is provided by the promise or achievement of rewards, and is generally the more effective way to properly motivate learners.

    a. Such rewards may involve financial gain, satisfaction of the self-concept, personal gain, or public recognition.

        1) Intangible positive motivations may include the desire for personal comfort and security, group approval, and the achievement of a favorable self image.

        2) Tangible positive motivation may include rewards that involve financial gain or public recognition.

4. **Negative motivations** are those that cause a learner to react with fear and anxiety.

    a. Negative motivations in the form of reproof and threats should be avoided with all but the most overconfident and impulsive learners.

5. **Tangible motivation** often comes in the form of financial rewards.

6. Learners seeking **intangible** rewards are motivated by the desire for personal comfort and security, group approval, and the achievement of a favorable self-image. Instructors often forget this important form of motivation.

7. Sources of motivation vary, but all offer some type of reward in exchange for performing work. It is important for an instructor to make the learner aware that a particular lesson can help him or her reach an important goal.

    a. If learners are unable to see the benefits or purpose of a lesson, they are less motivated.

    b. Confusion, disinterest, and uneasiness on the part of the learner could happen as a result of not knowing the objective of each period of instruction.

    c. If motivation is to be effective, learners must believe that their efforts will be suitably rewarded in a definite, tangible manner.

8. Understanding where a learner's motivation comes from may aid in maintaining motivation at the highest level possible.

9. To maintain motivation, an instructor must reward success by frequently presenting positive feedback.

    a. EXAMPLE: Praising incremental successes during training, relating daily accomplishments to lesson objectives, and commenting favorably on learner progress.

10. Learner anxiety can be minimized throughout training by emphasizing the benefits and pleasurable experiences that can be derived from flying, rather than by continuously citing the unhappy consequences of faulty performances.

11. Both drops in motivation and learning plateaus, which are a common source of frustration, are normal and can be overcome by reminding learners of their own goals and reassuring them that there will be results for their continued efforts.

3.3 AERONAUTICAL DECISION MAKING AND RISK MANAGEMENT

1. **Aeronautical decision making (ADM)** can be defined as a systematic approach to the mental process used by pilots to consistently determine the best course of action in response to a given set of circumstances.

2. One step in the ADM process for good decision making is to identify personal attitudes hazardous to safe flight.

   a. Examples of classical behavioral traps that experienced pilots may fall into are the compulsion to complete a flight as planned, the desire to please passengers, the pressure to meet schedules, and the determination to get the job done.

   b. At some time, many experienced pilots have fallen prey to dangerous tendencies or behavior problems that must be identified and eliminated, including

      1) Peer pressure
      2) Scud running
      3) Loss of positional or situational awareness
      4) Operating without adequate fuel reserves

   c. In order to gain a realistic perspective on your attitude toward flying, you should take a Self-Assessment Hazardous Attitude Inventory Test.

   d. ADM addresses the following five hazardous attitudes:

      1) **Antiauthority** – "Do not tell me what to do!"

         a) EXAMPLE: During a stall recovery, the CFI allows the learner to exceed maneuvering speed. An antiauthority attitude expressed by the CFI would be "The aircraft can handle a lot more than the maneuvering speed."

      2) **Impulsivity** – "Do something quickly!"

         a) EXAMPLE: On short final, the CFI realizes his learner has forgotten to lower the flaps and immediately adds full flaps. The impulsivity attitude expressed by the CFI would be "I have to extend the flaps to get this aircraft down."

      3) **Invulnerability** – "It will not happen to me."

         a) EXAMPLE: Before a flight, the CFI does not check to verify a learner has completed a pre-flight inspection. The invulnerability attitude expressed by the CFI would be "Nothing bad will happen on this flight."

      4) **Macho** – "I can do it."

         a) EXAMPLE: A pilot is on an instrument approach in which the aircraft in front of him have had to go around yet continues instead of diverting to an alternate. The macho attitude expressed by the pilot would be "I am better than others and can make it."

      5) **Resignation** – "What is the use?"

         a) EXAMPLE: A non-instrument-rated pilot continues into an area of known low visibility. The resignation attitude expressed by the pilot would be "What is the use? No matter what I do, it won't end well!"

3. In the ADM process, the first step in neutralizing a hazardous attitude is recognizing it.

   a. When you recognize a hazardous thought, you should label it as hazardous; then correct the attitude by stating the corresponding antidote.

   b. Hazardous attitudes, which contribute to poor pilot judgment, can be effectively counteracted by the appropriate antidote, as listed below.

      1) Antiauthority -- "Follow the rules. They are usually right."
      2) Impulsivity -- "Not so fast. Think first."
      3) Invulnerability -- "It could happen to me."
      4) Macho -- "Taking chances is foolish."
      5) Resignation -- "I am not helpless. I can make a difference."

4. **Stress** describes the body's response to a set of circumstances that induces a change in an individual's current physiological and/or psychological patterns of functioning, forcing the individual to adapt to these changes.

   a. Success in reducing stress associated with crisis management on the flight deck begins by making a personal assessment of stress in all areas of your life.

   b. To help manage flight deck stress, you should try to relax and think rationally at the first sign of stress.

5. The DECIDE process consists of six elements to help provide a pilot a logical way of approaching ADM.

   a. These elements are to

      1) **D**etect
      2) **E**stimate
      3) **C**hoose
      4) **I**dentify
      5) **D**o
      6) **E**valuate

   b. These elements represent a continuous-loop decision process that can be used to assist a pilot in the decision-making process when faced with a change in a situation that requires a judgment.

6. **Risk management** is a decision-making process designed to systematically identify hazards, assess the degree of risk, and determine the best course of action associated with each flight. This process relies on situational awareness, problem identification, and good judgment to reduce the risks associated with each flight.

   a. **Situational awareness** is defined as the accurate perception and understanding of all the factors and conditions within the four fundamental risk elements that affect safety before, during, and after the flight. Some obstacles to maintaining situational awareness include fatigue, stress, and workload.

b.　The four fundamental risk elements in the ADM process that comprise any given aviation situation are the

1)　**Pilot (PIC)** – The pilot's fitness to fly must be evaluated, including competency in the aircraft, currency, and flight experience.

2)　**Aircraft** – The aircraft performance, limitations, equipment, and airworthiness must be determined.

3)　**Environment** – Factors such as weather and airport conditions must be examined.

4)　**External pressures** – The purpose of the flight is a factor that influences the pilot's decision to begin or continue the flight.

c.　Risk management involves two broad steps: risk assessment and risk mitigation.

1)　Every flight has hazards and some level of risk associated with it. It is critical that pilots and especially learners are able to differentiate in advance between a low-risk flight and a high-risk flight and then establish a review process and develop risk mitigation strategies to address flights throughout that range.

2)　All identified risks should be addressed in proper risk management. Risks must be either accepted or mitigated in some way.

a)　Common mitigation strategies include taking along a more experienced pilot or flight instructor, delaying the flight, or canceling the flight altogether.

7.　**Single-pilot resource management (SRM)** is the art and science of managing the resources available to a single pilot to ensure the safe and successful outcome of a flight operation.

a.　Effective SRM instruction teaches learners to gather information, analyze it, and make decisions.

b.　SRM also teaches pilots to use available resources such as ATC, replicating the principles of CRM.

8.　To aid pilots in understanding SRM, the **5P checklist** was created. This checklist looks at five key elements in the SRM process: the Plan, Plane, Pilot, Passengers, and Programming.

a.　Each of these areas consists of a set of challenges and opportunities that face a single pilot, and each can substantially increase or decrease the risk of successfully completing the flight based on the pilot's ability to make informed and timely decisions.

b.　The 5 Ps are used to evaluate the pilot's current situation at key decision points during the flight or when an emergency arises. These decision points include

1)　Preflight

2)　Pretakeoff

3)　Hourly or at the midpoint of the flight

4)　Predescent

5)　Just prior to the final approach fix (for IFR operations) or just prior to entering the traffic pattern (for VFR operations)

c.　Each of the 5 Ps should be considered at each decision point during a flight.

9.   The discussion that follows is an in-depth look at each of the 5 Ps, along with considerations on how to effectively use them in your everyday piloting.

   a.   **The 5 Ps: Plan**

      1)   The plan can also be called the mission or the task. It contains the basic elements of cross-country planning: weather, route, fuel, current publications, etc.

      2)   The plan should be reviewed and updated several times during the course of the flight.

         a)   A delayed takeoff due to maintenance, fast-moving weather, and a short-notice temporary flight restriction (TFR) may all radically alter the plan.

         b)   The plan is always being updated and modified and is especially responsive to changes in the other four Ps.

      3)   Obviously, weather is a huge part of any plan.

         a)   The addition of real-time datalink weather information provided by advanced avionics gives the pilot a real advantage in inclement weather, but only if the pilot is trained to retrieve and evaluate the weather in real time without sacrificing situational awareness.

         b)   Pilots of aircraft without datalink weather or without the ability to effectively interpret it should get updated weather in flight through an FSS.

   b.   **The 5 Ps: Plane**

      1)   The plane consists of the usual array of mechanical and cosmetic issues that every aircraft pilot, owner, or operator can identify.

      2)   With the advent of advanced avionics, the plane has expanded to include database currency, automation status, and emergency backup systems that were unknown a few years ago.

      3)   Pilots must regularly review airplane system operations to ensure all systems are within operating limits and to spot potential risk factors while they are more easily manageable.

   c.   **The 5 Ps: Pilot**

      1)   Flying, especially when used for business transportation, can expose the pilot to high-altitude flying, long distance and endurance, and more challenging weather.

         a)   An advanced avionics aircraft, simply due to its advanced capabilities, can expose a pilot to even more of these stresses.

      2)   The 5P process helps a pilot to recognize before takeoff the physiological situation that may exist at the end of the flight and to continue updating personal conditions as the flight progresses.

         a)   Once risks are identified, the pilot is better equipped to make alternate plans that lessen the effects of these factors and provide a safer solution.

d. **The 5 Ps: Passengers**

   1) Passengers present a unique situation because, depending on the circumstances of the flight, these individuals can be co-pilots.

      a) Passengers can re-read and help you verify checklist items, keep your navigation materials organized and accessible, and assist with many other tasks.

      b) Obviously, in some circumstances, it would not be appropriate to utilize passengers in such a manner.

      c) Be careful to consider what roles your passengers could play in reducing your workload.

   2) Passengers can also create additional pressures on the pilot to complete a flight as planned or take unnecessary risks.

      a) You should plan for passenger pressures any time they will be on board. Planning for this in advance allows you to be ready to handle these situations with a programmed response.

e. **The 5 Ps: Programming**

   1) The advanced avionics in modern aircraft adds an entirely new dimension to the way general aviation (GA) aircraft are flown.

      a) The electronic instrument displays, GPS, and autopilot reduce pilot workload and increase pilot situational awareness.

      b) The pilot must be trained to properly use these avionics for them to be effective.

   2) Although the programming and operation of these devices are fairly simple and straightforward (unlike the analog instruments they replace), they tend to capture the pilot's attention and hold it for long periods of time.

      a) To avoid this phenomenon, the pilot should plan in advance when and where the programming for approaches, route changes, and airport information gathering should be accomplished, as well as times it should not.

      b) Pilot familiarity with the equipment, the route, the local air traffic control environment, and personal capabilities in using the automation should dictate when, where, and how the automation is programmed and used.

10. Risk can be reduced to the lowest possible level by using the concepts of ADM, risk management, situational awareness, and SRM.

3.4 EFFECTIVE COMMUNICATION

1. The process of communication is composed of three dynamically interrelated elements:

    a. A source (instructor)
    b. The symbols used in composing and transmitting the message (e.g., words)
    c. The receiver (learner)

2. Communication takes place when one person transmits ideas or feelings to another person or to a group of people.

    a. The effectiveness of communication is measured by the similarity between the idea transmitted and the idea received.

    b. Effective communication has taken place when, and only when, the receivers react with understanding and change their behavior accordingly.

    c. Instruction has taken place when a procedure has been explained and the desired learner response has occurred.

3. The effectiveness of persons acting in the role of communicators is related to at least three basic factors.

    a. First, their ability to select symbols that are meaningful to the listener.

    b. Second, communicators consciously or unconsciously reveal attitudes toward themselves, toward the ideas they are trying to transmit, and toward their receivers.

        1) Thus, to communicate effectively, instructors must reveal a positive attitude while delivering their message.

    c. Third, to be more likely to communicate effectively, communicators should speak or write from a broad background of accurate, up-to-date, stimulating material.

4. **Symbols** are oral and visual codes used to communicate.

    a. Ideas are communicated only when symbols are combined into meaningful wholes (e.g., sentences, paragraphs, chapters, etc.).

    b. Symbols are perceived through three sensory channels: visual, auditory, or kinesthetic (touching, doing, etc.).

        1) Instructors will be more successful in gaining and retaining learner attention by using a variety of these channels.

    c. The feedback an instructor gets from a learner needs to be monitored constantly in order to modify the symbols, as required, to optimize communication.

5. To understand the process of communication, three characteristics of receivers must be understood.

    a. First, they exercise their ability to question and comprehend the ideas that have been transmitted.

    b. Second, the receiver's attitude may be one of resistance, willingness, or of passive neutrality. Communicators must gain the receiver's attention and then retain it.

        1) The communicator will be more successful in this area by using a varied communicative approach.

    c. Third, the receiver's background, experience, and education frame the target at which communications must aim.

3.5 BARRIERS TO EFFECTIVE COMMUNICATION

1. Probably the greatest single barrier to effective communication is the lack of a common core of experience between communicator and receiver.

   a. A receiver's past experience with the words and things to which they refer determine how the receiver responds to what the communicator says.

   b. A communicator's words cannot communicate the desired meaning to another person unless the listener or reader has had some experience with the objects or concepts to which these words refer.

   c. In order for communication to be effective, the learner's understanding of the meaning of the words and symbols needs to be the same as the instructor's understanding and desired thought.

2. Confusion between the symbol (word or sign) and the symbolized object results when a word is confused with what it is meant to represent.

   a. Words and symbols do not always represent the same thing to each person.

   b. To communicate effectively, speakers and instructors should be aware of these differences and choose words or symbols that represent what is intended.

3. Overuse of abstractions should be avoided.

   a. **Concrete words** refer to objects that human beings can relate directly to their own experiences.

   b. **Abstract words** stand for ideas that cannot be directly experienced or things that do not call forth specific mental images.

      1) Abstractions thus serve as shorthand symbols that sum up large areas of experience.

   c. The danger with using abstract words is that they may not evoke in the listener's mind the specific items of experience the communicator intends.

   d. By using concrete words, the communicator narrows (and gains better control of) the image produced in the minds of the listeners and readers.

4. **External factors** may prevent a process or activity from being carried out properly and are composed of factors outside the control of the instructor yet may be overcome.

   a. **Physiological external factors** are any biological problem that may inhibit reception.

      1) EXAMPLE: Hearing loss, injury, or physical illness.

   b. **Environmental external factors** are caused by external physical conditions.

      1) EXAMPLE: Aircraft noise or vibration or lighting conditions.

   c. **Psychological external factors** are a product of how the instructor and learner feel at the time the communication process is occurring.

      1) EXAMPLE: If either the instructor or learner is not committed to the communication process, communication is impaired.

   d. The instructor must recognize when external factors are present and adapt the presentation to allow the learner to be more receptive to new ideas.

3.6 DEVELOPING COMMUNICATION SKILLS

1. Communication skills need to be developed; they do not occur automatically. Instructional communication often begins with roleplaying during training to be an instructor, continues during the actual instruction, and is enhanced by additional training.

2. **Roleplaying**

   a. In roleplaying, the learner is provided with a general description of a situation and applies a new skill or knowledge to perform the role.

      1) A flight instructor applicant can fly with an instructor playing a learner. The instructor can then duplicate learner responses. The instructor applicant can use this exercise to find a comfortable communication style in a less threatening environment.

3. **Instructional Communication**

   a. Instruction takes place when an instructor explains a procedure and determines the learner exhibits the desired response.

      1) An instructor giving a presentation on a well-known subject allows the learner to perform better in early lessons.

      2) Instructors should use personal experience to make lessons more valuable.

4. **Listening** is one way to become better acquainted with learners. There are several techniques to become better at listening.

   a. Listening can be described as hearing with comprehension.

   b. Some instructor tools to aid listening are thinking before answering, not interrupting, concentrating, and watching nonverbal behaviors.

   c. Learners and instructors can become better listeners by avoiding daydreaming, taking notes, and being emotionally calm.

5. **Questioning** can determine how well a learner has been taught.

   a. Using focused questions allows an instructor to concentrate on a desired area.
   b. Open-ended questions are designed to encourage full, meaningful answers.
   c. Closed-ended questions often only test rote knowledge.

3.7 INSTRUCTOR RESPONSIBILITIES

1. The job of flight instruction is to transfer knowledge. Flight instructors are responsible for producing the safest pilots possible with the overall focus on education and learning. Aviation instructors have five main responsibilities.

   a. Helping Learners

      1) Learning should be interesting. Though learners may be drawn to less difficult tasks, they ultimately devote more effort to activities that bring rewards.

      2) The use of standards, and measurement against standards, is key to helping learners learn.

      3) Knowing the objective of each period of instruction gives meaning and provides interest to learner and instructor.

    b.   Providing Adequate Instruction

        1)   Flight instructors should analyze the learner's personality, thinking, and ability to tailor their teaching technique to the learner.

        2)   Remain open-minded and seek other resources and information to develop enhanced teaching ability.

    c.   Demanding Adequate Standards of Performance

        1)   Evaluation of demonstrated ability during flight instruction must be based upon established standards of performance, suitably modified to apply to the learner's experience and stage of development as a pilot.

        2)   In evaluating learner demonstrations of piloting ability, it is important for the flight instructor to keep the learner informed of his or her progress.

            a)   EXAMPLE: This may be done as each procedure/maneuver is completed or summarized during postflight critiques.

    d.   Emphasizing the Positive

        1)   Emphasize the positive because positive instruction results in positive learning.

    e.   Ensuring Aviation Safety

        1)   The safety practices aviation instructors emphasize have a long-lasting effect on learners.

        2)   Emphasizing safety by example is one of the best actions an instructor can take to ensure aviation safety.

2.   Additional responsibilities of flight instructors include

    a.   Evaluation of learner piloting ability

        1)   In evaluating learner demonstrations of ability, it is important for the instructor to keep the learner informed of progress. This may be done as each procedure or maneuver is completed or summarized during a postflight or class critique.

        2)   An instructor should constantly monitor feedback from the learner in order to identify misunderstandings and tailor the presentation of information, periodically asking the learner to explain his or her understanding of added information.

    b.   Pilot supervision

    c.   Practical test recommendations

    d.   Flight instructor endorsements

        1)   Examples of all common endorsements can be found in the current issue of AC 61-65, Appendix A.

    e.   Additional training and endorsements

    f.   Pilot proficiency

    g.   See and avoid responsibility

    h.   Learner's pre-solo flight thought process

        1)   The learner needs to show consistency in the required solo tasks before attempting the first solo flight.

3.   It is a flight instructor's responsibility to teach the learner how to take charge during a flight. A pilot in command (PIC) must know when to tell any passengers, even a designated pilot examiner (DPE), when the PIC finds actions in the aircraft that distract and interfere with the safe conduct of the flight.

   a.   Instructor responsibilities include teaching the learner to divide his or her attention between the distracting task and maintaining control of the aircraft.

   b.   Properly interjected distractions may help learners learn to determine whether a distraction warrants further attention or action on their part.

4.   Flight instructors have a particular responsibility to provide guidance and restraint regarding the solo operations of their learners.

   a.   Before receiving an instructor endorsement for solo flight, a learner should be required to demonstrate the consistent ability to perform all of the fundamental maneuvers without the need of instructor assistance.

   b.   The learner should also be capable of handling ordinary problems that might occur, such as traffic pattern congestion, a change in the active runway, or unexpected crosswinds.

5.   **Minimizing Learner Frustrations**

   a.   Motivate Learners

      1)   More can be gained from wanting to learn than from being forced to learn.

      2)   Too often, learners do not realize how a particular lesson or course can help them reach an important goal.

      3)   When learners can see the benefits and purpose of the lesson or course, their enjoyment and efforts increase.

   b.   Keep Learners Informed

      1)   Learners feel insecure when they do not know what is expected of them or what is going to happen to them.

      2)   Instructors can minimize feelings of insecurity by telling learners what is expected of them and what they can expect in return.

      3)   Instructors keep learners informed in various ways, including giving them an overview of the course, keeping them posted on their progress, and giving them adequate notice of examinations, assignments, or other requirements.

   c.   Approach Learners as Individuals

      1)   When instructors limit their thinking to a group mentality without considering the individuals who make up that group, their efforts are directed at an average personality that really fits no one.

      2)   Each learner group has its own personality that stems from the characteristics and interactions of its members, but each individual within the group has a unique personality to constantly be considered.

d. Give Credit When Due

1) When learners do something extremely well, they normally expect their abilities and efforts to be noticed. Otherwise, they may become frustrated.

2) Praise or credit from the instructor is usually an ample reward and provides an incentive to do even better. Praise pays dividends in learner effort and achievement when deserved, but when given too freely, it becomes valueless.

e. Criticize Constructively

1) Although it is important to give praise and credit when deserved, it is equally important to identify mistakes and failures. It does not help to tell learners they have made errors and not provide explanations.

2) If a learner has made an earnest effort but is told that the work is unsatisfactory, with no other explanation, frustration occurs.

3) Errors cannot be corrected if they are not identified, and if they are not identified, they will probably be perpetuated through faulty practice. On the other hand, if the learner is briefed on the errors and is told how to correct them, progress can be made.

f. Be Consistent

1) Learners want to please their instructor—the same desire that influences much of the behavior of subordinates toward their superiors in industry and business.

2) Naturally, learners have a keen interest in knowing what is required to please the instructor. If the same thing is acceptable one day and unacceptable the next, the learner becomes confused. The instructor's philosophy and actions must be consistent.

g. Admit Errors

1) No one, including learners, expects an instructor to be perfect. The instructor can win the respect of learners by honestly acknowledging mistakes.

2) If the instructor tries to cover up or bluff, learners are quick to sense it. Such behavior tends to destroy learner confidence in the instructor.

3) If in doubt about some point, the instructor should admit it.

h. Assign Goals

1) Goals the learner considers difficult but possible usually provide a challenge and promote learning.

2) In a typical flight lesson, reasonable goals are listed in the lesson objectives and the desired levels of proficiency for the goals are included in statements that contain completion standards.

i. Learners will remain engaged if they are aware of the progress they are making.

1) One way to make learners aware of their progress is to repeat a demonstration or example and to show them the standards their performance must ultimately meet.

3.8 INSTRUCTOR PROFESSIONALISM

1. Although the term professionalism is widely used, it is rarely defined. In fact, no single definition can encompass all of the qualifications and considerations of true professionalism. The following are some of the major considerations:

    a. Professionals must be able to reason logically and accurately.

    b. Professionalism requires good decision-making ability.

        1) Professionals cannot limit actions and decisions to standard patterns and practice.
        2) Professionals commit themselves to continuous learning and development.

    c. Professionalism demands a code of ethics.

2. The professional flight instructor should be straightforward and honest.

    a. Anything less than a sincere performance is quickly detected and immediately destroys instructor effectiveness.

    b. Learner confidence tends to be destroyed if instructors bluff when in doubt.

    c. The well-prepared instructor instills not only confidence but good habits, since preparing well for a flight is a basic requirement for safe flying. Learners quickly become apathetic when they recognize that the flight instructor is inadequately prepared.

3. The attitude, movements, and general demeanor of the flight instructor contribute a great deal to his or her professional image.

    a. The instructor should avoid erratic movements, distracting speech habits, and capricious changes in mood. The professional image requires development of a calm, pleasant, thoughtful manner that puts the learner at ease.

4. The professional relationship between the instructor and the learner should be based on a mutual acknowledgment that both the learner and the instructor are important to each other and that both are working toward the same objective.

    a. Accepting lower-than-normal standards to please a learner will **not** help the learner-instructor relationship.

    b. Reasonable standards strictly enforced are not resented by an earnest learner.

    c. Learners must be treated with respect, regardless of whether they are quick to learn or require more time to absorb certain concepts.

5. The professional flight instructor should accept learners as they are with all of their faults and problems.

    a. However, (s)he should also build learner self-confidence, set challenges, and generally create an atmosphere for learning.

6. A flight instructor who is not completely familiar with current pilot certification and rating requirements cannot do a competent job of flight instruction.

    a. Flight instructors must strive to maintain the highest level of knowledge, training, and currency in their field.

    b. For a professional performance as a flight instructor, it is essential that the instructor maintain current copies of

        1) The Federal Aviation Regulations, especially Parts 1, 61, and 91;

        2) The *Aeronautical Information Manual*;

        3) Practical Test Standards or Airman Certification Standards; and

        4) Appropriate pilot training manuals.

    c. True performance as a professional is based on study and research.

7. Flight instructors fail to provide competent instruction when they permit learners to partially learn an important item of knowledge or skill.

    a. More importantly, such deficiencies may in themselves allow hazardous inadequacies to develop in the learner's ongoing piloting performance.

8. Aviation instructors should be constantly alert for ways to improve the services they provide to their learners, their effectiveness, and their qualifications.

9. Successful aviation instructors do not become complacent. This goal can be attained by reading an article or taking a course at a technical school.

QUESTIONS AND ANSWER EXPLANATIONS: All of the Fundamentals of Instructing knowledge test questions chosen by the FAA for release as well as additional questions selected by Gleim relating to the material in the previous outlines are provided on the following pages. These questions have been organized into the same subunits as the outlines. To the immediate right of each question are the correct answer and answer explanations. You should cover these answers and answer explanations while responding to the questions. Refer to the general discussion in the Introduction on how to take the FAA knowledge test.

Remember that the questions from the FAA knowledge test bank have been reordered by topic and organized into a meaningful sequence. Also, the first line of the answer explanation gives the citation of the authoritative source for the answer.

QUESTIONS

3.1 Human Needs

1. Before a learner can concentrate on learning, which human needs must be satisfied?

    A. Security.

    B. Biological.

    C. Psychological.

Answer (B) is correct. (FAA-H-8083-9B Chap 2)
    DISCUSSION: Physiological, or biological, needs consist of the need for air, food, water, and maintenance of the human body. Unless the biological needs are met, a person cannot concentrate fully on learning, self-expression, or any other tasks.
    Answer (A) is incorrect. The need for security is only a driving force once all of the physiological needs are met.
    Answer (C) is incorrect. Psychological needs, such as belonging and esteem, are only important after the basic biological and security needs are met.

2. After individuals are physically comfortable and have no fear for their safety, which human needs become the prime influence on their behavior?

    A. Esteem.

    B. Self-Actualization.

    C. Belonging.

Answer (C) is correct. (FAA-H-8083-9B Chap 2)
    DISCUSSION: When individuals are physically comfortable and do not feel threatened, they seek to satisfy their social needs of belonging, that is, to overcome feelings of loneliness and alienation.
    Answer (A) is incorrect. The need of esteem follows after the need of belonging. Generally speaking, a person must feel accepted by peers to develop stable, positive self-esteem.
    Answer (B) is incorrect. The needs of self-actualization are only applicable after all other human needs have been met.

3. Which of the learner's human needs offer the greatest challenge to an instructor?

    A. Physiological.

    B. Psychological.

    C. Self-Actualization.

Answer (C) is correct. (FAA-H-8083-9B Chap 2)
    DISCUSSION: When all of the foregoing needs are satisfied, the needs for self-actualization are activated. Self-actualization is a person's need to be and do what the person was "born to do." Helping a learner achieve his or her individual potential in aviation training offers the greatest challenge as well as reward to the instructor.
    Answer (A) is incorrect. Physiological needs are needs that the instructor has no direct impact on. These basic biological needs include the need for air, food, water, and maintenance of the human body. **Answer (B) is incorrect.** Psychological needs include the learner's need to belong, have positive self-esteem, cognitively know and understand, and emotionally be drawn to learning. While difficult to develop, these needs are not as difficult to encourage as self-actualization.

4. The need for realizing one's own potentialities, for continued development, and for being creative is defined as a(n)

    A. esteem need.

    B. social need.

    C. self-actualization need.

Answer (C) is correct. (FAA-H-8083-9B Chap 2)
    DISCUSSION: Self-actualization needs are the needs for realizing one's own potentialities, for continued development, and for being creative.
    Answer (A) is incorrect. Esteem needs relate to feeling good about one's self. **Answer (B) is incorrect.** Social needs are the needs to belong and to associate with other people.

3.2 Motivation

5. Which is generally the more effective way for an instructor to properly motivate learners?

    A. Maintain pleasant personal relationships with learners.

    B. Provide positive motivations by the promise or achievement of rewards.

    C. Reinforce their self-confidence by requiring no tasks beyond their ability to perform.

Answer (B) is correct. (FAA-H-8083-9B Chap 2)
    DISCUSSION: Providing positive motivation is generally considered the most effective way to properly motivate people. Positive motivations are provided by the promise or achievement of rewards.
    Answer (A) is incorrect. Maintaining pleasant personal relationships with learners (while desirable) is not the more effective way for an instructor to properly motivate learners. **Answer (C) is incorrect.** A learner who is not required to perform a task beyond present abilities will neither be motivated nor make any progress.

6. By understanding a learner's motivation, an instructor will

    A. Encourage positive behaviors.

    B. Make lessons interesting.

    C. Create open communication.

Answer (A) is correct. (FAA-H-8083-9B Chap 2)
    DISCUSSION: When an instructor understands a learner's motivation, (s)he can encourage positive behaviors by tailoring the lessons to match the motivation.
    Answer (B) is incorrect. Instructors need to do more than make lessons interesting. What one learner finds interesting another may not. Understanding each learner's motivation will encourage positive behaviors. **Answer (C) is incorrect.** Creating open lines of communication is helpful but may not always produce the behavior needed to complete tasks.

7. How can an instructor help a learner cope with fear and anxiety?

    A. By emphasizing the benefits and pleasurable experiences from flying.

    B. By minimizing fear by teaching the learner advanced maneuvers.

    C. By keeping the learner focused on achieving Practical Test Standards (PTS).

Answer (A) is correct. (FAA-H-8083-9B Chap 2)
    DISCUSSION: Learner anxiety can be minimized throughout training by emphasizing the benefits and pleasurable experiences that can be derived from flying, rather than by continuously citing the unhappy consequences of faulty performances.
    Answer (B) is incorrect. Anxiety for learners is usually associated with certain types of flight operations and maneuvers. Instructors should introduce these maneuvers with care so that learners know what to expect and what their reactions should be. **Answer (C) is incorrect.** The PTS should not be introduced to the learner prior to the last 3 hours of training prior to the practical test.

8. Motivations in the form of reproof and threats should be avoided with all but the learner who is

    A. overconfident and impulsive.

    B. avidly seeking group approval.

    C. experiencing a learning plateau.

Answer (A) is correct. (FAA-H-8083-9B Chap 2)
    DISCUSSION: Educational experts have shown that negative motivation is useful only for a learner who is overconfident and impulsive. Otherwise, negative motivation in the form of reproof and threats tends to discourage learner behavior.
    Answer (B) is incorrect. Group approval is a strong motivating force. Use of reproofs and threats with a learner seeking group approval would only alienate him or her from the group. **Answer (C) is incorrect.** One of the reasons a learner has reached a learning plateau is due to a lack of motivation. Use of reproofs and threats would only cause a learner to remain at the plateau longer.

9. Confusion, disinterest, and uneasiness on the part of the learner could happen as a result of not knowing the

    A. importance of each period of instruction.

    B. objective of each period of instruction.

    C. subject of each period of instruction.

Answer (B) is correct. (FAA-H-8083-9B Chap 8)
    DISCUSSION: Knowing the objective of each period of instruction gives meaning and interest to the learner as well as the instructor. Not knowing the objective of the lesson often leads to confusion, disinterest, and uneasiness on the part of the learner.
    Answer (A) is incorrect. Confusion, disinterest, and uneasiness on the part of the learner could happen as a result of not knowing the objective of each period of instruction, not its importance. **Answer (C) is incorrect.** Confusion, disinterest, and uneasiness on the part of the learner could happen as a result of not knowing the objective of each period of instruction, not its subject. The subject of the instructional period will be obvious if it has been planned appropriately.

10. Which statement is true regarding sources of motivation?

- A. A desire for monetary gain is the main source of motivation for each individual.
- B. All sources of motivation offer some type of reward in exchange for performing work.
- C. Sources of motivation are normal and can be overcome by reminding learners of their own goals.

Answer (B) is correct. (FAA-H-8083-9B Chap 2)
DISCUSSION: Sources of motivation vary, but all offer some type of reward in exchange for performing work.
Answer (A) is incorrect. While the desire for monetary gain is a source of motivation to some, there are many different sources of motivation, and each individual may have a different one. Sources of motivation all offer some type of reward in exchange for performing work. **Answer (C) is incorrect.** Drops in motivation, not sources of motivation, can be overcome by reminding learners of their own goals. Sources of motivation all offer some type of reward in exchange for performing work.

11. Motivations that cause a learner to react with fear and anxiety are

- A. tangible.
- B. negative.
- C. difficult to identify.

Answer (B) is correct. (FAA-H-8083-9B Chap 2)
DISCUSSION: Negative motivations may produce fears and may thus be seen by learners as threats. Negative motivation generally intimidates learners and should be avoided.
Answer (A) is incorrect. Motivations, whether tangible or intangible, can be either positive or negative. **Answer (C) is incorrect.** Motivations, whether very subtle or difficult to identify, can be either positive or negative.

12. When learners are unable to see the benefits or purpose of a lesson, they will

- A. be less motivated.
- B. not learn as quickly.
- C. be expected to increase their efforts.

Answer (A) is correct. (FAA-H-8083-9B Chap 2)
DISCUSSION: Learners will be less motivated if they are unable to see the benefits or purpose of a lesson. It is important for the instructor to make the learner aware that a particular lesson can help him or her reach an important goal.
Answer (B) is incorrect. While a learner may not learn as quickly when (s)he is unable to see the benefits or purpose of a lesson, (s)he will become less motivated. **Answer (C) is incorrect.** The frustration of working without a known goal will likely decrease, not increase, their efforts.

13. Which statement is true concerning motivations?

- A. Motivations must be tangible to be effective.
- B. Motivations may be very subtle and difficult to identify.
- C. Negative motivations often are as effective as positive motivations.

Answer (B) is correct. (FAA-H-8083-9B Chap 2)
DISCUSSION: Motivations may be subtle, subconscious, and difficult to identify. A learner may be motivated without even being aware (s)he is being influenced.
Answer (A) is incorrect. Intangible motivations can be as effective (or even more effective) than tangible motivations. Rewards such as accomplishment, fame, and peer acceptance are intangible, but they are among the best positive motivators. **Answer (C) is incorrect.** Negative motivation tends to discourage the learner.

14. For a motivation to be effective, learners must believe their efforts will be rewarded in a definite manner. This type of motivation is

- A. subtle.
- B. negative.
- C. tangible.

Answer (C) is correct. (FAA-H-8083-9B Chap 2)
DISCUSSION: Learners, like any worker, need and want tangible returns for their efforts. These rewards must be constantly apparent to the learner during instruction.
Answer (A) is incorrect. The learner is often unaware of the application of subtle motivation and thus feels unrewarded for his or her effort. **Answer (B) is incorrect.** Negative motivations are not as effective as positive motivations, as they tend to intimidate learners and cause unpleasant experiences.

15. An instructor can most effectively maintain a high level of learner motivation by

    A. making each lesson a pleasurable experience.

    B. relaxing the standards of performance required during the early phase of training.

    C. continually challenging the learner to meet the highest objectives of training that can be established.

Answer (A) is correct. (FAA-H-8083-9B Chap 2)
    DISCUSSION: An instructor can most effectively maintain a high level of motivation by making each lesson a pleasant experience for a learner. People avoid negative experiences, but they will seek out and want to repeat positive experiences.
    Answer (B) is incorrect. Relaxing the standards of performance required during the early phase of training may actually reduce a learner's motivation. Reasonable standards strictly enforced are not resented by an earnest learner.
    Answer (C) is incorrect. Performance standards should be set to the learner's potential and not his or her current ability or to unrealistically high objectives. Improvement must be fostered.

16. In order to maintain learner motivation and progress, the instructor should

    A. make each lesson a pleasant experience.

    B. make each lesson easy for learner achievement.

    C. repeat each lesson until the learner is confident.

Answer (A) is correct. (FAA-H-8083-9B Chap 2)
    DISCUSSION: All learners desire to experience a secure, pleasant, and safe environment. It is easier to motivate the learner once they realize what is being learned may promote these objectives. An unpleasant training experience will inhibit the learning experience.
    Answer (B) is incorrect. Each lesson should be a pleasurable experience to maintain learner motivation. Making each lesson easy defeats the purpose of instruction and sacrifices the standards of lesson performance. **Answer (C) is incorrect.** Although repetition of skills is essential, repeating each lesson would decrease learner motivation. Once the learner has completed the stated lesson objectives to the required standards, the next challenge, learning block, or lesson should be attempted.

17. How can drops in motivation be overcome?

    A. By reminding learners of their own goals and reassuring them there will be rewards for their continued efforts.

    B. By praising incremental successes during training, relating daily accomplishments to lesson objectives, and commenting favorably on learner progress.

    C. By making each lesson a pleasurable experience.

Answer (A) is correct. (FAA-H-8083-9B Chap 2)
    DISCUSSION: Drops in motivation, which are a common source of frustration, are normal and can be overcome by reminding learners of their own goals and reassuring them that there will be rewards for their continued efforts.
    Answer (B) is incorrect. Praising incremental successes during training, relating daily accomplishments to lesson objectives, and commenting favorably on learner progress are ways to maintain motivation, not to overcome a drop in motivation. **Answer (C) is incorrect.** While an instructor should strive to make each lesson a pleasurable experience, this will not guarantee that learners will not experience a drop in motivation.

18. Examples of tangible positive motivation may include

    A. rewards such as accomplishment, personal comfort, and peer acceptance.

    B. penalties in the form of reproof and threats.

    C. rewards that involve financial gain or public recognition.

Answer (C) is correct. (FAA-H-8083-9B Chap 2)
    DISCUSSION: Examples of positive motivations that are tangible may involve financial gain or public recognition.
    Answer (A) is incorrect. Rewards such as accomplishment, personal comfort, and peer acceptance, while positive, are types of intangible motivators. **Answer (B) is incorrect.** Motivations in the form of reproof and threats are defined as negative motivations.

3.3 Aeronautical Decision Making and Risk Management

19. What is the systematic approach to the mental process used by pilots to determine the best course of action in response to a given set of circumstances?

    A. Pilot Judgment Chain.

    B. Aeronautical Decision Making.

    C. Crew Resource Management.

Answer (B) is correct. (FAA-H-8083-9B Chap 1)
    DISCUSSION: Aeronautical Decision Making is defined as the systematic approach to the mental process used by pilots to determine the best course of action in response to a given set of circumstances.
    Answer (A) is incorrect. This approach is the definition of Aeronautical Decision Making, not the Pilot Judgment Chain. **Answer (C) is incorrect.** Crew Resource Management pertains to team management concepts on the flight deck, as well as those that affect flight attendants, maintenance personnel, and others. This question describes Aeronautical Decision Making.

20. The aeronautical decision making (ADM) process identifies several steps involved in good decision making. One of these steps is

    A. making a rational evaluation of the required actions.

    B. identifying personal attitudes hazardous to safe flight.

    C. developing a "can do" attitude.

Answer (B) is correct. (AC 60-22)
    DISCUSSION: The ADM process addresses all aspects of decision making on the flight deck and identifies several steps involved in good decision making. One of these steps is to identify personal attitudes hazardous to safe flight.
    Answer (A) is incorrect. Making a rational evaluation of the required actions is a step in good judgment, not a step in good decision making. **Answer (C) is incorrect.** The "can do," or macho, attitude is one of the personal hazardous attitudes to identify in the steps involved in good decision making.

21. Which of the following identifies accurate perception of the aircraft and environmental factors that affect the aircraft and passengers during a specific period of time?

    A. CRM.

    B. Situational Awareness.

    C. ADM.

Answer (B) is correct. (FAA-H-8083-9B Chap 1)
    DISCUSSION: Situational awareness is defined as an accurate perception and understanding of all the factors and conditions within the four fundamental risk elements that affect safety before, during, and after the flight.
    Answer (A) is incorrect. Crew Resource Management (CRM) refers to the application of team management concepts on the flight deck environment, including cabin crew, maintenance personnel, and others. It is situational awareness that involves the accurate perception and understanding of all the factors and conditions within the four fundamental risk elements that affect safety before, during, and after the flight. **Answer (C) is incorrect.** Aeronautical Decision Making (ADM) is defined as the systematic approach to the mental process used by pilots to determine the best course of action in response to a given set of circumstances. It is situational awareness that involves the accurate perception and understanding of all the factors and conditions within the four fundamental risk elements that affect safety before, during, and after the flight.

22. One of the risk elements in the Aeronautical Decision Making process is?

    A. Fuel on board.

    B. Passengers.

    C. Aircraft.

Answer (C) is correct. (FAA-H-8083-9B Chap 1)
    DISCUSSION: The four fundamental risk elements incorporated into aeronautical decision making are the pilot, the aircraft, the environment, and the type of operation that comprises any given aviation situation.
    Answer (A) is incorrect. Fuel on board is not one of the risk elements included in the aeronautical decision making process. The pilot, the aircraft, the environment, and the type of operation are the four fundamental risk elements included in ADM. **Answer (B) is incorrect.** The passengers are not considered to be one of the risk elements included in aeronautical decision making. The pilot, the aircraft, the environment, and the type of operation are the four fundamental risk elements included in ADM.

23. Risk management, as part of the aeronautical decision making (ADM) process, relies on which features to reduce the risks associated with each flight?

    A. Application of stress management and risk element procedures.

    B. The mental process of analyzing all information in a particular situation and making a timely decision on what action to take.

    C. Situational awareness, problem recognition, and good judgment.

Answer (C) is correct. (AC 60-22)
    DISCUSSION: Risk management is that part of the ADM process which relies on situational awareness, problem recognition, and good judgment to reduce risks associated with each flight.
    Answer (A) is incorrect. Risk management relies on situational awareness, problem recognition, and good judgment, not the application of stress management and risk-element procedures, to reduce the risks associated with each flight. **Answer (B) is incorrect.** Judgment, not risk management, is the mental process of analyzing all information in a particular situation and making a timely decision on what action to take.

24. Examples of classic behavioral traps that experienced pilots may fall into are to

    A. promote situational awareness and then necessary changes in behavior.

    B. complete a flight as planned, please passengers, meet schedules, and "get the job done."

    C. assume additional responsibilities and assert PIC authority.

Answer (B) is correct. (AC 60-22)
    DISCUSSION: Pilots have been known to fall into a number of classic behavioral traps. Pilots, particularly those with considerable experience, as a rule always try to complete a flight as planned, please passengers, meet schedules, and do what it takes to "get the job done."
    Answer (A) is incorrect. To promote situational awareness and then to make necessary changes in behavior are part of learning good decision making, not classical behavioral traps. **Answer (C) is incorrect.** Assuming additional responsibilities and asserting PIC authority are not examples of classical behavioral traps.

25. Hazardous attitudes occur to every pilot to some degree at some time. What are some of these hazardous attitudes?

    A. Antiauthority, impulsivity, macho, resignation, and invulnerability.

    B. Poor situational awareness, snap judgments, and lack of a decision making process.

    C. Poor risk management and lack of stress management.

Answer (A) is correct. (AC 60-22)
    DISCUSSION: The five hazardous attitudes addressed in the ADM process are antiauthority, impulsivity, invulnerability, macho, and resignation.
    Answer (B) is incorrect. Poor situational awareness and snap judgments are indications of the lack of a decision-making process, not hazardous attitudes. **Answer (C) is incorrect.** Poor risk management and lack of stress management lead to poor ADM and are not considered hazardous attitudes.

26. In the aeronautical decision making (ADM) process, what is the first step in neutralizing a hazardous attitude?

    A. Recognizing hazardous thoughts.

    B. Recognizing the invulnerability of the situation.

    C. Making a rational judgment.

Answer (A) is correct. (AC 60-22)
    DISCUSSION: Hazardous attitudes, which contribute to poor pilot judgment, can be effectively counteracted by redirecting that hazardous attitude so that appropriate action can be taken. Recognition of hazardous thoughts is the first step in neutralizing them in the ADM process.
    Answer (B) is incorrect. Invulnerability is a hazardous attitude. The first step in neutralizing a hazardous attitude is to recognize it. **Answer (C) is incorrect.** Before a rational judgment can be made, the hazardous attitude must be recognized then redirected so that appropriate action can be taken.

27. Success in reducing stress associated with a crisis on the flight deck begins with

    A. eliminating the more serious life and flight deck stress issues.

    B. knowing the exact cause of the stress.

    C. assessing stress areas in one's personal life.

Answer (C) is correct. (AC 60-22)
    DISCUSSION: If you hope to succeed in reducing stress associated with crisis management on the flight deck, it is essential to begin by making a personal assessment of stress in all areas of your life.
    Answer (A) is incorrect. To eliminate the more serious life and flight deck stress issues, you must first make an assessment of stress in all areas of your life to identify those stressors. **Answer (B) is incorrect.** To know the exact cause of the stress, you must first make an assessment of stress in all areas of your life to identify stressors and the causes of them.

28. The DECIDE process consists of six elements to help provide a pilot a logical way of approaching aeronautical decision making. These elements are to

    A. estimate, determine, choose, identify, detect, and evaluate.

    B. determine, evaluate, choose, identify, do, and eliminate.

    C. detect, estimate, choose, identify, do, and evaluate.

Answer (C) is correct. (AC 60-22)
    DISCUSSION: The DECIDE model, comprised of six elements, is intended to provide a pilot with a logical way of approaching decision making. These six elements, using the acronym DECIDE, are detect, estimate, choose, identify, do, and evaluate.
    Answer (A) is incorrect. One of the elements of the DECIDE process is "do," not "determine." **Answer (B) is incorrect.** Two of the elements of the DECIDE process are "detect," not "determine," and "estimate," not "eliminate."

29. If a pilot wanted to mitigate risk during a cross-country flight in MVFR conditions, the pilot could

    A. Take a pilot who is IFR-rated.

    B. Continue the flight as planned.

    C. Stay out of controlled airspace.

Answer (A) is correct. (FAA-H-8083-9B Chap 1)
    DISCUSSION: Risk assessment is only part of the risk management equation. After determining the level of risk, the pilot needs to mitigate, or reduce, the risk. In this example, the pilot could reduce the risk by taking a qualified IFR-rated pilot along on the trip in case the weather deteriorated below VFR minimums.
    Answer (B) is incorrect. Continuing the flight as planned is acceptance, not mitigation, of the risk of flying in MVFR conditions. **Answer (C) is incorrect.** Deciding to stay out of controlled airspace should be an immediate red flag, as it signals that the pilot may try to push his or her limits and continue into weather that could present additional hazards. Risk mitigation is about reducing total risk, not adding additional potential risks to the planned flight.

30. A pilot's inexperience in direct crosswinds greater than 10 knots is an example of which of the fundamental risk elements?

    A. The pilot in command.

    B. The aircraft.

    C. The external pressures.

Answer (A) is correct. (FAA-H-8083-9B Chap 1)
    DISCUSSION: The pilot is one of the risk factors in a flight. The pilot must ask, "Am I ready for this trip?" in terms of experience, currency, and physical and emotional condition. If the pilot has experience with 10 knots of direct crosswind, it could be unsafe to exceed a 10-knot crosswind component without additional training. Therefore, the crosswind experience level is that pilot's personal limitation until additional training with a CFI provides the pilot with additional experience for flying in crosswinds that exceed 10 knots.
    Answer (B) is incorrect. The pilot's lack of experience level in crosswinds that exceed 10 knots is a personal limitation and risk factor, not one having to do with the aircraft itself. **Answer (C) is incorrect.** The pilot's lack of experience level in crosswinds that exceed 10 knots is a personal limitation and risk factor, not one having to do with external pressures associated with a planned flight.

31. The antidote for the antiauthority hazardous attitude is

    A. "Follow the rules. They are usually right."

    B. "It could happen to me."

    C. "I am not helpless. I can make a difference."

Answer (A) is correct. (FAA-H-8083-9B Chap 1)
    DISCUSSION: The antidote for the antiauthority hazardous attitude is "Follow the rules. They are usually right."
    Answer (B) is incorrect. "It could happen to me" is the antidote for the invulnerability hazardous attitude. **Answer (C) is incorrect.** "I am not helpless. I can make a difference" is the antidote for the resignation hazardous attitude.

32. Which of the following aircraft risks can be mitigated during the preflight inspection?

    A. Urgency of completing the flight.

    B. Weather en-route.

    C. Fuel quantity.

Answer (C) is correct. (FAA-H-8083-9B Chap 1)
    DISCUSSION: As part of a preflight inspection, the pilot in command should check the fuel quantity to ensure that the amount is accurate compared with what was ordered and what was planned for during the preflight planning phase.
    Answer (A) is incorrect. The urgency of completing the flight is a risk factor associated with external pressures, not the aircraft. This risk factor should be dealt with during the pilot's evaluation of the planned flight, not during the preflight inspection. **Answer (B) is incorrect.** The weather en-route for a planned flight is an environmental risk factor, not one associated with the aircraft. This risk factor should be dealt with during the preflight planning phase rather than during the preflight inspection.

33. The macho attitude can be described by which of the following statements?

    A. "Do something quickly!"

    B. "I can do it."

    C. "Do not tell me what to do!"

Answer (B) is correct. (AC 60-22)
    DISCUSSION: "I can do it" is an example of a macho attitude. It is characteristic of an individual who thinks (s)he is superior to others.
    Answer (A) is incorrect. The impulsivity attitude is expressed by taking action quickly with little thought for the consequences. A macho attitude is displayed by someone who thinks "I can do it." **Answer (C) is incorrect.** "Do not tell me what to do!" is the thought had by one who displays the antiauthority attitude. A macho attitude is displayed by someone who thinks "I can do it."

34. What is the antidote to the hazardous attitude of invulnerability?

    A. "It could happen to me."

    B. "Not so fast. Think first."

    C. "Taking chances is foolish."

Answer (A) is correct. (AC 60-22)
    DISCUSSION: To properly counteract the attitude of invulnerability, the antidote is thinking or saying "It could happen to me."
    Answer (B) is incorrect. "Not so fast. Think first." describes the antidote to the hazardous attitude of impulsivity. **Answer (C) is incorrect.** A macho attitude can be neutralized by thinking "Taking chances is foolish."

35. During a stall recovery, the instructor allows the learner to exceed maneuvering speed. Which best illustrates an 'anti-authority' reaction by the instructor?

    A. There has not been a problem doing this in the past.

    B. The aircraft can handle a lot more than the maneuvering speed.

    C. The learner should know how to recover from a stall by this time.

Answer (B) is correct. (AC 60-22)
    DISCUSSION: An example of the antiauthority ("Don't tell me what to do!") attitude would be an instructor allowing a learner to exceed maneuvering speed during a stall recovery. The specific antiauthority attitude expressed by the instructor is "The aircraft can handle a lot more than the maneuvering speed."
    Answer (A) is incorrect. This attitude falls closer to the hazardous attitude of invulnerability ("It won't happen to me"). There might not have been a problem in the past, but it could happen. **Answer (C) is incorrect.** The hazardous attitude in this answer selection is resignation ("What's the use?"). The instructor in this case should instead ask himself or herself "How can I teach this learner how and when to recover from a stall?"

36. The body's response to a set of circumstances that induces a change in an individual's current physiological and/or psychological patterns of functioning forcing the individual to adapt to these changes is

    A. risk management.

    B. aeronautical decision making.

    C. stress.

Answer (C) is correct. (AC 60-22)
    DISCUSSION: Stress describes the body's response to a set of circumstances that induces a change in an individual's current physiological and/or psychological patterns of functioning, forcing the individual to adapt to these changes.
    Answer (A) is incorrect. Risk management is the part of the decision-making process that relies on situational awareness, problem recognition, and good judgment to reduce risks associated with each flight, not stress. **Answer (B) is incorrect.** Aeronautical decision making is a systematic approach to the mental process used by pilots to consistently determine the best course of action in response to a given set of circumstances. Stress describes the body's response to a set of circumstances that induces a change in an individual's current physiological and/or psychological patterns of functioning, forcing the individual to adapt to these changes.

37. To help manage flight deck stress, you should

    A. evaluate the effect(s) of the action taken to counter the change.

    B. recall the antidote "I am not helpless. I can make a difference."

    C. try to relax and think rationally at the first sign of stress.

Answer (C) is correct. *(AC 60-22)*
    DISCUSSION: To help manage flight deck stress, you should try to relax and think rationally at the first sign of stress.
    Answer (A) is incorrect. Evaluating the effect(s) of the action taken to counter the change describes the sixth element of the DECIDE model, evaluate. **Answer (B) is incorrect.** The antidote "I am not helpless. I can make a difference" will not help reduce stress, but instead will help counteract the tendency to display an attitude of resignation.

38. The likely cause of a pilot ignoring the requirements for minimum fuel reserve is most likely overconfidence, disregard for applicable regulations, or

    A. lack of flight planning.

    B. acute fatigue.

    C. learning plateau.

Answer (A) is correct. *(FAA-H-8083-9B Chap 1)*
    DISCUSSION: Operating without adequate fuel reserves or ignoring minimum fuel reserve requirements is generally the result of overconfidence, lack of flight planning, or disregarding applicable regulations.
    Answer (B) is incorrect. Acute fatigue, a normal occurrence of everyday living, is the tiredness felt after long periods of physical and mental strain, including strenuous muscular effort, immobility, heavy mental workload, strong emotional pressure, monotony, and lack of sleep. **Answer (C) is incorrect.** A learning plateau is a phenomenon where progress appears to cease or slow down for a significant period of time before once again increasing.

39. Which of the following are five variables that can affect a pilot's decision-making process during single-pilot operations?

    A. Plan, pilot, precision, practice, process.

    B. Plan, weather, maintenance, pilot, ATC.

    C. Pilot, plan, programming, plane, passengers.

Answer (C) is correct. *(FAA-H-8083-9B Chap 1)*
    DISCUSSION: The plan, plane, pilot, passengers, and programming are all variables that should be evaluated during a flight or an emergency to help make sound decisions.
    Answer (A) is incorrect. Precision, practice, and process are not part of the 5P check. **Answer (B) is incorrect.** In the 5P checklist, weather is part of the plan and maintenance is part of the plane. ATC is part of CRM.

40. Single-pilot resource management (SRM) teaches pilots to use all available resources. Which principle does this replicate?

    A. Higher-order thinking skills (HOTS).

    B. Crew resource management (CRM).

    C. Aeronautical decision making (ADM).

Answer (B) is correct. *(FAA-H-8083-9B Chap 1)*
    DISCUSSION: Using all available resources is a component of CRM.
    Answer (A) is incorrect. HOTS is a result of problem-based learning. **Answer (C) is incorrect.** Using all available resources is a component of ADM, which leads to good SRM.

41. What should be done with the "plan" in the 5P method?

    A. It may be discarded once in flight.

    B. It should be followed for the entire flight.

    C. It should be reviewed and updated throughout the flight.

Answer (C) is correct. *(FAA-H-8083-9B Chap 1)*
    DISCUSSION: The plan should be reviewed and updated throughout the flight after assessments are done. The plan should allow for changes to be made as flight conditions change.
    Answer (A) is incorrect. The plan should not be discarded. It should be consulted and reviewed as the flight continues. Changes should be made as necessary. **Answer (B) is incorrect.** The existing plan does not need to be followed throughout the entire flight. It should allow for assessments and changes as flight conditions change.

3.4 Effective Communication

42. The effectiveness of communication between instructor and learner is measured by the

    A. degree of dynamic, interrelated elements.

    B. similarity between the idea transmitted and the idea received.

    C. relationship between communicative and dynamic elements.

Answer (B) is correct. (FAA-H-8083-9B Chap 4)
    DISCUSSION: Communication takes place when one person transmits ideas or feelings to another person or group of people. Its effectiveness is measured by the similarity between the idea transmitted and the idea received.
    Answer (A) is incorrect. The process, not the effectiveness, of communication is composed of three dynamic, interrelated elements -- the source, the symbols, and the receiver. **Answer (C) is incorrect.** The relationship between the communicative elements (source, symbols, and receiver) is dynamic. There are no dynamic elements.

43. Oral and visual codes used to communicate are called what?

    A. Signals.

    B. Sensory channels.

    C. Symbols.

Answer (C) is correct. (FAA-H-8083-9B Chap 4)
    DISCUSSION: Symbols are defined as oral and visual codes used to communicate.
    Answer (A) is incorrect. Symbols, not signals, are defined as oral and visual codes used to communicate. **Answer (B) is incorrect.** Sensory channels are ways through which symbols are perceived. Oral and visual codes used to communicate are symbols.

44. Effective communication has taken place when, and only when, the

    A. information is transmitted and received.

    B. receivers react with understanding and change their behavior accordingly.

    C. receivers have the ability to question and comprehend ideas that have been transmitted.

Answer (B) is correct. (FAA-H-8083-9B Chap 4)
    DISCUSSION: The rule of thumb among communicators is that communication succeeds only in relation to the reaction of the receiver. Effective communication has taken place only when the receivers react with understanding and change their behavior.
    Answer (A) is incorrect. Information may be transmitted and received without effective communication. Only when the receiver reacts to the information being transmitted and received with understanding, and changes his or her behavior accordingly, has effective communication taken place. **Answer (C) is incorrect.** The ability to question and comprehend ideas that have been transmitted is only one characteristic of a receiver.

45. When has instruction taken place?

    A. When a procedure has been explained, and the desired learner response has occurred.

    B. When the learner hears what is presented.

    C. When all the required material has been presented.

Answer (A) is correct. (FAA-H-8083-9B Chap 4)
    DISCUSSION: Instruction has taken place when the instructor has explained a particular procedure and subsequently determined that the desired learner response has occurred.
    Answer (B) is incorrect. Instruction has taken place when the instructor has explained a particular procedure and subsequently determined that the desired learner response has occurred, not only when the learner hears what is presented. **Answer (C) is incorrect.** Instruction has taken place when the instructor has explained a particular procedure and subsequently determined that the desired learner response has occurred, not only when all the required material has been presented.

46. To communicate effectively, instructors must

    A. recognize the level of comprehension.

    B. provide an atmosphere which encourages questioning.

    C. reveal a positive attitude while delivering their message.

Answer (C) is correct. (FAA-H-8083-9B Chap 4)
    DISCUSSION: Communicators consciously or unconsciously reveal attitudes toward themselves, the ideas they are trying to transmit, and their receivers. These attitudes must be positive if the communicators are to communicate effectively.
    Answer (A) is incorrect. An instructor can recognize the level of a learner's comprehension in the application step of the teaching process, not during the communication process. **Answer (B) is incorrect.** While an instructor should provide an atmosphere that encourages questioning, the learner must exercise his or her ability to ask questions to communicate effectively.

47. To be more likely to communicate effectively, an instructor should speak or write from a background of

    A. technical expertise.

    B. knowing the ideas presented.

    C. up-to-date, stimulating material.

Answer (C) is correct. (FAA-H-8083-9B Chap 4)
    DISCUSSION: A basic factor of a communicator's effectiveness is the ability to speak or write from a broad background of accurate, up-to-date, and stimulating material.
    Answer (A) is incorrect. A speaker or writer with technical expertise may depend on technical jargon. Reliance on technical language can impede effective communication, especially when the receiver lacks a similar background. **Answer (B) is incorrect.** Just knowing the ideas presented does not ensure that effective communication will take place. A communicator must be able to make the receiver react with understanding and change his or her behavior accordingly.

48. In the communication process, the communicator will be more successful in gaining and retaining the receiver's attention by

    A. being friendly and informative.

    B. using a varied communicative approach.

    C. using a variety of audiovisual aids in class.

Answer (B) is correct. (FAA-H-8083-9B Chap 4)
    DISCUSSION: The most successful communicator will use the variety of channels that best communicates the necessary ideas and techniques, i.e., a varied communicative approach.
    Answer (A) is incorrect. Effective, engaging communication is more complex than merely being friendly. The source, the symbols, and the receiver are all interrelated in the communication process. **Answer (C) is incorrect.** Audiovisual aids can often further the learning, not the communication, process by supporting, supplementing, or reinforcing important ideas. By presenting the material in a new manner, instructional aids can even improve communication between instructor and learner.

49. Communication takes place when

    A. one person transmits ideas or feelings to another person or to a group of people.

    B. symbols are used to transmit messages.

    C. the instructor takes into account the learner's background, experience, and education.

Answer (A) is correct. (FAA-H-8083-9B Chap 4)
    DISCUSSION: Communication takes place when one person transmits ideas or feelings to another person or to a group of people.
    Answer (B) is incorrect. While symbols are used to transmit messages, the receiver has to have the same understanding of the symbol as the communicator for communication to take place. **Answer (C) is incorrect.** Knowledge of the learner's background does not guarantee communication will take place. Communication takes place when one person transmits ideas or feelings to another person or to a group of people.

50. The three dynamically interrelated elements that compose the process of communication are

    A. Visual, auditory, and kinesthetic.

    B. Source, symbol, and receiver.

    C. Background, experience, and education.

Answer (B) is correct. (FAA-H-8083-9B Chap 4)
    DISCUSSION: The process of communication is composed of a source, the symbols used in transmitting the message, and the receiver.
    Answer (A) is incorrect. The three sensory channels through which symbols are perceived are the visual, auditory, and kinesthetic channels. The process of communication, however, is composed of a source, the symbols used in transmitting the message, and the receiver. **Answer (C) is incorrect.** The process of communication is composed of a source, the symbols used in transmitting the message, and the receiver.

51. What is true of symbols?

    A. Ideas can be communicated by presenting individual symbols.

    B. The three sensory channels that symbols are perceived through are words, signs, visual aids.

    C. Instructors should use a variety of sensory channels to be more successful in gaining and retaining learner attention.

Answer (C) is correct. (FAA-H-8083-9B Chap 4)
    DISCUSSION: Instructors will be more successful in gaining and retaining learner attention by using a variety of sensory channels.
    Answer (A) is incorrect. Ideas are communicated only when symbols are combined into meaningful wholes (e.g., sentences, paragraphs, chapters, etc.). Instructors will be more successful in gaining and retaining learner attention by using a variety of sensory channels. **Answer (B) is incorrect.** Symbols are perceived through three sensory channels: visual, auditory, or kinesthetic, not words, signs, or visual aids.

3.5 Barriers to Effective Communication

52. Probably the greatest single barrier to effective communication in the teaching process is a lack of

    A. respect for the instructor.

    B. personality harmony between instructor and learner.

    C. a common experience level between instructor and learner.

Answer (C) is correct. (FAA-H-8083-9B Chap 4)
    DISCUSSION: The greatest single barrier to effective communication is the lack of common experience between the communicator and the receiver. Those with the least in common usually find it difficult to communicate.
    Answer (A) is incorrect. While lack of respect for the instructor is a barrier to communication, it is not as great and as prevalent as a lack of common experience between the communicator and the receiver. **Answer (B) is incorrect.** While lack of personality harmony is a barrier to communication, it is not as great and as prevalent as a lack of common experience between the communicator and the receiver.

53. A communicator's words cannot communicate the desired meaning to another person unless the

    A. words have meaningful referents.

    B. words give the meaning that is in the mind of the receiver.

    C. listener or reader has had some experience with the objects or concepts to which these words refer.

Answer (C) is correct. (FAA-H-8083-9B Chap 4)
    DISCUSSION: Since a common core of experience is basic to effective communication, a communicator's words cannot communicate the desired meaning to another person unless the listener or the reader has had some experience with the objects or concepts to which these words refer.
    Answer (A) is incorrect. The words must have not only meaningful referents, but the exact same meaningful referents in order for the communicator and the receiver to share a desired meaning. **Answer (B) is incorrect.** Words only arouse desired meanings if the communicator generates the desired response in the mind of the receiver. The nature of this response is determined by the receiver's past experiences with the words and the concepts to which they refer.

54. Which of the following is an example of a problem with using abstract words?

    A. They may stand for ideas that cannot be directly experienced by the learner.

    B. They tend to confuse the listener between the symbol and the symbolized object.

    C. They reduce the effectiveness of role-playing methods.

Answer (A) is correct. (FAA-H-8083-9B Chap 4)
    DISCUSSION: Abstract words stand for ideas that cannot be directly experienced; i.e., they do not call forth the specific mental image in the mind of the learner that the instructor intends. The word "aircraft" is an abstract word. It does not call to mind a specific aircraft in the imaginations of various learners.
    Answer (B) is incorrect. Confusion between the symbol and the symbolized object is a barrier to communication separate and distinct from the use of abstract words. **Answer (C) is incorrect.** Reducing the effectiveness of role-playing methods is not among the problems of using abstract words.

55. The danger in using abstract words is that they

    A. sum up vast areas of experience.

    B. call forth different mental images in the minds of the receivers.

    C. will not evoke the specific items of experience in the listener's mind that the communicator intends.

Answer (C) is correct. (FAA-H-8083-9B Chap 4)
    DISCUSSION: The purpose of abstract words is not to bring forth specific ideas in the mind of the receiver but to serve as shorthand symbols that sum up vast areas of experience. The danger in using abstract words is that they will not evoke the specific items in the listener's mind that the communicator intends.
    Answer (A) is incorrect. The purpose, not the danger, of using abstract words is to use them as shorthand symbols that sum up vast areas of experience. **Answer (B) is incorrect.** Abstract words do not call forth mental images; on the contrary, they stand for ideas that cannot be directly experienced.

56. By using abstractions in the communication process, the communicator will

    A. bring forth specific items of experience in the minds of the receivers.

    B. be using words which refer to objects or ideas that human beings can experience directly.

    C. not evoke in the listener's or reader's mind the specific items of experience the communicator intends.

Answer (C) is correct. (FAA-H-8083-9B Chap 4)
    DISCUSSION: Abstract words are necessary and useful. Their purpose is not to bring forth specific items of experience in the minds of receivers but to serve as shorthand symbols that refer to thoughts or ideas. The danger is that an abstract term might not evoke in the listener's mind the specific item of experience the communicator intended.
    Answer (A) is incorrect. Abstract words are not used to bring forth specific items of experience in the minds of the receivers. **Answer (B) is incorrect.** Concrete, not abstract, words refer to objects or ideas that human beings can experience directly.

57. What should you use in order to remove barriers to effective communication?

- A. Abstract terminology since concepts described in this way are universal and common to most learners.
- B. Language emphasizing that the learner should make an appropriate response for each situation.
- C. Concrete terms that refer to objects or concepts related to the learner's own experiences.

Answer (C) is correct. (FAA-H-8083-9B Chap 4)
   DISCUSSION: Concrete terms referring to objects that people can relate directly to their own experiences are essential to removing barriers to effective communication. Concrete terms specify an idea that can be perceived or a thing that can be visualized.
   Answer (A) is incorrect. Abstract terminology describes ideas that cannot be directly experienced by learners. It does not call forth mental images in the minds of learners. **Answer (B) is incorrect.** A barrier to effective communication may be that the language and words used rarely convey the same meaning from the mind of the instructor to the mind of the listener.

58. What is required for communication to be effective?

- A. The learner's past experience needs to be the same as the instructor's.
- B. The learner's understanding of the meaning of symbols needs to be the same as the instructor's intended meaning.
- C. The instructor should explain technical terms that he uses in speech.

Answer (B) is correct. (FAA-H-8083-9B Chap 4)
   DISCUSSION: A learner's understanding of the meaning of words and symbols needs to be the same as the instructor's understanding of the words and symbols. This requires the instructor to spend time making sure the learners understand that terminology and the correct or intended use.
   Answer (A) is incorrect. A learner and instructor will never have exactly the same experiences in life. Because past experience varies greatly among each individual, the learner's understanding of the meaning of the words needs to be the same as the instructor's understanding. **Answer (C) is incorrect.** While an instructor should explain technical terms (s)he uses, the learner still needs to understand what they mean and how and when they apply to a given situation.

59. What is the term for when a symbol is different from the intended meaning?

- A. External factors.
- B. Confusion.
- C. Abstraction.

Answer (B) is correct. (FAA-H-8083-9B Chap 4)
   DISCUSSION: Confusion between the symbol and the symbolized object results when a word is confused with what it is meant to represent.
   Answer (A) is incorrect. External factors may prevent a process or activity from being carried out properly and are composed of factors outside the control of the instructor. **Answer (C) is incorrect.** Abstractions serve as shorthand symbols that sum up large areas of experience.

60. Because words and symbols do not always represent the same thing to each person, speakers and instructors should

- A. use technical terms to accurately explain the subject being covered.
- B. employ words and symbols that are concrete to narrow the image being produced in the listener's mind.
- C. choose words and symbols that represent what is intended.

Answer (C) is correct. (FAA-H-8083-9B Chap 4)
   DISCUSSION: To communicate effectively, speakers and instructors should choose words and symbols that represent what is intended. Thus, confusion will be avoided.
   Answer (A) is incorrect. Technical terms do not necessarily accurately explain the subject being covered. This requires the listener to have background knowledge of what is being presented. **Answer (B) is incorrect.** Concrete words and symbols, while narrowing the images produced in the mind of a listener, can still confuse a learner if they do not represent what is intended.

61. External factors may prevent a process or activity from being carried out properly and are composed of what three factors outside the control of the instructor?

- A. Physiological, Psychological, Environmental.
- B. Psychological, Physiological, Biological.
- C. Physical, Environmental, Psychological.

Answer (A) is correct. (FAA-H-8083-9B Chap 4)
   DISCUSSION: The three factors that compose external factors are physiological, environmental, and psychological.
   Answer (B) is incorrect. Any biological problem that may inhibit symbol reception is known as a physiological external factor. The three factors that compose external factors are physiological, environmental, and psychological. **Answer (C) is incorrect.** Any physical problem, such as hearing loss, injury, or illness, is a type of a physiological external factor. The three factors that compose external factors are physiological, environmental, and psychological.

ed as

d learner
process is

physical

iological

Answer (C) is correct. *(FAA-H-8083-9B Chap 4)*
   DISCUSSION: Physiological external factors are defined as any biological problem that may inhibit reception.
   Answer (A) is incorrect. Physiological external factors are defined as any biological problem that may inhibit reception. Psychological external factors are a product of how the instructor and learner feel at the time the communication process is occurring. **Answer (B) is incorrect.** Physiological external factors are defined as any biological problem that may inhibit reception. External factors caused by external physical conditions are defined as environmental external factors.

ditions are

Answer (A) is correct. *(FAA-H-8083-9B Chap 4)*
   DISCUSSION: Environmental factors could include aircraft noise, vibration, or lighting conditions.
   Answer (B) is incorrect. Physiological factors could include hearing loss, injury, or physical illness. **Answer (C) is incorrect.** If either the instructor or learner is not committed to the communication process, communication is impaired.

yed in the
ngaged in
d?

Answer (B) is correct. *(FAA-H-8083-9B Chap 4)*
   DISCUSSION: If the learner is not committed to the communication process, as demonstrated by seeming distracted or not engaged, communication is impaired. This type of external factor is a psychological factor.
   Answer (A) is incorrect. Examples of physiological external factors could include hearing loss, injury, or physical illness. **Answer (C) is incorrect.** Examples of environmental external factors could include aircraft noise, vibration, or lighting conditions.

ning a better
me a better

Answer (B) is correct. *(FAA-H-8083-9B Chap 4)*
   DISCUSSION: Thinking before answering gives the listener time to process what the speaker has said and give appropriate feedback.
   Answer (A) is incorrect. Interrupting can lead to frustration from the speaker. The speaker can feel his or her thoughts or questions are not being heard. **Answer (C) is incorrect.** Daydreaming gives the impression the listener was not actually listening to the speaker.

dure is
esired

Answer (A) is correct. *(FAA-H-8083-9B Chap 4)*
   DISCUSSION: Instructional communication occurs when an instructor explains a procedure and determines that the learner exhibits the desired response. The instructor can determine that instructional communication has taken place by the learner's response.
   Answer (B) is incorrect. Questioning is a technique to develop communication skills. **Answer (C) is incorrect.** Roleplaying is a technique to develop better communication skills.

a learner has been taught. What type of questions should be used?

A. Open-ended questions.
B. Focused questions.
C. All of the answers are correct.

Answer (C) is correct. *(FAA-H-8083-9B Chap 4)*
   DISCUSSION: Both open-ended and focused questions can help an instructor determine how well the learner has learned. Open-ended questions allow a larger discussion to take place. Focused questions allow the instructor to stay within a single topic to determine the extent of the learner's understanding.
   Answer (A) is incorrect. Focused questions are also useful for determining how well a learner has learned. **Answer (B) is incorrect.** Open-ended questions are also useful for determining how well a learner has learned.

3.7 Instructor Responsibilities

68. Evaluation of demonstrated ability during flight instruction must be based upon

    A. the progress of the learner.

    B. the instructor's opinion concerning the maneuver(s).

    C. established standards of performance.

Answer (C) is correct. (FAA-H-8083-9B Chap 8)
    DISCUSSION: Evaluation of demonstrated learner ability during flight instruction must be based upon established standards of performance, suitably modified to apply to the learner's experience and stage of development as a pilot.
    Answer (A) is incorrect. Evaluation must be based on established standards of performance, not the progress of the learner. **Answer (B) is incorrect.** Evaluation must be based on established standards of performance, not on the instructor's opinion.

69. Evaluation of demonstrated ability during flight instruction must be based upon

    A. the instructor's background and experience relating to learner pilots at this stage of training.

    B. the progress of the learner, considering the time and experience attained since beginning training.

    C. established standards of performance, suitably modified to apply to the learner's experience.

Answer (C) is correct. (FAA-H-8083-9B Chap 8)
    DISCUSSION: Evaluation of demonstrated learner ability during flight instruction must be based upon established standards of performance, suitably modified to apply to the learner's experience and stage of development as a pilot.
    Answer (A) is incorrect. Evaluation should be based on established standards of performance and modified based on the learner's experience, not the instructor's experience. **Answer (B) is incorrect.** Evaluation should be based on established standards of performance, not the learner's progress since beginning training, modified based on the learner's experience.

70. It is important that an instructor enhance a learner's acceptance of further instruction by

    A. keeping the learner informed of the progress made.

    B. constantly reminding the learner of the learning objectives that lie ahead.

    C. setting standards beyond the learner's abilities.

Answer (A) is correct. (FAA-H-8083-9B Chap 8)
    DISCUSSION: In assessing piloting ability, it is important for the flight instructor to keep the learner informed of progress. This may be done as each procedure or maneuver is completed or summarized during post-flight critiques. Post-flight critiques should be in a written format such as notes to aid the flight instructor in covering all areas that were noticed during the flight or lesson.
    Answer (B) is incorrect. Keeping a learner informed of progress made to date is a more effective motivator than drawing attention to the tasks that the learner has not yet addressed. **Answer (C) is incorrect.** Performance standards should be realistic and achievable.

71. In evaluating learner demonstrations of piloting ability, it is important for the flight instructor to

    A. remain silent and observe.

    B. keep the learner informed of progress.

    C. explain errors in performance immediately.

Answer (B) is correct. (FAA-H-8083-9B Chap 8)
    DISCUSSION: In evaluating learner demonstrations of piloting ability, it is important for the flight instructor to keep the learner informed of his or her progress. This may be done as each procedure/maneuver is completed or summarized during post-flight critiques.
    Answer (A) is incorrect. In evaluating learner demonstrations of piloting ability, it is important for the flight instructor to keep the learner informed of his or her progress, not remain silent and observe. **Answer (C) is incorrect.** Learners should be allowed to make mistakes and correct them on their own; errors should not be pointed out immediately because learners learn by correcting their mistakes. The error can be explained at the completion of the procedure/maneuver or during a post-flight critique.

72. Goals learners consider difficult, but possible, tend to

    A. provide a challenge and promote learning.

    B. cause frustration and lead to failure.

    C. be appropriate only for learners lacking motivation.

Answer (A) is correct. (FAA-H-8083-9B Chap 2)
    DISCUSSION: Assignment of goals the learner considers difficult, but possible, usually provides a challenge and promotes learning. Motivation also declines when a learner believes the instructor is making unreasonable demands for performance and progress.
    Answer (B) is incorrect. The assignment of impossible or unreasonable goals discourages the learner, diminishes effort, and retards the learning process. **Answer (C) is incorrect.** All learners will benefit from the assignment of reasonable goals that offer a challenge to complete.

73. The use of distractions by a flight instructor

   A. will teach the learner to divide his or her attention between the distracting task and maintaining control of the aircraft.

   B. will be of little value to more experienced learners.

   C. will allow learners to develop concentration skills so they can ignore distracting passengers.

Answer (A) is correct. (FAA-H-8083-9B Chap 9)
   DISCUSSION: Instructor responsibilities include teaching the learner to divide his or her attention between the distracting task and maintaining control of the aircraft.
   Answer (B) is incorrect. Pilots at all skill levels should be aware of the increased risk of entering into an inadvertent stall or spin while performing tasks that are secondary to controlling the aircraft. **Answer (C) is incorrect.** The proper use of distractions will not develop concentration skills that allow learners to ignore distracting passengers.

74. Examples of all common endorsements can be found in the current issue of

   A. AC 61-67, Appendix A.

   B. AC 91-67, Appendix A.

   C. AC 61-65, Appendix A.

Answer (C) is correct. (FAA-H-8083-9B Chap 9)
   DISCUSSION: Examples of all common endorsements can be found in the current issue of AC 61-65, Appendix A.
   Answer (A) is incorrect. Examples of all common endorsements can be found in the current issue of AC 61-65, not AC 61-67, Appendix A. **Answer (B) is incorrect.** Examples of all common endorsements can be found in the current issue of AC 61-65, not AC 91-67, Appendix A.

75. Before endorsing a learner for solo flight, the instructor should require the learner to demonstrate consistent ability to perform

   A. all maneuvers specified in the Student Pilot Guide.

   B. all of the fundamental maneuvers.

   C. slow flight, stalls, emergency landings, takeoffs and landings, and go-arounds.

Answer (B) is correct. (FAA-H-8083-9B Chap 9)
   DISCUSSION: Before endorsing a learner for solo flight, the instructor should require the learner to demonstrate the consistent ability to perform all of the fundamental maneuvers.
   Answer (A) is incorrect. Before endorsing a learner for solo flight, the instructor should require the learner to demonstrate the consistent ability to perform all of the fundamental maneuvers, not all maneuvers specified in the Student Pilot Guide (which contains no maneuvers). **Answer (C) is incorrect.** Before endorsing a learner for solo flight, the instructor should require the learner to demonstrate the consistent ability to perform all of the fundamental maneuvers, not just slow flight, stalls, emergency landings, takeoffs, landings, and go-arounds.

76. The learner should be capable of handling problems that might occur, such as traffic pattern congestion, change in active runway, or unexpected crosswinds prior to

   A. the first solo cross-country flight.

   B. initial solo.

   C. being recommended for a Recreational or Private Pilot Certificate.

Answer (B) is correct. (FAA-H-8083-9B Chap 9)
   DISCUSSION: Flight instructors have a responsibility to provide guidance and restraint regarding the solo operations of their learners. Before receiving an instructor endorsement for solo flight, a learner should be required to demonstrate the consistent ability to perform all of the fundamental maneuvers and should be capable of handling ordinary problems that might occur, such as traffic pattern congestion, a change in the active runway, or unexpected crosswinds.
   Answer (A) is incorrect. The learner should be capable of handling problems that might occur prior to initial solo, not the first solo cross-country flight. **Answer (C) is incorrect.** The learner should be capable of handling problems that might occur prior to initial solo, not being recommended for a recreational or private pilot certificate.

77. What is one of the best actions an instructor can take to emphasize aviation safety?

   A. By setting the example.

   B. By informing the learner of his or her progress as each procedure is completed.

   C. By analyzing the learner's personality, thinking, and ability to tailor his or her teaching technique to the learner.

Answer (A) is correct. (FAA-H-8083-9B Chap 8)
   DISCUSSION: Emphasizing safety by example is one of the best actions an instructor can take to ensure aviation safety.
   Answer (B) is incorrect. Informing the learner of his or her progress as each procedure is completed is an example of evaluating the learner's piloting ability. Emphasizing safety by example is one of the best actions an instructor can take to ensure aviation safety. **Answer (C) is incorrect.** Analyzing a learner's personality, thinking, and ability and then tailoring a teaching technique to fit the learner is an example of providing adequate instruction.

78. What are the five main responsibilities of aviation instructors?

- A. Helping learners, providing adequate instruction, emphasizing the positive, providing pilot endorsements, and ensuring aviation safety.
- B. Helping learners, providing adequate instruction, demanding adequate standards of performance, emphasizing the positive, and ensuring aviation safety.
- C. Helping learners, providing adequate instruction, emphasizing the positive, practical test recommendations, and ensuring aviation safety.

Answer (B) is correct. (FAA-H-8083-9B Chap 8)
DISCUSSION: The five main responsibilities of aviation instructors include helping learners, providing adequate instruction, demanding adequate standards of performance, emphasizing the positive, and ensuring aviation safety.
Answer (A) is incorrect. Providing pilot endorsements, while a responsibility of an aviation instructor, is not one of the five main responsibilities. **Answer (C) is incorrect.** Practical test recommendations, while a responsibility of an aviation instructor, is not one of the five main responsibilities.

79. Which statement is true regarding flight instructor responsibilities?

- A. The flight instructor should motivate learners by using harsh criticism if a learner needs a behavioral change.
- B. The flight instructor should prepare the learner to become a safe pilot who takes a professional approach to flying.
- C. The flight instructor should avoid admitting personal errors, so learner confidence in the instructor is not undermined.

Answer (B) is correct. (FAA-H-8083-9B Chap 8)
DISCUSSION: The flight instructor should prepare the learner to become a safe pilot who takes a professional approach to flying. This encompasses all of an aviation instructor's main responsibilities: help learners to learn through adequate instruction, demanding appropriate standards of performance in a positive manner while prioritizing aviation safety.
Answer (A) is incorrect. Constructive criticism is advantageous to any learner when required. However, criticism that is harsh or deemed unfair will destroy a learner's confidence in the instructor. **Answer (C) is incorrect.** As a role model to learners, admitting when an error has occurred is intrinsic to an instructor's credibility and integrity. Learner confidence is destroyed when an instructor fails to acknowledge personal errors.

80. The use of standards, and measurement against those standards, is key to

- A. ensuring aviation safety.
- B. pilot supervision.
- C. helping learners.

Answer (C) is correct. (FAA-H-8083-9B Chap 8)
DISCUSSION: The use of standards, and measurement against standards, is key to helping learners.
Answer (A) is incorrect. The use of standards, and measurement against standards, is key to helping learners, not to ensuring aviation safety. **Answer (B) is incorrect.** The use of standards, and measurement against standards, is key to helping learners, not pilot supervision.

81. Which would more likely result in learners becoming frustrated?

- A. Giving the learners meaningless praise.
- B. Telling learners their work is unsatisfactory with no explanation.
- C. An instructor freely admitting mistakes causing lack of trust.

Answer (B) is correct. (FAA-H-8083-9B Chap 8)
DISCUSSION: It does not help to tell learners they have made errors and not provide explanations. If a learner has made an earnest effort but is told that the work is unsatisfactory, with no other explanation, frustration occurs. Errors cannot be corrected if they are not identified, and if they are not identified, they will probably be perpetuated through faulty practice. On the other hand, if the learner is briefed on the errors and is told how to correct them, progress can be made.
Answer (A) is incorrect. While you are not providing effective instruction by offering a learner meaningless praise, you are also not creating frustration on the part of the learner. This instructional error offers many other negative consequences, though, and should be avoided. **Answer (C) is incorrect.** While failing to admit your own errors might frustrate a learner pilot, freely acknowledging your mistakes to the learner is more likely to increase rather than decrease trust on the part of the learner. You are also acting as a good example to the learner pilot by acknowledging and talking through your errors.

82. What is one method of keeping learners aware of their progress?

    A. Learners should keep attempting a maneuver even if they are making the same mistake.

    B. Repeating a demonstration, showing the learners the standard their performance must ultimately meet.

    C. Learners are usually aware of their progress without instructor intervention.

Answer (B) is correct. (FAA-H-8083-9B Chap 3)
    DISCUSSION: One way to make learners aware of their progress is to repeat a demonstration or example and to show them the standards their performance must ultimately meet.
    Answer (A) is incorrect. They should be told as soon after the performance as possible and should not be allowed to practice mistakes. It is more difficult to unlearn a mistake, and then learn the skill correctly, than to learn correctly in the first place. **Answer (C) is incorrect.** Mistakes are not always apparent. A learner may know that something is wrong but not know how to correct it. In any case, the instructor provides a helpful and often critical function in making certain that the learners are aware of their progress.

3.8 Instructor Professionalism

83. Which statement is true regarding true professionalism as an instructor?

    A. Anything less than sincere performance destroys the effectiveness of the professional instructor.

    B. To achieve professionalism, actions and decisions must be limited to standard patterns and practices.

    C. A single definition of professionalism would encompass all of the qualifications and considerations which must be present.

Answer (A) is correct. (FAA-H-8083-9B Chap 8)
    DISCUSSION: Professionalism demands a code of ethics. Professionals must be true to themselves and to those they serve. Anything less than sincere performance will be detected by learners and immediately destroy instructor effectiveness.
    Answer (B) is incorrect. Professionalism requires good judgment. Professionals cannot limit their actions and decisions to standard patterns and practice. **Answer (C) is incorrect.** Professionalism is so multi-dimensional that no single definition can encompass all of the qualifications and considerations.

84. Aviation instructors should be constantly alert for ways to improve the services they provide to their learners, their effectiveness, and their

    A. appearance.

    B. qualifications.

    C. demeanor.

Answer (B) is correct. (FAA-H-8083-9B Chap 8)
    DISCUSSION: Professional aviation instructors must never become complacent or satisfied with their own qualifications and abilities. Aviation instructors should be constantly alert for ways to improve the services they provide to their learners, their effectiveness, and their qualifications.
    Answer (A) is incorrect. While an instructor's personal appearance is important to maintaining a professional image, aviation instructors should be constantly alert for ways to improve the services they provide to their learners, their effectiveness, and their qualifications. **Answer (C) is incorrect.** While an instructor's demeanor is important to maintaining a professional image, aviation instructors should be constantly alert for ways to improve the services they provide to their learners, their effectiveness, and their qualifications.

85. Professional aviation instructors need to commit themselves to

    A. maintaining minimal qualifications and standards.

    B. continuous professional development.

    C. sharing responsibility for phases of training.

Answer (B) is correct. (FAA-H-8083-9B Chap 8)
    DISCUSSION: Professional aviation instructors need to commit to continuous, lifelong learning and professional development through study, service, and membership in professional organizations.
    Answer (A) is incorrect. Simply maintaining the minimum qualifications and standards required to become an aviation instructor is the antithesis of continued professional development. **Answer (C) is incorrect.** The professional aviation instructor is the primary figure in aviation training and bears all responsibility for all phases of required training.

86. True performance as a professional is based on study and

    A. perseverance.

    B. research.

    C. attitude.

Answer (B) is correct. (FAA-H-8083-9B Chap 8)
    DISCUSSION: True performance as a professional is based on study and research.
    Answer (A) is incorrect. True performance as a professional is based on study and research, not perseverance. **Answer (C) is incorrect.** True performance as a professional is based on study and research, not attitude.

87. Learner confidence tends to be destroyed if instructors

    A. bluff whenever in doubt about some point.

    B. continually identify learner errors and failures.

    C. direct and control the learner's actions and behavior.

Answer (A) is correct. (FAA-H-8083-9B Chap 8)
    DISCUSSION: No one, including learners, expects an instructor to be perfect. An instructor can gain the respect of learners by honestly acknowledging mistakes. If the instructor tries to cover up or bluff, learners will be quick to sense it and lose their confidence in the instructor.
    Answer (B) is incorrect. Identifying the learner's errors and failures helps the learner to progress and gain confidence. **Answer (C) is incorrect.** Directing the learner's actions and behavior is a basic responsibility of the flight instructor.

88. Learners quickly become apathetic when they

    A. realize material is being withheld by the instructor.

    B. understand the objectives toward which they are working.

    C. recognize that the instructor is not adequately prepared.

Answer (C) is correct. (FAA-H-8083-9B Chap 2)
    DISCUSSION: Learners become apathetic when they recognize that the instructor has made inadequate preparations for the instruction being given or when the instruction appears to be deficient, contradictory, or insincere.
    Answer (A) is incorrect. Learners will lose respect for the instructor (not become apathetic) when they realize material is being withheld by the instructor. **Answer (B) is incorrect.** It is optimal that both the learner and instructor understand the objectives so that they may work cooperatively toward them.

89. Which is true regarding professionalism as an instructor?

    A. Professionalism demands a code of ethics.

    B. To achieve professionalism, actions and decisions must be limited to standard patterns and practices.

    C. Professionalism does not require extended training and preparation.

Answer (A) is correct. (FAA-H-8083-9B Chap 8)
    DISCUSSION: Professionalism demands a code of ethics. Professionals must be true to themselves and to those they serve. Anything less than a sincere performance will be detected by learners and immediately destroy instructor effectiveness.
    Answer (B) is incorrect. Professionalism requires good judgment. Professionals cannot limit their actions and decisions to standard patterns and practices. **Answer (C) is incorrect.** Professionalism is achieved only after extended training and preparation.

90. Which statement is true regarding the achievement of an adequate standard of performance?

    A. A flight instructor should devote major effort and attention to the continuous evaluation of learner performance.

    B. Flight instructors can affect a genuine improvement in the learner-instructor relationship by not strictly enforcing standards.

    C. Flight instructors fail to provide competent instruction when they permit learners to partially learn an important item of knowledge or skill.

Answer (C) is correct. (FAA-H-8083-9B Chap 8)
    DISCUSSION: Flight instructors fail to provide competent instruction when they permit their learners to partially learn an important item of knowledge or skill. More importantly, such deficiencies may in themselves allow hazardous inadequacies in the learner's later piloting performance.
    Answer (A) is incorrect. A flight instructor should devote major effort and attention to all areas of the teaching process, not only to the evaluation of learner performance. **Answer (B) is incorrect.** It is a fallacy to believe that a flight instructor can affect a genuine improvement in the learner-instructor relationship by not strictly enforcing standards. Reasonable standards strictly enforced are not resented by an earnest learner.

91. The professional relationship between the instructor and the learner should be based on what?

    A. A predetermined code of ethics.

    B. A mutual acknowledgment that both the learner and the instructor are working toward the same objective.

    C. The knowledge that the instructor will maintain the highest level of knowledge, training, and currency during training.

Answer (B) is correct. (FAA-H-8083-9B Chap 8)
    DISCUSSION: The professional relationship between the instructor and the learner should be based on a mutual acknowledgment that both the learner and the instructor are important to each other and that both are working toward the same objective.
    Answer (A) is incorrect. While professionalism demands a code of ethics, this is not what a professional relationship is based on. **Answer (C) is incorrect.** A relationship is two-sided and does not rest solely on the instructor to be knowledgeable and prepared. The professional relationship between the instructor and the learner should be based on a mutual acknowledgment that both the learner and the instructor are working toward the same objective.

STUDY UNIT FOUR

TEACHING METHODS

(10 pages of outline)

4.1 LECTURE METHOD

1. The lecture is used primarily for

    a. Introducing learners to new subject material,
    b. Summarizing ideas,
    c. Showing relationships between theory and practice, and
    d. Reemphasizing main points.

2. The following are four types of lecture methods:

    a. The illustrated talk, in which the speaker relies heavily on visual aids to convey his or her ideas to the listeners;

    b. The briefing, in which the speaker presents a concise array of facts to the listeners, who do not expect elaboration or supporting material;

    c. The formal speech, in which the speaker's purpose is to inform, persuade, or entertain; and

    d. The teaching lecture, for which the instructor must plan and deliver an oral presentation in a manner that helps the learners reach the desired learning outcomes.

3. One advantage of a teaching lecture is that the instructor can present many ideas in a relatively short time. Facts and ideas that have been logically organized can be concisely presented in rapid sequence.

    a. Thus, a teaching lecture is the most economical of all teaching methods in terms of the time required to present a given amount of material.

4. One disadvantage of a teaching lecture is that the instructor does not receive a direct reaction (either words or actions) from the learners.

    a. Thus, the instructor must develop a keen perception for subtle responses from the class and must be able to interpret the meaning of these indirect reactions and adjust the lesson accordingly.

        1) These reactions could be in the form of facial expressions, manner of taking notes, and apparent interest or lack of interest in the lesson.

    b. The instructor must recognize that the lecture method is least useful for evaluating learner performance.

        1) A distinguishable characteristic of an informal lecture is active participation from the learner. This can be accomplished through the use of questions.

5.   The following four steps should be followed in preparing a lecture:

   a.   Establish the objective and desired outcomes,

   b.   Research the subject,

   c.   Organize the material, and

   d.   Plan productive classroom activities.

6.   The teaching lecture is best delivered extemporaneously–but from a written outline.

   a.   Because the exact words used to express an idea are chosen at the moment of delivery, the lecture can be personalized or suited to the moment more easily than one that is read or spoken from memory.

7.   In the teaching lecture, use simple rather than complex words whenever possible.

   a.   Picturesque slang and colloquialisms, if they suit the subject, can add variety and vividness to a teaching lecture.

   b.   Errors in grammar and use of vulgarisms detract from an instructor's dignity and reflect upon the intelligence of the learners.

4.2   COOPERATIVE OR GROUP LEARNING METHOD

1.   Cooperative group learning is an instructional strategy used to organize learners into small groups so that they can work together to maximize their own and each other's learning.

   a.   The most significant characteristic of group learning is that it continually requires active participation of the learner.

   b.   The main reason that learners are put in cooperative learning groups is so they can individually achieve greater success than if they were to study alone.

   c.   Learners in cooperative learning groups tend to interact and achieve in ways and at levels that are rarely found with other instructional strategies.

2.   Instructor planning is key to achieving meaningful learning.

   a.   Instructors must determine and outline clear lesson objectives and completion standards. Evidence of mastery of targeted content and skills must be stated to inform learners of the intended results.

3.   Instructors should organize small heterogeneous groups of learners and promote individual accountability.

   a.   The main advantage of heterogeneous groups is that learners tend to interact and achieve in ways and at levels that are rarely found with other instructional strategies.

   b.   Heterogeneous groups lead learners to learn to work together, to seek more support for opinions, to tolerate each other's viewpoints, and to consider viewpoints dissimilar to their own.

4.   Instructors should provide clear, complete instructions of what learners are expected to do. Sufficient time and the appropriate materials should also be supplied.

4.3 GUIDED DISCUSSION METHOD

1. Fundamentally, the guided discussion method of teaching is the reverse of the lecture method. The instructor uses questions to guide and stimulate discussion among learners. The instructor does not present new ideas.

    a. The instructor should treat everyone impartially, encourage questions, and exercise patience and tact.

2. In the guided discussion, learning is achieved through the skillful use of questions.

    a. Questions facilitate discussion, which in turn develops an understanding of the subject.

3. Questions used in a guided discussion can be broken into several types, each with its usefulness in the guided discussion:

    a. **Overhead** -- the question is directed to the entire group to stimulate thought and response from each group member.

    b. **Rhetorical** -- the question stimulates thought, but the instructor will answer it himself or herself. This is normally used in a lecture, not a guided discussion.

    c. **Direct** -- the question is addressed to an individual for a response.

    d. **Reverse** -- the instructor answers a learner's question by redirecting the question for that learner to provide the answer.

    e. **Relay** -- the reverse question is addressed to the entire group, not the individual.

4. In preparing questions, the instructor should remember that the purpose is to bring about discussion, not merely to get answers.

    a. Leadoff questions should be open-ended; i.e., they should start with "how" or "why."

    b. Avoid questions that begin with "what," "when," or "does" because they only require short, categorical answers such as "yes," "no," "green," "one," etc.

5. Each question, in order to be effective, should

    a. Have a specific purpose,
    b. Be clear in meaning,
    c. Contain a single idea,
    d. Stimulate thought,
    e. Require definite answers, and
    f. Relate to previously taught information.

6. When it appears the learners have adequately discussed the ideas that support a particular part of the lesson, the instructor should summarize what they have accomplished.

    a. This interim summary is one of the most effective tools available to the instructor.

        1) This summary can be made immediately after the discussion of each learning outcome.

        2) It consolidates what learners learned, emphasizes how much they know already, and points out any aspects they missed.

7. Unless the learners have some knowledge to exchange with each other, they cannot reach the desired learning outcomes.

    a. Learners without some background in a subject should not be asked to discuss that subject.

8.   Planning a guided discussion is similar to planning a lecture. The instructor should

   a.   Select an appropriate topic.
   b.   State the lesson objective.
   c.   Conduct adequate research on the topic.
   d.   Organize main and supporting points.
   e.   Plan at least one lead-off question.

9.   Instructors should prepare learners for a guided discussion. Learners should be encouraged to accept responsibility for contributing to the discussion.

10.   Guiding a discussion can be classified into three parts: introduction, discussion, and conclusion.

   a.   The introduction should include an attention element, a motivation element, and an overview of key points.

   b.   Discussion should be started with a lead-off question. Depending on how difficult the question is, the learners may need more time to think about the answer. The instructor should listen attentively and use "how" and "why" to follow up.

   c.   A guided discussion should be concluded by summarizing the material.

4.4 DEMONSTRATION/PERFORMANCE METHOD

1.   The demonstration/performance method is based on the principle that we learn by doing.

   a.   It is the most commonly used teaching method of flight instructors.

   b.   This is the ideal method for teaching a skill that requires practice, such as using a flight computer or performing crosswind landings.

2.   The demonstration/performance method of instruction has five essential steps in their respective order:

   a.   **Explanation** -- the instructor must clearly explain the objectives of the particular lesson to the learner.

      1)   Additionally, the precise steps to be completed and the desired end result should be explained.

      2)   Learners should be given the opportunity to ask questions to understand the requirements fully.

      3)   EXAMPLE: An instructor describes the steps (power settings, flap configurations, etc.) needed to successfully perform a short-field landing. Using the Practical Test Standards (PTS)/Airman Certification Standards (ACS) as a guide, the instructor explains what the completion requirements are.

   b.   **Demonstration** -- the instructor must show the learner how to perform a skill.

      1)   Demonstrations not closely representing the explanation should be immediately acknowledged and explained so learners do not replicate improper techniques.

      2)   EXAMPLE: An instructor demonstrates and completes a short-field landing within the given tolerances.

    c.   **Learner performance** -- the learner must act and do.

        1)   To learn skills, learners must practice.

        2)   Through doing, learners learn to follow correct procedures and to reach established goals.

        3)   EXAMPLE: A learner practices short-field landings under the supervision of an instructor.

    d.   **Instructor supervision** -- the instructor coaches, as necessary, the learner's practice.

        1)   Both learner performance and instructor supervision are performed concurrently.

        2)   EXAMPLE: During a short-field landing by the learner, the instructor follows along on the controls during the demonstration of the maneuver and coaches as needed.

    e.   **Evaluation** -- the instructor judges the learner performance.

        1)   From the measurement of learner achievement, the instructor determines the effectiveness of the instruction.

        2)   EXAMPLE: During a post-flight debriefing, the instructor explains the learner's performance.

3.   The **drill and practice** method is derived from the law of exercise and predicts that connections are strengthened via practice.

    a.   In this method, learning continues through each occurrence. Discipline and repetition are used to focus on the skill being developed.

4.   The **telling and doing technique** is a form of the demonstration/performance method of instruction that includes specific variations for flight instruction.

    a.   This technique consists of performing several steps in proper order.

        1)   Instructor tells -- instructor does/shows
        2)   Learner tells -- instructor does/shows
        3)   Learner tells -- learner does/shows
        4)   Learner does/shows -- instructor evaluates

    b.   The telling and doing technique should be followed by the drill and practice method, promoting learning through repetition because the things that are most often repeated are best remembered.

        1)   The human mind rarely retains, evaluates, and applies new concepts or practices after a single exposure. Learners do not learn to perform crosswind landings during one instructional flight. They learn by applying what they have been told and shown.

        2)   Every time practice occurs, learning continues.

4.5 PROBLEM-BASED LEARNING

1. Problem-based learning (PBL) describes a type of learning environment in which lessons are structured to confront learners with problems encountered in real life that force them to reach real-world solutions.

   a. A characteristic of PBL is that there is no single solution to the given problem.

      1) These types of "authentic" problems allow the learner to "make meaning" of the information based on past experience and personal interpretation.

   b. Benefits of PBL include helping the learner gain a deeper understanding of the information. Learners will also improve their ability to recall information in this type of learning.

   c. Effective PBL problems

      1) Relate to the real world, stimulating learner desire to solve them
      2) Require learners to make decisions
      3) Are open ended and not limited to one correct answer
      4) Are connected both to previously learned and new knowledge
      5) Reflect the lesson objective(s)
      6) Challenge the learner to think critically

   d. PBL promotes higher-order thinking skills (HOTS). An instructor should incorporate analysis, synthesis, and evaluation into PBL lessons.

   e. The three types of **problem-based instruction** are **scenario-based training**, the **collaborative problem-solving method**, and the **case study method**.

2. **Scenario-Based Training (SBT) Method**

   a. SBT is a realistic situation that allows the learner to rehearse mentally for a situation and requires practical application of various pieces of knowledge.

      1) Scenarios often describe a story beginning with a reason to fly because a pilot's decisions may differ depending on the motivation to fly.

   b. SBT scenarios challenge learners to manage available resources, exercise sound judgment, and make timely decisions with the goal of reducing accidents. The overall learning objective is for the learner to be more prepared to make good decisions based on a variety of real-world situations.

   c. SBT is a powerful tool because the future is unpredictable and there is no way to train a pilot for every combination of events that may happen in the future.

   d. A good scenario

      1) Is not a test,
      2) Will not have only one correct answer,
      3) Does not offer an obvious answer,
      4) Should not promote errors, and
      5) Should promote situational awareness and opportunities for decision making.

   e. EXAMPLE: "A newly rated private pilot is heading out on a cross-country flight to see his son graduate from college. He has already gotten a late start because of poor weather at his home field. Halfway through his flight he encounters low visibility and increased turbulence. ATC and AWOS both confirm the weather is IMC at his destination airport and several others nearby. What will he do now?"

3. **Collaborative Problem-Solving Method**

   a. The collaborative problem-solving method combines collaboration with problem solving when the instructor provides a problem to a group of two or more people working together who then solve the problem.

   b. This type of instruction is similar to SBT in that it includes open ended "what if" questions.

4. **Case Study Method**

   a. This method uses a written or oral account of a real-world situation that contains an educational message for the learner.

   b. The instructor presents the case to the learners who then analyze it, reach conclusions, and offer possible solutions. Case studies require learners to use critical thinking skills.

   c. A good resource for source material for the creation of case studies can be found at the National Transportation Safety Board's (NTSB) website.

      1) The flight instructor will have the learner analyze the information and suggest possible reasons for the accident. This analysis will both reinforce positive decision-making skills and provide the learner with the consequences of improper decision making.

5. Operational pitfalls are classic behavioral traps that can ensnare the unwary pilot. Pilots, particularly those with considerable experience, try to complete a flight as planned, please passengers, and meet schedules. This basic drive to demonstrate achievements can have an adverse effect on safety.

   a. These tendencies ultimately may lead to practices that are dangerous and sometimes illegal.

      1) Learners develop awareness and learn to avoid many of these operational pitfalls through effective ADM training. The scenarios and examples provided by instructors during ADM instruction should involve these pitfalls.

   b. Lack of effective ADM training may lead to overconfidence, disregard for applicable regulations, or disregard of flight planning.

      1) An overconfident pilot may not properly plan for minimum fuel reserves during preflight planning or may neglect the preflight planning altogether.

4.6 ELECTRONIC LEARNING (E-LEARNING)

1. Electronic learning (e-learning) is defined as any type of education that involves an electronic component (e.g., Internet, stand-alone software, simulators, etc.).

    a. Advantages of e-learning include less time spent on instruction and higher levels of mastery and retention.

        1) E-learning often seems more enjoyable from the learner standpoint because it allows learners to feel as if they are in control of what they are learning and at a rate that is comfortable for them.

    b. **Distance learning**, the use of electronic media to deliver instruction when the instructor and learner are separated, is another advantage of e-learning.

    c. Improper or excessive use of e-learning should be avoided. It will always be the responsibility of the instructor to monitor and oversee learner progress and to intervene when necessary.

    d. Limitations of e-learning include

        1) Lack of peer interaction and personal feedback,
        2) Lack of instructor control and oversight, and
        3) Costs associated with equipment/programs.

2. **Computer-assisted learning (CAL)** is a specific form of e-learning that integrates a personal computer with multimedia software to create a training device.

    a. The major advantage of CAL is that it is interactive in that the computer will respond in different ways depending on learner input.

        1) Some of the more advanced CAL applications allow learners to progress through a series of interactive segments in which the presentation varies as a result of their responses.

            a) CAL responds quickly to learner input.
            b) When CAL is combined with multimedia, learners can control the pace of instruction.

    b. Other advantages of CAL include the fact that learners can progress at a rate that is comfortable for them and are often able to access material at locations and times convenient to them.

    c. Both initial and recurrent training can be accomplished with CAL.

        1) Aviation companies that incorporate CAL reduce the amount of manpower, and associated costs, needed to train employees.

    d. CAL can be used to test a learner's achievement, compare results with past performance, and indicate a learner's weak or strong areas.

        1) EXAMPLE: In preparing for an FAA knowledge test, learners may use test prep software to practice tests, evaluate scores, and review missed questions.

    e. CAL should be thought of and used as a reference aid, not as the sole means of accomplishing a training program.

    f. Instructors should remain actively involved with the learners by using close supervision, questions, exams, or guided discussions to constantly assess learner progress.

3. Simulation, role playing, and video gaming are other forms of e-learning that, while not thought of as primary means of instruction, are still valuable tools for aviation training.

   a. Many flight schools incorporate flight simulation into a learner's training regimen to have them practice scenarios that would otherwise be unwise or unsafe to perform in an actual aircraft.

   b. Depending on the type of device, use of flight simulators can be credited for actual flight time.

4.7 INTEGRATED METHOD OF FLIGHT INSTRUCTION

1. Integrated flight instruction is flight instruction during which learners are taught to perform flight maneuvers, both by outside visual references and by inside reference to flight instruments for the same operations. As an instructor, your primary goal is safety. You must develop the habit of constantly monitoring the learner's performance and the aircraft's performance while maintaining an appropriate scan for traffic.

   a. For this type of instruction to be fully effective, the use of instrument references should begin the first time each new maneuver is introduced.

   b. It is also important for the learner to learn the feel of the aircraft while conducting maneuvers.

      1) EXAMPLE: Determining, by feeling, that the aircraft is out of trim or in an unusual attitude.

   c. Learners who have been taught by means of integrated flight instruction will develop the habit of continuously monitoring both their own performance and that of the aircraft.

2. The habitual attention to instrument indications leads to improved pilot competency, operating efficiency of the aircraft, and an overall increase in safety.

   a. EXAMPLE: Landings will be improved due to more precise airspeed control, and average cruising flight performance increases by holding precise headings and altitudes.

   b. The ability to fly in instrument meteorological conditions (IMC) is not the objective of this type of primary training yet will provide a good foundation for later training for an instrument rating.

3. During the conduct of integrated flight instruction, you are responsible for collision avoidance while the learner is flying by simulated instruments, i.e., under the hood.

   a. You must guard against diverting your attention to the learner's performance for extended periods.

4. At the same time, you must be sure that the learner develops, from the first lesson, the habit of looking for other traffic when (s)he is not operating under simulated instrument conditions.

   a. Any observed tendency of a learner to enter a maneuver without clearing the area must be corrected immediately.

4.8 THE POSITIVE APPROACH IN FLIGHT INSTRUCTION

1.   In flight instruction, an effective positive approach will point out the pleasurable features of flying before the unpleasant possibilities are discussed.

2.   EXAMPLE of a positive first flight lesson:

   a.   A preflight inspection familiarizing the learner with the airplane and its components

   b.   A perfectly normal flight to a nearby airport and back

      1)   The instructor calls the learner's attention to how easy the trip was in comparison with other ways to travel and the fact that no critical incidents were encountered or expected.

3.   EXAMPLE of a negative first flight lesson:

   a.   An exhaustive indoctrination on preflight procedures with emphasis on the potential for disastrous mechanical failures in flight.

   b.   Instructions on the dangers of taxiing an airplane too fast.

   c.   A series of stalls with emphasis on the difficulties in recovering from them. (The side effect of this performance is likely to be airsickness.)

   d.   A series of simulated forced landings, stating that every pilot should always be prepared to cope with an engine failure.

4.9 TESTING THE LIMITS OF LEARNER KNOWLEDGE

1.   Presenting learners with problems that require them to make a decision to test the limits of their understanding is an effective way to help them acquire knowledge. Some examples may include the following:

   a.   Ask learners to recite or practice newly acquired knowledge.

   b.   Ask questions that probe learner understanding and prompt them to think about what they have learned in different ways.

   c.   Present opportunities for learners to apply what they know to solving problems or making decisions.

   d.   Demonstrate the benefits of understanding and being able to apply knowledge.

   e.   Introduce new topics that support the objectives of the lesson whenever possible.

2.   Fatigue is one of the most treacherous hazards to flight safety as it may not be apparent to a pilot until serious errors are made.

   a.   The amount of training any learner can absorb without incurring debilitating fatigue varies.

   b.   Complex operations tend to induce fatigue more rapidly than simpler procedures do, regardless of the physical effort involved.

   c.   Fatigue is the primary consideration in determining the length and frequency of flight instruction periods, and flight instruction should be continued only as long as the learner is alert, receptive to instruction, and performing at a level consistent with experience.

QUESTIONS AND ANSWER EXPLANATIONS: All of the Fundamentals of Instructing knowledge test questions chosen by the FAA for release as well as additional questions selected by Gleim relating to the material in the previous outlines are provided on the following pages. These questions have been organized into the same subunits as the outlines. To the immediate right of each question are the correct answer and answer explanations. You should cover these answers and answer explanations while responding to the questions. Refer to the general discussion in the Introduction on how to take the FAA knowledge test.

Remember that the questions from the FAA knowledge test bank have been reordered by topic and organized into a meaningful sequence. Also, the first line of the answer explanation gives the citation of the authoritative source for the answer.

QUESTIONS

4.1 Lecture Method

1. In the teaching process, which method of presentation is suitable for presenting new material, for summarizing ideas, and for showing relationships between theory and practice?

   A. Lecture method.

   B. Integrated instruction method.

   C. Demonstration/performance method.

Answer (A) is correct. (FAA-H-8083-9B Chap 5)
   DISCUSSION: The lecture is used primarily to introduce learners to new material. It is also valuable for summarizing ideas, showing relationships between theory and practice, and reemphasizing main points. The lecture is the most efficient teaching method in terms of time and scale, if not in other ways.
   Answer (B) is incorrect. The integrated method of flight instruction is designed to teach learners to perform maneuvers both by outside visual references and by reference to flight instruments. **Answer (C) is incorrect.** The demonstration/performance method is better suited to teaching a skill (i.e., flight instruction).

2. What is one advantage of a lecture?

   A. A lecture is effective in showing relationships between theory and practice.

   B. Excellent when additional research is required.

   C. Allows for maximum attainment of certain types of learning outcomes.

Answer (A) is correct. (FAA-H-8083-9B Chap 5)
   DISCUSSION: In a lecture, the instructor can present many ideas in a relatively short time. Facts and ideas that have been logically organized can be concisely presented in rapid sequence. Lecturing is unquestionably the most economical of all teaching methods in terms of time required to present a given amount of material.
   Answer (B) is incorrect. One advantage of the lecture is that it can be used to present information without requiring learners to do additional research. **Answer (C) is incorrect.** A disadvantage, not an advantage, of a lecture is that the lecture does not enable the instructor to estimate the learner's progress; thus, learning may not be maximized.

3. When an instructor is teaching in a lecture environment (s)he should

   A. maintain a consistent tone of voice and pace of speaking.

   B. try to use simple rather than complex words.

   C. move from the unknown to the known.

Answer (B) is correct. (FAA-H-8083-9B Chap 5)
   DISCUSSION: In the teaching lecture, simple rather than complex words should be used whenever possible. The instructor should not, however, use substandard English. Errors in grammar and vulgarisms detract from an instructor's dignity and insult the intelligence of the learners.
   Answer (A) is incorrect. Instructors should attempt to add life to the lecture by varying the tone of voice and pace of speaking. **Answer (C) is incorrect.** Instructors should always move from the known to the unknown.

4. During a teaching lecture, what would detract from an instructor's dignity and reflect upon the learner's intelligence?

    A. Use of figurative language.

    B. Errors in grammar and use of vulgarisms.

    C. Using picturesque slang and colloquialisms.

Answer (B) is correct. (FAA-H-8083-9B Chap 5)
    DISCUSSION: During a teaching lecture, errors in grammar and the use of vulgarisms detract from an instructor's dignity and reflect upon the learner's intelligence.
    Answer (A) is incorrect. Figurative language, when used properly, can add interest and color to a lecture. **Answer (C) is incorrect.** Picturesque slang and colloquialisms, if they suit the subject, can add variety and vividness to a lecture.

5. Which teaching method is most economical in terms of the time required to present a given amount of material?

    A. Briefing.

    B. Teaching lecture.

    C. Demonstration/performance.

Answer (B) is correct. (FAA-H-8083-9B Chap 5)
    DISCUSSION: The teaching lecture is unquestionably the most economical of all teaching methods in terms of the time required to present a given amount of material. The instructor can concisely present many ideas that have been logically organized in rapid sequence.
    Answer (A) is incorrect. Although a briefing is a type of lecture, it is used to present a concise array of facts to the listeners who do not expect elaboration or supporting material. **Answer (C) is incorrect.** The demonstration/performance method is the least, not the most, economical in terms of time required to present a given amount of material.

6. Which is a true statement regarding the teaching lecture?

    A. Delivering the lecture in an extemporaneous manner is not recommended.

    B. Instructor receives direct feedback from learners which is easy to interpret.

    C. Instructor must develop a keen perception for subtle responses and be able to interpret the meaning of these reactions.

Answer (C) is correct. (FAA-H-8083-9B Chap 5)
    DISCUSSION: In the teaching lecture, the instructor must develop a keen perception for subtle responses from the class (e.g., facial expressions, manner of taking notes, and apparent interest or lack of interest in the lesson) and must be able to interpret the meaning of these reactions and adjust the lesson accordingly.
    Answer (A) is incorrect. The lecture is best delivered extemporaneously but from a written outline. The lecture can thus be personalized to suit different audience moods. **Answer (B) is incorrect.** In the teaching lecture, the instructor's feedback is not as direct as other teaching methods and therefore is harder, not easier, to interpret.

7. What is the most appropriate statement regarding the teaching lecture?

    A. The instructor must develop a keen perception for subtle responses from the class.

    B. The instructor receives direct feedback from learners which is obvious and easily interpreted.

    C. The instructor cannot offer learners with varied backgrounds a common understanding.

Answer (A) is correct. (FAA-H-8083-9B Chap 5)
    DISCUSSION: In the teaching lecture, the instructor must develop a keen perception for subtle responses from the class (e.g., facial expressions, manner of taking notes, and apparent interest or lack of interest in the lesson) and must be able to interpret the meaning of these reactions and adjust the lesson accordingly.
    Answer (B) is incorrect. Instructor feedback in a teaching lecture is not as direct as in other teaching methods and therefore is harder, not easier, to interpret. **Answer (C) is incorrect.** The lecture method is well suited for communicating a common understanding of essential principles and facts to learners with varied backgrounds.

8. The first step in preparing a lecture is to

A. research the subject.

B. develop the main ideas or key points.

C. establish the objective and desired outcome.

Answer (C) is correct. (FAA-H-8083-9B Chap 5)
 DISCUSSION: The following four steps, in order, should be used in preparing a lecture:

1. Establish the objectives and desired outcomes.
2. Research the subject.
3. Organize the material.
4. Plan productive classroom activities.

 Answer (A) is incorrect. Researching the subject is the second, not the first, step in preparing a lecture. **Answer (B) is incorrect.** Developing the main ideas or key points is the third, not the first, step in preparing a lecture.

9. The distinguishing characteristic of an informal lecture is the

A. use of visual aids.

B. learner's participation.

C. requirement for informal notes.

Answer (B) is correct. (FAA-H-8083-9B Chap 5)
 DISCUSSION: The distinguishing characteristic of an informal lecture is the active learner participation. A formal lecture does not include learner participation.
 Answer (A) is incorrect. Visual aids can be used in either the formal or informal lecture. **Answer (C) is incorrect.** The requirement for informal notes is not the distinguishing characteristic of an informal lecture. Notes may or may not be used in the formal or informal lecture.

10. An instructor can inspire active learner participation during informal lectures through the use of

A. questions.

B. visual aids.

C. encouragement.

Answer (A) is correct. (FAA-H-8083-9B Chap 5)
 DISCUSSION: An instructor can inspire learner participation during informal lectures through the use of questions. In this way, the learners are encouraged to make contributions that supplement the lecture.
 Answer (B) is incorrect. Visual aids emphasize and enhance the lecture but do not help get the learners actively involved. **Answer (C) is incorrect.** Encouragement aids learning in all situations, not just participation during lectures.

4.2 Cooperative or Group Learning Method

11. An instructional strategy which organizes learners into small groups so that they can work together to maximize their own and each other's learning is called

A. workshop learning.

B. heterogeneous group learning.

C. cooperative or group learning.

Answer (C) is correct. (FAA-H-8083-9B Chap 5)
 DISCUSSION: Cooperative group learning is an instructional strategy that organizes learners into small groups so that they can work together to maximize their own and each other's learning.
 Answer (A) is incorrect. Workshop learning may take place individually; it does not necessarily involve groups. **Answer (B) is incorrect.** Cooperative group learning is an instructional strategy that organizes learners into small groups so that they can work together to maximize their own and each other's learning. Heterogeneous groups are recommended for effective cooperative group learning.

12. The most significant characteristic of group learning is that learners tend to

A. actively participate in the learning process.

B. allow the instructor to actively engage the group.

C. passively participate in the learning process.

Answer (A) is correct. (FAA-H-8083-9B Chap 5)
 DISCUSSION: Many positive characteristics have been attributed to group learning, the most significant of which is that it continually requires active participation in the learning process by the learner.
 Answer (B) is incorrect. The most significant characteristic of group learning is that it continually requires active participation of the learner, not the instructor. The instructor must allow groups to work by themselves if the learners are to maximize each other's learning. **Answer (C) is incorrect.** Group learning requires active, not passive, participation of the learner.

13. The main reason that learners are put in cooperative learning groups is so they

    A.   learn and help each other.

    B.   can individually achieve greater success than if they were to study alone.

    C.   learn that teamwork is essential if all members are to learn equally well.

Answer (B) is correct. (FAA-H-8083-9B Chap 5)
    DISCUSSION: The main reason that learners are put in cooperative learning groups is so they can individually achieve greater success than if they were to study alone.
    Answer (A) is incorrect. While learners do learn and help each other, the main reason that learners are put in cooperative learning groups is so they can individually achieve greater success than if they were to study alone. **Answer (C) is incorrect.** While teamwork is essential to group learning, it is unlikely that all members will learn equally well. Learners are put in cooperative learning groups so they can individually achieve greater success than if they were to study alone.

14. The main advantage(s) with heterogeneous groups are that learners tend to

    A.   think for themselves since they are in a group of dissimilar learners.

    B.   interact and achieve in ways and at levels that are rarely found with other instructional strategies.

    C.   interact and achieve since they are in a group of similar learners.

Answer (B) is correct. (FAA-H-8083-9B Chap 5)
    DISCUSSION: Instructors should organize small heterogeneous groups of learners who have different academic abilities, ethnic backgrounds, race, and gender. The main advantage of heterogeneous groups is that learners tend to interact and achieve in ways and at levels that are rarely found with other instructional strategies.
    Answer (A) is incorrect. Heterogeneous groups lead learners to learn to work together, to seek more support for opinions, and to tolerate each other's viewpoints, not to think for themselves. **Answer (C) is incorrect.** Heterogeneous groups contain dissimilar, not similar, learners.

15. To achieve meaningful learning on the part of all in a group, instructors must

    A.   interact with individuals in the group so as to ensure lesson objectives are being met.

    B.   determine and outline clearly what the lesson objectives and completion standards are.

    C.   consider the background abilities of learners.

Answer (B) is correct. (FAA-H-8083-9B Chap 5)
    DISCUSSION: To achieve meaningful learning, instructors must determine and outline clear lesson objectives and completion standards.
    Answer (A) is incorrect. Interaction with individuals in a group does not guarantee lesson objectives are being met. By providing clear lesson objectives and explaining the completion standards, meaningful learning can be achieved. **Answer (C) is incorrect.** The background of the learner is not a factor in group learning as all individuals will be sharing ideas and potentially new thoughts. To achieve meaningful learning, instructors must determine and outline clear lesson objectives and completion standards.

16. During cooperative group learning, an instructor should supply learners with

    A.   Sufficient time and appropriate materials.

    B.   An open-ended outline for the lesson.

    C.   Vague instructions to facilitate the discussion.

Answer (A) is correct. (FAA-H-8083-9B Chap 5)
    DISCUSSION: Sufficient time and appropriate materials facilitate an engaging group discussion and allow learners to be thoughtful with their comments and answers.
    Answer (B) is incorrect. An open-ended outline will not provide an organized group discussion. **Answer (C) is incorrect.** Vague instructions may lead the discussion away from the desired outcome.

4.3 Guided Discussion Method

17. In a guided discussion, learning is achieved through the

    A. skillful use of questions.

    B. use of questions, each of which contains several ideas.

    C. use of reverse questions directed to the class as a whole.

Answer (A) is correct. (FAA-H-8083-9B Chap 5)
    DISCUSSION: The guided discussion method relies on the learners to provide ideas, experiences, opinions, and information. The instructor guides the discussion by use of questions aimed at drawing out what the learners know. Thus, learning is achieved through the skillful use of questions.
    Answer (B) is incorrect. In a guided discussion, each question used should contain only one, not several, ideas. **Answer (C) is incorrect.** A relay, not reverse, question is redirected to the class as a whole.

18. A question directed to an entire group to stimulate thought and response from each group member is identified as

    A. Relay.

    B. Overhead.

    C. Rhetorical.

Answer (B) is correct. (FAA-H-8083-9B Chap 5)
    DISCUSSION: In the guided discussion, learning is produced through skillful use of questions. To begin a guided discussion, the instructor should use an overhead question. This type of question is directed to the entire group to stimulate thought and response from each learner.
    Answer (A) is incorrect. A relay question responds to a learner's question by redirecting it back to the rest of the group. **Answer (C) is incorrect.** A rhetorical question is similar in nature to an overhead question, but the instructor answers the question. This is more commonly used in lecturing than in guided discussion.

19. In a guided discussion, leadoff questions should usually begin with

    A. why.

    B. what.

    C. when.

Answer (A) is correct. (FAA-H-8083-9B Chap 5)
    DISCUSSION: In preparing questions, the instructor should remember that the purpose is to bring about discussion, not merely to get only short categorical answers (e.g., yes, no, one, etc.). Thus, leadoff questions should usually begin with "how" or "why."
    Answer (B) is incorrect. A question beginning with "what" usually requires only a short categorical answer and will not encourage a discussion. **Answer (C) is incorrect.** A question beginning with "when" usually requires a short answer and will not encourage a discussion.

20. To begin a guided discussion, instructors should ask a leadoff question that begins with

    A. who or when.

    B. what.

    C. why or how.

Answer (C) is correct. (FAA-H-8083-9B Chap 5)
    DISCUSSION: Leadoff questions should usually begin with "how" or "why." For example, it is better to ask "Why does an aircraft normally require a longer takeoff run at Denver than at New Orleans?" than "Would you expect an aircraft to require a longer takeoff run at Denver or at New Orleans?" Learners can answer the second question by merely saying "Denver," but the first question is likely to start a discussion of air density, engine efficiency, and the effect of temperature on performance.
    Answer (A) is incorrect. Leadoff questions should contain "why" or "how," not "who" or "when." The former type of question creates a chance for deeper thought on the part of the learner, which can stimulate a more productive discussion. **Answer (B) is incorrect.** Leadoff questions should contain "why" or "how," not "what." The former type of question creates a chance for deeper thought on the part of the learner, which can stimulate a more productive discussion.

21. Which question would be best as a leadoff question for a guided discussion on the subject of torque?

    A. Does torque affect an airplane?

    B. How does torque affect an airplane?

    C. What effect does torque have on an airplane in a turn?

Answer (B) is correct. (FAA-H-8083-9B Chap 5)
    DISCUSSION: In preparing questions to lead off a guided discussion, the instructor should remember that the purpose is to bring about discussion, not merely answers. Avoid questions that require only short, categorical (i.e., yes or no) answers. Leadoff questions should usually begin with "how" or "why."
    Answer (A) is incorrect. A question beginning with "does" only requires a yes or no answer and will not encourage a discussion. **Answer (C) is incorrect.** A question beginning with "what" only requires a short, categorical answer and will not encourage a discussion.

22. When it appears learners have adequately discussed the ideas presented during a guided discussion, one of the most valuable tools an instructor can use is

    A. a session of verbal testing.

    B. a written test on the subject discussed.

    C. an interim summary of what the learners accomplished.

Answer (C) is correct. (FAA-H-8083-9B Chap 5)
    DISCUSSION: When it appears the learners have discussed the ideas that support a particular part of the lesson, the instructor should summarize what the learners have accomplished. This interim summary is one of the most effective tools available to the instructor in a guided discussion. To bring ideas together and help in transition, an interim summary should be made after the discussion of each desired learning outcome.
    Answer (A) is incorrect. A session of verbal testing goes against the intention of the guided discussion, where the instructor aims to "draw out" what the learners know in a structured but personable manner. **Answer (B) is incorrect.** A written test on the subject without an instructor summary would be testing learner opinions and experiences rather than facts.

23. Which statement about the guided discussion method of teaching is true?

    A. The lesson objective becomes apparent at the application level of learning.

    B. Learners without a background in the subject can also be included in the discussion.

    C. Unless the learners have some knowledge to exchange with each other, they cannot reach the desired learning outcomes.

Answer (C) is correct. (FAA-H-8083-9B Chap 5)
    DISCUSSION: Throughout the time the instructor prepares the learners for their discussion (e.g., early lectures, homework assignments), the learners should be made aware of the lesson objectives. This gives them the background for a fruitful guided discussion. Learners without some background in a subject should not be asked to discuss that subject.
    Answer (A) is incorrect. The lesson objective should be known while the learners are preparing for the guided discussion, or at least during the introduction, not afterward at the application level of learning. **Answer (B) is incorrect.** Learners with no background in the subject will not be able to contribute to an effective discussion.

24. During a guided discussion, learners should be encouraged to

    A. Take notes and listen to the discussion.

    B. Ask questions and contribute to the discussion.

    C. Meet with other learners.

Answer (B) is correct. (FAA-H-8083-9B Chap 5)
    DISCUSSION: Learners should take responsibility and become involved in the discussion to enhance learning. Asking questions and adding statements and knowledge is one way to do so.
    Answer (A) is incorrect. Taking notes and listening to the discussion apply to the lecture method. **Answer (C) is incorrect.** Meeting with other learners to discuss is part of the cooperative group learning method.

25. When planning a guided discussion, instructors should

    A. Use multiple vague topics.

    B. Have learners begin the discussion.

    C. Prepare learners and encourage contribution to the discussion.

Answer (C) is correct. (FAA-H-8083-9B Chap 5)
    DISCUSSION: Having learners prepare for a guided discussion aids in the learners' contributions to the discussion. If learners have researched the topic and prepared questions, they will be able to confidently add to the discussion.
    Answer (A) is incorrect. Using multiple or vague topics can lead the discussion down paths that are not desired for the lesson. **Answer (B) is incorrect.** Requiring learners to begin the guided discussion may lead the lesson in the incorrect direction. Instructors should open the guided discussion with an open-ended question appropriate to the lesson.

4.4 Demonstration/Performance Method

26. The drill and practice method of instruction is based on which of the following learning principles (Thorndike's Laws)?

A. Primary.

B. Effect.

C. Exercise.

Answer (C) is correct. (FAA-H-8083-9B Chap 5)
DISCUSSION: The drill and practice method is based on Thorndike's Law of exercise, which holds that connections are strengthened with continued practice. It promotes learning through repetition because those things most often repeated are best remembered.
Answer (A) is incorrect. Primacy, the state of being first, is an important learning principle, but it is not the basis of the drill and practice method. Primacy often creates a strong, almost unshakable impression and underlies the reason an instructor must teach correctly the first time and the learner must learn correctly the first time. For example, a learner learns a faulty technique. Now the instructor must correct the bad habit and reteach the correct technique. Relearning is more difficult than initial learning. **Answer (B) is incorrect.** Effect is an important learning principle, but it is not the basis of the drill and practice method. All learning involves the formation of connections, and connections are strengthened or weakened according to the law of effect. Responses to a situation that are followed by satisfaction are strengthened, while responses followed by discomfort are weakened, either strengthening or weakening the connection of learning, respectively. Thus, learning is strengthened when accompanied by a pleasant or satisfying feeling and weakened when associated with an unpleasant feeling.

27. Which method of presentation is desirable for teaching a skill such as ground school lesson on the flight computer?

A. Lecture/application.

B. Presentation/practice.

C. Demonstration/performance.

Answer (C) is correct. (FAA-H-8083-9B Chap 5)
DISCUSSION: The demonstration/performance method of teaching is based on the principle that you learn by doing. Learners learn physical or mental skills best by actually performing them under supervision. Learning to use a flight computer is an ideal application of this teaching method.
Answer (A) is incorrect. The lecture method is not suitable to teach flight computer use because the lecture does not provide for learner participation and, as a consequence, lets the instructor do all the work. **Answer (B) is incorrect.** Presentation/practice is not a method of presentation.

28. Learners should be given the opportunity to ask questions during which step of the demonstration/performance method?

A. Instructor supervision.

B. Evaluation.

C. Explanation.

Answer (C) is correct. (FAA-H-8083-9B Chap 5)
DISCUSSION: Learners should be given the opportunity to ask questions so as to understand the requirements fully during the explanation stage.
Answer (A) is incorrect. Instructor supervision occurs when the instructor watches learner performance and coaches as necessary. **Answer (B) is incorrect.** Evaluation occurs at the end of a task, and any questions relating to the desired outcome of the task should have already been asked.

29. What are the essential steps in the demonstration/performance method of teaching?

A. Demonstration, practice, and evaluation.

B. Demonstration, learner performance, and evaluation.

C. Explanation, demonstration, learner performance, instructor supervision, and evaluation.

Answer (C) is correct. (FAA-H-8083-9B Chap 5)
DISCUSSION: The demonstration/performance method of teaching is based on the principle that we learn by doing. Thus, it is used by flight instructors in teaching procedures and maneuvers. The five essential steps are

1. Explanation
2. Demonstration
3. Learner performance
4. Instructor supervision
5. Evaluation

Answer (A) is incorrect. The five, not three, essential steps in the demonstration/performance method of teaching are explanation, demonstration, learner performance (not practice), instructor supervision, and evaluation. **Answer (B) is incorrect.** The five, not three, essential steps in the demonstration/performance method of teaching are explanation, demonstration, learner performance, instructor supervision, and evaluation.

30. What is the last step in the demonstration/performance method?

   A. Summary.

   B. Evaluation.

   C. Learner performance.

Answer (B) is correct. (FAA-H-8083-9B Chap 5)
   DISCUSSION: The demonstration/performance method of teaching is based on the principle that we learn by doing. Thus, it is used by flight instructors in teaching procedures and maneuvers. The five essential steps are

1. Explanation
2. Demonstration
3. Learner performance
4. Instructor supervision
5. Evaluation

   Answer (A) is incorrect. Summary is not a step in the demonstration/performance method. **Answer (C) is incorrect.** Learner performance is the third, not last, step in the demonstration/performance method.

31. The basic demonstration/performance method of instruction consists of several steps in proper order. They are

   A. instructor tells--learner does; learner tells--learner does; learner does--instructor evaluates.

   B. instructor tells--instructor does; learner tells--instructor does; learner does--instructor evaluates.

   C. instructor tells--instructor does; learner tells--instructor does; learner tells--learner does; learner does--instructor evaluates.

Answer (C) is correct. (FAA-H-8083-9B Chap 9)
   DISCUSSION: The telling and doing technique of flight instruction (basically the demonstration/performance method) is very effective and valuable in teaching procedures and maneuvers. First, the instructor explains, then demonstrates. Then the learner performs, first by explaining as the instructor does, then by explaining and doing it him/herself while the instructor supervises. Finally, the instructor evaluates how the learner performs.
   Answer (A) is incorrect. It omits the first step, which is instructor tells--instructor does. The second step is learner tells--instructor does, not vice versa. **Answer (B) is incorrect.** It omits the third step of learner tells--learner does.

32. A post-flight debriefing is an example of which step in the demonstration/performance method?

   A. Instructor supervision.

   B. Evaluation.

   C. Explanation.

Answer (B) is correct. (FAA-H-8083-9B Chap 5)
   DISCUSSION: During a post-flight debriefing, the instructor explains the learner's performance. This is known as evaluation.
   Answer (A) is incorrect. Instructor supervision occurs when the instructor watches learner performance and coaches as necessary. **Answer (C) is incorrect.** Explanation is the first step in the demonstration/performance method and occurs before a task is performed. A post-flight debriefing would not occur during this step.

33. The telling and doing technique promotes learning because

   A. learners learn more by passively watching a task rather than engaging in it themselves.

   B. things that are most often repeated are best remembered.

   C. it consists of one simple step to remember; that of the instructor telling and doing.

Answer (B) is correct. (FAA-H-8083-9B Chap 9)
   DISCUSSION: The telling and doing technique promotes learning through repetition because those things most often repeated are best remembered.
   Answer (A) is incorrect. Learners do not learn better by passively watching. An engaged learner with proper supervision and who gets evaluated learns better; this happens in the telling and doing technique. **Answer (C) is incorrect.** The telling and doing technique consists of four steps, not one. They are as follows: instructor tells--instructor does/shows, learner tells--instructor does/shows, learner tells--learner does/shows, and learner does/shows--instructor evaluates. The telling and doing technique promotes learning through repetition because those things most often repeated are best remembered.

34. In the demonstration/performance method of instruction, which two separate actions are performed concurrently?

   A. Instructor explanation and demonstration.

   B. Learner performance and instructor supervision.

   C. Instructor explanation and learner demonstration.

Answer (B) is correct. (FAA-H-8083-9B Chap 5)
   DISCUSSION: In the demonstration/performance method of instruction, learner performance and instructor supervision are performed concurrently. As the learner practices, the instructor supervises and coaches as necessary.
   Answer (A) is incorrect. During the explanation phase, the instructor explains to the learner the actions they are to perform. This is accomplished during the preflight discussion. The demonstration is done in the airplane as the instructor shows the learner how to perform a maneuver. **Answer (C) is incorrect.** Instructor supervision, not explanation, and learner performance, not demonstration, are performed concurrently.

4.5 Problem-Based Learning

35. The overall learning objective of scenario-based training (SBT) is

A. that learners will improve their ability to recall previously learned information.

B. for the learner to be more prepared to make good decisions based on a variety of real world situations.

C. to promote situational awareness and opportunities for decision making.

Answer (B) is correct. (FAA-H-8083-9B Chap 5)
DISCUSSION: The overall learning objective of scenario-based training is for the learner to be more prepared to make good decisions based on a variety of real-world situations.
Answer (A) is incorrect. A benefit of problem-based learning is that learners will improve their ability to recall information. **Answer (C) is incorrect.** A good scenario should promote situational awareness and opportunities for decision making.

36. Problem-based learning (PBL) can lead to

A. Rote understanding of information.

B. Higher-order thinking skills (HOTS).

C. One correct answer.

Answer (B) is correct. (FAA-H-8083-9B Chap 5)
DISCUSSION: PBL should lead to HOTS. PBL can demonstrate that the learner has surpassed the rote level of learning.
Answer (A) is incorrect. The goal of PBL is to surpass the rote level of understanding. **Answer (C) is incorrect.** PBL can lead to multiple correct answers due to the promotion of HOTS.

37. The three types of problem-based learning instruction are

A. Scenario-based training, the collaborative problem-solving method, and the case study method.

B. Scenario-based training, the critical thinking method, and the case study method.

C. Scenario-based training, the cooperative problem-solving method, and the case study method.

Answer (A) is correct. (FAA-H-8083-9B Chap 5)
DISCUSSION: The three types of PBL instruction are scenario-based training, the collaborative problem-solving method, and the case study method.
Answer (B) is incorrect. The critical thinking method is not a type of problem-based learning. **Answer (C) is incorrect.** The collaborative problem-solving method, not the cooperative problem-solving method, is one of the three types of problem-based learning.

38. What is a characteristic of an effective scenario?

A. It should not promote errors.

B. It should be in the form of a test.

C. It should include an account of a real world situation that contains an educational message.

Answer (A) is correct. (FAA-H-8083-9B Chap 5)
DISCUSSION: A effective scenario should not promote errors.
Answer (B) is incorrect. A good scenario should not be in the form of a test. **Answer (C) is incorrect.** An account of a real-world situation that contains an educational message is a case study method.

39. "A type of learning environment in which lessons are structured to confront learners with problems encountered in real life that force them to reach real world solutions" is the definition of what?

A. Problem-Based Learning.

B. Case Study Method.

C. Collaborative Problem-Solving Method.

Answer (A) is correct. (FAA-H-8083-9B Chap 5)
DISCUSSION: Problem-Based Learning (PBL) describes a type of learning environment in which lessons are structured to confront learners with problems encountered in real life that force them to reach real-world solutions.
Answer (B) is incorrect. A written or oral account of a real-world situation that contains an educational message is the definition of the case study method. **Answer (C) is incorrect.** The collaborative problem-solving method combines collaboration with problem solving when the instructor provides a problem to a group of two or more people working together who then solve the problem.

40. Which of the following is true concerning effective problem-based learning?

A. Effective PBL problems are open ended and not limited to one correct answer.

B. Effective PBL problems are only connected to previously learned information.

C. Effective PBL problems begin with a reason to fly because a pilot's decisions will differ depending on the motivation.

Answer (A) is correct. (FAA-H-8083-9B Chap 5)
DISCUSSION: Effective PBL problems are open ended and not limited to one correct answer.
Answer (B) is incorrect. Effective PBL problems are connected both to previously learned and new knowledge.
Answer (C) is incorrect. A good scenario usually tells a story that begins with a reason to fly because a pilot's decisions will differ depending on the motivation to fly.

41. A written or oral account of a real world situation that contains an educational message for the learner describes what?

A. The Collaborative Problem-Solving Method.

B. The Scenario-Based Training Method.

C. The Case Study Method.

Answer (C) is correct. (FAA-H-8083-9B Chap 5)
DISCUSSION: The case study method is a written or oral account of a real-world situation that contains an educational message for the learner.
Answer (A) is incorrect. The collaborative problem-solving method combines collaboration with problem solving when the instructor provides a problem to a group of two or more people working together who then solve the problem. **Answer (B) is incorrect.** The scenario-based training method is a realistic situation that allows the learner to rehearse mentally for a situation and requires practical application of various pieces of knowledge.

4.6 Electronic Learning (E-Learning)

42. Which statement is true regarding e-learning?

A. The instructor need not be actively involved with the learner when using a form of e-learning.

B. E-learning can be used as the sole means of instruction for a learner.

C. An advantage of e-learning includes higher levels of mastery and retention.

Answer (C) is correct. (FAA-H-8083-9B Chap 5)
DISCUSSION: Advantages of e-learning include less time spent on instruction and higher levels of mastery and retention.
Answer (A) is incorrect. Instructors should still be actively involved with learners using e-learning so as to monitor and oversee learner progress. **Answer (B) is incorrect.** E-learning, while having many advantages, should not be solely relied upon to ensure proper knowledge transfer has taken place.

43. What is one reason why flight schools use flight simulation in training learners?

A. All flight simulation time can be credited for actual flight time.

B. Learners can practice scenarios that would be unwise or unsafe to perform in real-life.

C. Instructor oversight is not required when learners perform maneuvers on a flight simulator.

Answer (B) is correct. (FAA-H-8083-9B Chap 5)
DISCUSSION: Many flight schools incorporate flight simulation into a learner's training regimen to have them practice scenarios that would otherwise be unwise or unsafe to perform in an actual aircraft.
Answer (A) is incorrect. Not all time spent on a simulator may be credited toward actual flight time. Credit toward logging actual flight time also depends on the type of device being used for simulation. **Answer (C) is incorrect.** Instructors should still be on hand to oversee all types of e-learning, including that of flight simulation.

44. The capabilities of the most recently developed computer-assisted learning (CAL) applications allow the presentation to be customized based on the user's

A. responses.

B. previous experience.

C. wants and desires.

Answer (A) is correct. (FAA-H-8083-9B Chap 5)
DISCUSSION: Some of the more recent CAL applications allow learners to progress through a series of interactive segments where the presentation varies as a result of their responses.
Answer (B) is incorrect. The presentation can be varied based on the user's responses, not his or her previous experience. **Answer (C) is incorrect.** The presentation can be varied by the user's responses, not his or her wants and desires.

45. Which method allows a learner to control the pace of instruction?

   A. Simulation.

   B. Role playing games.

   C. Computer-assisted learning (CAL).

Answer (C) is correct. (FAA-H-8083-9B Chap 5)
    DISCUSSION: Real interactivity with CAL means the learner is fully engaged with the instruction by doing something meaningful, which makes the subject of study come alive. For example, the learner controls the pace of instruction, reviews previous material, jumps forward, and receives instant feedback.
    Answer (A) is incorrect. Simulation gives the learner a stake in the outcome, placing him or her in the shoes of a character in a real-world scenario. This valuable teaching method does not offer a learner direct control over the pace of instruction. **Answer (B) is incorrect.** Role playing games give the learner a stake in the outcome, placing him or her in the shoes of a character in a real-world scenario. This valuable teaching method does not offer a learner direct control over the pace of instruction.

46. Among the many advantages of computer-assisted learning (CAL) over other forms of instruction is that the computer can respond in different ways depending on the learner's

   A. age.

   B. mathematical ability.

   C. input.

Answer (C) is correct. (FAA-H-8083-9B Chap 5)
    DISCUSSION: The major advantage of CAL is that it is interactive—the computer responds in different ways, depending on learner input. When using CAL, the instructor should remain actively involved with the learners by using close supervision, questions, examinations, quizzes, or guided discussions on the subject matter to constantly assess learner progress.
    Answer (A) is incorrect. The learner's age is not a factor used by the computer to determine a response. **Answer (B) is incorrect.** The learner's mathematical ability is not a factor used by the computer to determine a response.

47. Which statement is true regarding e-learning?

   A. A major limitation of e-learning is that it can be conducted from alternate locations.

   B. Improper or excessive use of e-learning should be avoided.

   C. E-learning requires a learner to learn at the pace provided by the monitoring instructor.

Answer (B) is correct. (FAA-H-8083-9B Chap 5)
    DISCUSSION: Improper or excessive use of e-learning should be avoided. It will always be the responsibility of the instructor to monitor and oversee learner progress and to intervene when necessary.
    Answer (A) is incorrect. A major advantage, not limitation, of e-learning is that users can be in alternate locations from an instructor. This is termed distance learning. **Answer (C) is incorrect.** E-learning allows learners to feel as if they are in control of what they are learning and at a rate that is comfortable for them, not at a pace required by an instructor.

48. Which statement is true regarding Computer-Assisted Learning, or CAL?

   A. CAL will not be able to indicate a learner's weak or strong areas.

   B. CAL is used by flight schools so learners can practice scenarios that are unwise to perform in an actual aircraft.

   C. The learner controls the pace and content of instruction.

Answer (C) is correct. (FAA-H-8083-9B Chap 5)
    DISCUSSION: With CAL, the learner controls the pace and content of the instruction.
    Answer (A) is incorrect. Many CAL programs can and will indicate a learner's weak or strong areas. An example of this is software used in preparing for an FAA knowledge test. **Answer (B) is incorrect.** Flight simulation, not CAL, is used to practice scenarios that are unwise or unsafe to perform in an actual aircraft.

49. The major advantage of Computer-Assisted Learning (CAL) is that it is interactive; the computer will respond in different ways depending on learner

   A. background.

   B. input.

   C. training.

Answer (B) is correct. (FAA-H-8083-9B Chap 5)
    DISCUSSION: The major advantage of CAL is that it is interactive in that the computer will respond in different ways depending on learner input.
    Answer (A) is incorrect. The computer responds based on the learner's input, not background. The choice of CAL training may depend on the learner's academic or experimental background. **Answer (C) is incorrect.** The computer responds based on the learner's input, not training.

4.7   Integrated Method of Flight Instruction

50. Which of the following is the primary objective of integrated flight instruction?

    A. To develop the learner's habit of constantly monitoring both his or her performance and the aircraft's performance.

    B. To develop a proper scan while relating the instrument indications to the horizon.

    C. To develop multitasking skills.

Answer (A) is correct. (FAA-H-8083-9B Chap 9)
    DISCUSSION: It is important for the learner to establish the habit of observing and relying on flight instruments from the beginning of flight training. It is equally important for the learner to learn the feel of the airplane while conducting maneuvers, such as being able to feel when the airplane is out of trim or in a nose-high or nose-low attitude. Learners who have been required to perform all normal flight maneuvers by reference to instruments, as well as by outside references, develop from the start the habit of continuously monitoring their own and the aircraft's performance.
    Answer (B) is incorrect. The primary objective of integrated flight instruction is to develop the habit of constantly monitoring the pilot's own performance and the aircraft's performance. **Answer (C) is incorrect.** The primary objective of integrated flight instruction is to develop the habit of constantly monitoring the pilot's own performance and the aircraft's performance.

51. During integrated flight instruction, the instructor must be sure the learner

    A. develops the habit of looking for other traffic.

    B. is able to control the aircraft for extended periods under IMC.

    C. can depend on the flight instruments when maneuvering by outside references.

Answer (A) is correct. (FAA-H-8083-9B Chap 9)
    DISCUSSION: If learners are allowed to believe that the instructor assumes all responsibility for avoiding other traffic, they cannot develop the habit of keeping a constant watch, which is essential to safety. Any observed tendency of a learner to enter flight maneuvers without first making a careful check for other possible air traffic must be corrected immediately.
    Answer (B) is incorrect. The ability to control the aircraft for extended periods under IMC is not the objective of integrated flight instruction. **Answer (C) is incorrect.** The instructor must be sure not to let the learner focus his attention on the instruments at the expense of looking for other traffic.

52. What is integrated flight instruction?

    A. Flight instruction during which the learner learns by sole reference to the flight instruments.

    B. Flight instruction that combines the use of flight simulation with actual flight.

    C. Flight instruction during which learners are taught to perform flight maneuvers by outside visual references and reference to flight instruments.

Answer (C) is correct. (FAA-H-8083-9B Chap 9)
    DISCUSSION: Integrated flight instruction is flight instruction during which learners are taught to perform flight maneuvers, both by outside visual references and by inside reference to flight instruments for the same operations.
    Answer (A) is incorrect. Integrated flight instruction is not accomplished by sole reference to the flight instruments. It also includes outside visual references for the same operations or maneuvers. **Answer (B) is incorrect.** Simulation, not integrated flight instruction, uses flight simulators in conjunction with actual flight to train learners.

53. For integrated flight instruction to be fully effective, what must take place?

    A. A learner must rely on the instructor for collision avoidance.

    B. The use of instrument references should begin the first time each new maneuver is introduced.

    C. Learners must already have learned the feel of the aircraft while conducting maneuvers.

Answer (B) is correct. (FAA-H-8083-9B Chap 9)
    DISCUSSION: For integrated flight instruction to be fully effective, the use of instrument references should begin the first time each new maneuver is introduced.
    Answer (A) is incorrect. A learner should develop the habit of scanning for other traffic from the first flight lesson. The learner will rely on the instructor to ensure adequate collision avoidance while flying by simulated instruments, but this is not a factor in effectively conducting integrated flight instruction. **Answer (C) is incorrect.** Feel for the aircraft during a maneuver is learned during integrated flight training and is not necessary for effective integrated flight training.

54. Foremost among the objectives of integrated flight instruction is

A. encouraging habit patterns for observing and referencing the flight instruments.

B. developing the learner's ability to operate in IMC.

C. ensuring the learner is completely dependent on the instruments during VFR flight.

Answer (A) is correct. (FAA-H-8083-9B Chap 9)
DISCUSSION: The early establishment of proper habits of instrument cross-check, instrument interpretation, and aircraft control are highly useful to the learner. The habitual attention to instrument indications leads to improved landings because of more precise airspeed control. Effective use of instruments also results in superior cross-country navigation, better coordination of the aircraft, and generally a better overall pilot competency level.
Answer (B) is incorrect. The habits formed during integrated flight instruction provide a firm foundation for later training for an instrument rating but are not intended to provide the skills required to operate in IMC. **Answer (C) is incorrect.** Integrated flight instruction ensures the learner is able to operate the aircraft using visual references as well as the flight instruments.

55. Which of the following statements about integrated flight instruction is true?

A. Devote certain training lessons entirely to instrument or visual flight.

B. Instruction in the control of an aircraft by outside visual references is integrated with instruction in the use of flight instrument indications for the same operations.

C. Introduce maneuvers using visual references, then repeat the maneuvers using only the instruments.

Answer (B) is correct. (FAA-H-8083-9B Chap 9)
DISCUSSION: Integrated flight instruction is flight instruction during which learners are taught to perform flight maneuvers both by outside visual references and by reference to flight instruments. For this type of instruction to be fully effective, the use of instrument references should begin the first time each new maneuver is introduced. No distinction in the pilot's operation of the flight controls is permitted, regardless of whether outside references or instrument indications are used for the performance of the maneuver. When this training technique is used, instruction in the control of an aircraft by outside visual references is integrated with instruction in the use of flight instrument indications for the same operations.
Answer (A) is incorrect. In integrated flight instruction, learners must learn to use both the visual references and flight instruments simultaneously. **Answer (C) is incorrect.** In integrated flight instruction, learners must learn to use both the visual references and flight instruments simultaneously.

56. What is a benefit of learning to habitually give attention to instrument indications during primary training?

A. Cruising performance will increase by holding precise headings and altitudes.

B. Learners will be completely prepared for their instrument checkride.

C. Learners will be more likely to watch for other traffic.

Answer (A) is correct. (FAA-H-8083-9B Chap 9)
DISCUSSION: A benefit of habitually giving attention to instrument indications is better cruising performance because a learner will hold more precise headings and altitudes.
Answer (B) is incorrect. Additional training on the specifics of flying solely by reference to flight instruments will be needed. Giving habitual attention to instrument indications during primary flight training will, however, provide a basis for future training for an instrument rating. **Answer (C) is incorrect.** Instructors must be careful that learners develop the habit of looking for other traffic when operating by reference to instruments, even during VFR conditions. It can actually be a disadvantage if a learner focuses solely on an aircraft's instruments during primary flight training.

4.8   The Positive Approach in Flight Instruction

57. Which is an example of a positive approach in the first flight lesson of a learner with no previous aviation experience?

    A.   Conducting a thorough preflight.

    B.   A normal flight to a nearby airport and return.

    C.   Instruction in the care which must be taken when taxiing an airplane.

Answer (B) is correct. (FAA-H-8083-9B Chap 8)
   DISCUSSION: A normal flight to a nearby airport and back shows the learner some of the pleasant aspects of aviation. Such an introductory lesson leaves a positive impression in the new learner's mind. Positive teaching results in positive learning.
   Answer (A) is incorrect. In the first flight lesson of a learner with no aviation experience, conducting a thorough, exhaustive preflight is an example of a negative, not a positive, approach. The learner may question whether learning to fly is a good idea or not. **Answer (C) is incorrect.** In the first flight lesson of a learner with no aviation experience, instruction in the care that must be taken when taxiing an airplane is an example of a negative, not a positive, approach. The learner may question whether learning to fly is a good idea or not.

58. Which statement is true regarding positive or negative approaches in aviation instructional techniques?

    A.   A learner with normal abilities should not be affected by an instructor who emphasizes emergency procedures early in training.

    B.   A positive approach, to be effective, will point out the pleasurable features of aviation before the unpleasant possibilities are discussed.

    C.   The introduction of emergency procedures before the learner is acquainted with normal operations is likely to be neither discouraging nor affect learning.

Answer (B) is correct. (FAA-H-8083-9B Chap 8)
   DISCUSSION: Flight instructor success depends, in large measure, on the ability to frame instructions so that learners develop a positive image of flying. A positive approach, to be effective, will point out the pleasurable features of aviation before the unpleasant possibilities are discussed. A negative approach generally results in negative learning because the learner's perceptual process would be adversely affected by fear.
   Answer (A) is incorrect. An instructor who emphasizes emergency procedures early in training will most likely have a negative effect on the learning process regardless of a learner's abilities. The learner new to aviation is still quite impressionable. **Answer (C) is incorrect.** The introduction of emergency procedures before the learner is acquainted with normal operations most likely will be discouraging or threatening and will adversely affect learning.

4.9   Testing the Limits of Learner Knowledge

59. Which of the following is the primary consideration when determining the length and frequency of flight instruction periods?

    A.   Inattention.

    B.   Fatigue.

    C.   Distractibility.

Answer (B) is correct. (FAA-H-8083-9B Chap 2)
   DISCUSSION: Fatigue is the primary consideration in determining the length and frequency of flight instruction periods. Flight instruction should be continued only as long as the learner is alert, receptive to instruction, and performing at a level consistent with experience.
   Answer (A) is incorrect. Inattention is one of the symptoms of fatigue; it is not the same as fatigue. **Answer (C) is incorrect.** Distractibility is one of the symptoms of fatigue; it is not the same as fatigue.

60. Asking learners about problems or decisions that test the limits of their knowledge is

    A.   ineffective, only promoting rote level learning.

    B.   beneficial to gauge understanding and determines that the learner is able to apply the knowledge.

    C.   an effective method to help learners acquire knowledge.

Answer (C) is correct. (FAA-H-8083-9B Chap 3)
   DISCUSSION: To help learners acquire knowledge, the instructor should ask learners questions about problems or decisions that test the limits of their knowledge.
   Answer (A) is incorrect. For learners to fully understand a task or concept, instructors must push the limits of the learners' knowledge. This technique encourages learning beyond merely the rote level of learning. **Answer (B) is incorrect.** Asking questions about problems or decisions to test the limits of a learner's knowledge is beneficial to gauge understanding but is not a determination that the learner has the ability to apply the knowledge.

STUDY UNIT FIVE

PLANNING INSTRUCTIONAL ACTIVITY

(9 pages of outline)

5.1 COURSE DEVELOPMENT

1. A course of training is a complete series of studies leading to attainment of a goal, such as a certificate of completion, graduation, etc.

2. A determination of objectives and standards is necessary before any important instruction can be presented. Any instructional activity must be competently planned and organized if it is to achieve the desired learning outcomes.

   a. The broad overall objective of any pilot training is to qualify the learner to be a competent, efficient, safe pilot.

   b. There are two types of objectives in aviation: performance-based objectives and decision-based objectives.

3. **Performance-based objectives** are used to set measurable, reasonable standards that describe the required learner performance.

   a. They provide a way of stating what performance level is desired of a learner before progressing to the next stage of instruction.

   b. Written objectives are clear, measurable, and repeatable.

   c. These objectives consist of three elements: description of the skill or behavior, conditions, and criteria.

      1) **Description of the skill or behavior:** desired outcome of training stated in concrete terms that can be measured.

         a) EXAMPLE: "The learner should be able to repeat the steps to a proper engine start."

      2) **Conditions:** used to explain the rules under which the skill or behavior is to be demonstrated.

         a) EXAMPLE: "Using an approved airplane checklist and referencing the Pilot's Operating Handbook (POH), perform a normal engine start."

      3) **Criteria:** the standards used to measure the accomplishment of the objective. The performance-based objectives must fit the desired outcome for a particular lesson, and the criteria should be stated so that there is no question whether the objective has been met.

         a) EXAMPLE: "Using an approved airplane checklist and referencing the POH, perform a normal engine start. Engine power should be reduced to below 1000 RPM after the engine is engaged, and fuel pump adjustments should be made as required in the POH."

   d. Practical Test Standards (PTS)/Airman Certification Standards (ACS) provide specific performance-based objectives based on the standards that must be met for the issuance of a particular aviation certificate or rating.

4. **Decision-based objectives** allow for a more dynamic training environment and are designed to develop pilot judgment and ADM skills.

    a.   Combined with traditional task and maneuver training, decision-based objectives facilitate a higher level of learning and application and thus reduce improper pilot decision making and increase overall flight safety.

5. Once the instructor establishes the overall training objectives, (s)he must identify the blocks of learning that make up the necessary parts of the total objective.

    a.   You must ensure that each block of learning identified is truly an integral part of the overall objective.

        1)   The blocks of learning should represent units of learning that can be measured and evaluated.

        2)   Extraneous blocks of instruction are expensive frills, especially in flight instruction, and detract from the completion of the final objective.

        3)   EXAMPLE: A learner is preparing for their first solo flight, and the instructor starts teaching about cross country procedures.

    b.   The blocks of learning must be developed and arranged in their proper sequence.

        1)   In this way, a learner can master the segments of the overall pilot performance requirements individually and can progressively combine these with other related segments until their sum meets the final objective.

    c.   Learners will master segments of blocks individually and can progressively combine these with other related segments until the overall training objectives are reached.

        1)   EXAMPLE: Flight training may be divided into the following major blocks: achievement of the knowledge and skills necessary for solo flight, achievement of the knowledge and skills necessary for solo cross-country flight, and achievement of the knowledge and skills appropriate for achieving a private pilot certificate.

    d.   Using this approach provides the learner with a boost of self-confidence as each block is successfully completed.

6. A training syllabus is an abstract or digest of the course of training. It consists of the blocks of learning to be completed in the most efficient order.

    a.   All syllabi should stress well-defined objectives, content, and completion standards for each lesson.

    b.   The order of training can and should be altered when necessary to suit the progress of the learner and the demands of special circumstances, such as weather conditions.

        1)   However, it is often preferable to skip to a completely different part of the syllabus when the conduct of a scheduled lesson is impossible, rather than proceeding to the next lesson, which may be predicated completely on skills to be developed during the lesson being postponed.

        2)   EXAMPLE: If a learner is having a difficult time with normal approach and landings, it might be wise for the instructor to skip the next proposed lesson on short field landings and instead review another area of training. This would enable the learner to gain confidence and reinforce skills needed to perform normal landings.

5.2 ORGANIZATION OF TRAINING MATERIAL

1.   Once a determination of objectives and standards has been made, an instructor must formulate a plan of action to lead learners through the course in a logical manner toward the desired goal. One effective way to organize a lesson is by introduction, development, and conclusion.

   a.   The **introduction** sets the stage for everything to come. The introduction can be divided into three subparts:

   1)   **Attention** -- The instructor must gain each learner's attention and focus it on the subject.

   a)   EXAMPLE: Stories, video clips, questions, or jokes can be used to gain learner attention.

   2)   **Motivation** -- The instructor should offer specific reasons why they need to learn the material. This motivation should appeal to each learner personally and accentuate the desire to learn.

   a)   EXAMPLE: The instructor may talk about where the knowledge in the lesson was or will be applied in real life or remind learners of an upcoming test on the material.

   3)   **Overview** -- Each lesson introduction should contain an overview that tells the learner(s) what is to be covered during the period.

   a)   The overview is presented as a clear, concise presentation of the objective.

   b.   The **development** is the main part of the lesson during which the instructor organizes the explanations and demonstrations in a manner that helps the learners achieve the desired learning outcomes.

   1)   The instructor must logically organize the material to show the relationships of the main points to each other. This is done by developing the main points in one of the following ways:

   a)   Chronologically (from past to present or present to past)
   b)   From simple to complex
   c)   From known to unknown (i.e., using a learner's previous experiences and knowledge to acquire new concepts)
   d)   From most frequently used (most familiar) to least frequently used

   c.   The **conclusion** retraces the important elements of the lesson and relates them to the objective.

   1)   This reinforces learning and improves retention of what has been learned.
   2)   New ideas should not be introduced in the conclusion because doing so at this point in the lesson will only confuse learners.

5.3 LESSON PLAN

1. Each lesson of the training syllabus includes an objective, content, and completion standards.

2. A lesson plan is an organized outline that is developed for a single instructional period.

    a. A properly constructed lesson plan will provide an outline that tells the instructor what to do, in what order to do it, and what teaching procedure to use.

    b. The lesson plan must be appropriate for the particular learner.

        1) Standard lesson plans may not be effective for learners requiring a different approach.

        2) Therefore, the main concern in developing a lesson plan is the learner.

3. A lesson plan should be prepared in writing for each instructional period to show what specific knowledge and/or skills will be taught during a lesson.

    a. A so-called mental outline is not a lesson plan.

    b. Another instructor should be able to take the lesson plan and know what to do in conducting the same period of instruction.

4. Lesson plans are designed to ensure that each learner receives the best possible instruction under existing circumstances. Lesson plans help instructors keep a constant check on their own activity, as well as that of learners.

5. Steps to ensuring a quality lesson:

    a. Determine the objective of the lesson,
    b. Instructor research,
    c. Determine the method of instruction,
    d. Identify the lesson planning format,
    e. Decide how to organize the lesson and supporting material,
    f. Assemble training aids, and
    g. Write the lesson plan outline.

6. The following are some important characteristics of a well-planned lesson:

    a. Unity: Each lesson is a unified segment of instruction.

    b. Content: The lesson should contain new material.

    c. Scope: The scope is balanced and reasonable.

    d. Practicality: The lesson is planned in terms of the conditions under which the training is conducted.

    e. Flexibility: Always allow for a degree of flexibility.

    f. Relation to the course of training: The lesson is planned and taught so that it relates to the course objectives clearly.

    g. Instructional steps: The lesson follows the steps of the teaching process.

7. In flight training, a brief review of earlier lessons is usually necessary.

8. The teaching process organizes materials the instructor wishes to teach in a manner the learner can easily understand. Each lesson should also fall logically into the four steps of the traditional teaching process: preparation, presentation, application, and review/evaluation. The steps of the teaching process may also be referred to as preparation, presentation, application, and assessment.

9.   An adequate lesson plan, when properly developed, should

   a.   Ensure a wise selection of material and the elimination of unimportant details.

   b.   Make certain that due consideration is given to each part of the lesson.

   c.   Aid the instructor in presenting the material in a suitable sequence for efficient learning.

   d.   Provide an outline of the teaching procedure to be used.

   e.   Serve as a means of relating the lesson to the objectives of the course of training.

   f.   Give the inexperienced instructor confidence.

   g.   Promote uniformity of instruction regardless of the instructor or the date on which the lesson is given.

10.   Each lesson plan should contain the following items: lesson objective, content, schedule, equipment, instructor's actions, learner's actions, and completion standards. The illustration below is an example of a traditional training lesson plan.

LESSON	Ground reference maneuvers	LEARNER		DATE	/ /

OBJECTIVE	To develop the learner's skill in planning and following a pattern over the ground compensating for wind drift at varying angles.
CONTENT	Use of ground references to control path Observation and control of wind effect Control of airplane attitude, altitude, and heading
SCHEDULE	Preflight discussion :10 Instructor demonstrations :25 Learner practice :45 Postflight critique :10
EQUIPMENT	Chalkboard for preflight discussion IFR visor for maneuvers reviewed
INSTRUCTOR'S ACTIONS	Preflight—discuss lesson objective. Diagram "S" turns, eight along a road, and rectangular course on a chalkboard. Inflight—demonstrate elements. Demonstrate following a road, "S" turns, eights along a road, and rectangular course, coach learner practice. Postflight—critique learner performance and make study assignment.
LEARNER'S ACTIONS	Preflight—discuss lesson objective and resolve questions. Inflight—review previous maneuvers including power-off stalls and flight at minimum controllable airspeed. Perform each new maneuver as directed. Postflight—ask pertinent questions.
COMPLETION STANDARDS	Learner should demonstrate competency in maintaining orientation, airspeed within 10 knots, altitude within 100 feet, and headings within 10 degrees, and in making proper correction for wind drift.

11. The figure below is an example of a ground lesson plan in contrast to the sample flight lesson plan on the previous page.

LESSON PLAN

Introduction (3 minutes)

A _____ Relate aircraft accident in which a multi-engine ran off the end of the runway. This could have been avoided by correctly computing the landing distance. Relate similar personal experience of the same type of mishap.

B _____ Tell learners how landing distance can affect them (any aircraft, plus future application).

C _____ Explain what will be learned. Explain how the lesson will proceed. Define landing distance and explain the normal landing distance chart. Then, demonstrate how to solve for landing distance. The learners will practice the procedure at least once with supervision and at least once with as little help as possible. Next, the learners will be evaluated according to the standards. Finally, the lesson will conclude with questions and answers, followed by a brief summary.

Body (29 minutes)

D _____ Define landing distance. Explain the normal landing distance chart to include the scale and interpolation. Ensure learners can see demonstrations and encourage questions. Demonstrate the procedure using °C with a headwind and °F with a tailwind. Show the normal landing distance chart with given data in the following order:
1. temperature
2. pressure altitude
3. gross weight
4. headwind-tailwind component
5. read ground roll distance from graph

E _____ Review standards. Hand out chart and practice problems. Remind learners to use a pencil, to make small tick marks, and to work as accurately as possible. Explain that they should follow the procedure on the chart to work the practice problems. Encourage learners to ask questions. Check progress of each learner continually so they develop skill proficiency within acceptable standards. Reteach any area(s) of difficulty to the class as they go along.

F _____ Review procedure again from the chart. Reemphasize standards of acceptable performance including time available. Prepare area for evaluation by removing the task step chart and practice problem sheets, and by handing out the evaluation problems. Ask learners to work the three problems according to conditions and standards specified. Terminate evaluation after 6 minutes. Evaluate each learner's performance and tactfully reveal results. Record results for use in reteaching any area(s) of difficulty in the summary.

Conclusion (3 minutes)

G _____ Review lessons with emphasis on any weak area(s).

H _____ Remind learners that landing distance will be an important consideration in any aircraft they fly.

I _____ Advise learners that this lesson will be used as a starting point for the next lesson. Assign study materials for the next lesson.

12. The objectives of each lesson, content to support these objectives, and completion standards should be clearly stated.

    a. The objective is the reason for the lesson -- what the learner is expected to know or be able to do at the end of the lesson.

    b. Keeping the learner informed of lesson objectives and completion standards minimizes learner insecurity.

13. When planning time for learner performance, a primary consideration is the length of the practice session.

    a. A beginning learner reaches a point where additional practice is not only unproductive but may be harmful. As a learner gains experience, longer periods of practice become profitable.

        1) **Overlearning** is the continued study of a skill after initial proficiency has been achieved. Practice proceeds beyond the point at which the act can be performed with the required degree of excellence.

        2) One common effect of overlearning is the development of automated routines rather than development of concept application skills. Automatic responses can be undesirable.

    b. As a learner gains experience, longer periods of practice are profitable.

14. Lesson plans are designed to ensure each learner receives the best possible instruction under the existing conditions.

    a. Understanding learning styles and approaches can help instructors make adjustments in how material is presented if their personal style differs from the particular way an individual learns.

15. The **VAK** model is based on the three main sensory receptors.

    a. **V**isual style: use charts, graphs, and audiovisual tools.

    b. **A**uditory style: have learners verbalize questions.

    c. **K**inesthetic style: use skill demonstrations.

16. A blank lesson plan is provided on page 197 so you may make copies for your use.

5.4 SCENARIO-BASED TRAINING LESSON PLANNING

1. For scenario-based training (SBT) to be effective, it is vital that the instructor and learner establish the following information:

    a. Flight scenario:

        1) Scenario destination(s)
        2) Desired learning outcomes
        3) Desired level of learner performance
        4) Possible inflight scenario changes

    b. Nonflight scenario:

        1) Narrative of the task goal
        2) Desired learning outcomes
        3) Desired level of learner performance
        4) Possible scenario changes

2. SBT teaches learners to assess situations and react appropriately.

3. The overall learning objective is for the learner to be ready to exercise sound judgment and make good decisions. The instructor should create lessons appropriate to the stage of learning, help the learner become a confident planner, and help the learner understand the knowledge requirements present in real-world applications.

The Main Points To Remember About Scenario-Based Training

- SBT is situated in a real context and is based on the idea that knowledge cannot be gained and fully integrated independent of its context.

- SBT accords with a performance improvement and behavior change philosophy of the learning function.

- SBT is different from traditional instructional design; one must be aware of the differences to successfully employ SBT.

- Most learning solutions should employ both traditional training and SBT.

- Traditional learning elements should enhance the SBT elements.

- It is essential to place boundaries around scenarios to make the transitions between scenarios and traditional learning as efficient as possible.

- Open-ended qualitative learner feedback is key to successful scenario revision, but revisions should not further complicate the scenario unless highly justified.

5.5 INSTRUCTIONAL AIDS AND TRAINING TECHNOLOGY

1. Instructional aids are useful tools that emphasize, support, supplement, or reinforce the key points or concepts in a lesson and assist an instructor in the teaching-learning process.

    a. Instructional aids include models, chalkboards, charts, and projected material (e.g., videotapes, movies, slides, etc.).

2. Reasons for using instructional aids include the following:

    a. Helping learners remember important information,

    b. Gaining and holding learner attention,

    c. Clarifying the relationship between material objects and concepts,

    d. Assisting in solving language barriers, and

    e. Giving support when topics involve the use of more senses (i.e., sight, hearing, or a combination of others).

3. The following four-step procedure should be used to determine if and when instructional aids are necessary:

    a. Clearly establish the lesson objective, being certain what must be communicated.

    b. Gather the necessary data by researching for support material.

    c. Organize the material into an outline or lesson plan. The outline should include all key points to be presented.

    d. Finally, determine what ideas should be supported with instructional aids. They should be

        1) Compatible with the learning outcomes to be achieved.
        2) Designed to cover the key points in a lesson.
        3) Visible throughout the lesson.

4. Instructional aids used in the teaching/learning process should not be used as a crutch by the instructor.

5. Interactive video is a type of computer software that responds quickly to certain choices and commands by the user.

    a. The questions or directions are programmed using a branching technique, which provides several possible courses of action for the user to choose in order to move from one sequence to another.

QUESTIONS AND ANSWER EXPLANATIONS: All of the Fundamentals of Instructing knowledge test questions chosen by the FAA for release as well as additional questions selected by Gleim relating to the material in the previous outlines are provided on the following pages. These questions have been organized into the same subunits as the outlines. To the immediate right of each question are the correct answer and answer explanations. You should cover these answers and answer explanations while responding to the questions. Refer to the general discussion in the Introduction on how to take the FAA knowledge test.

Remember that the questions from the FAA knowledge test bank have been reordered by topic and organized into a meaningful sequence. Also, the first line of the answer explanation gives the citation of the authoritative source for the answer.

QUESTIONS

5.1 Course Development

1. In planning any instructional activity, the first consideration should be to

    A. determine the overall objectives and standards.

    B. establish common ground between the instructor and learner.

    C. identify the blocks of learning which make up the overall objective.

Answer (A) is correct. (FAA-H-8083-9B Chap 7)
    DISCUSSION: The first step in planning any instructional activity is to determine the overall objectives and standards. If the instructor does not have a logical view of what is to be achieved, then the learners will not.
    Answer (B) is incorrect. Establishing a common ground between the instructor and learner is the purpose of a lesson introduction, not the first step in planning instructional activity. **Answer (C) is incorrect.** The second, not the first, consideration in planning for any instructional activity is to identify the blocks of learning that make up the overall objective.

2. Which statement is true concerning extraneous blocks of instruction during a course of training?

    A. They are usually necessary parts of the total objective.

    B. They detract from the completion of the final objective.

    C. They assist in the attainment of the lesson's objective.

Answer (B) is correct. (FAA-H-8083-9B Chap 7)
    DISCUSSION: While identifying the blocks of learning to be used in the course, the instructor must examine each carefully to see that it is truly an integral part of the structure. Extraneous blocks of instruction can detract from, rather than assist, in the completion of the final objective.
    Answer (A) is incorrect. Extraneous blocks of instruction are unnecessary parts of the total objective. **Answer (C) is incorrect.** Extraneous blocks of instruction detract, not assist, in the attainment of the lesson's objective.

3. In a syllabus with the objective leading to the first solo flight, a block of learning that contains cross-country procedures

    A. is a required part of the objective.

    B. would detract from the completion of the objective.

    C. would assist in the attainment of the objective.

Answer (B) is correct. (FAA-H-8083-9B Chap 7)
    DISCUSSION: The major learning blocks leading to the first solo flight objective require cross-country procedures to be scheduled after achieving the knowledge and skills necessary for solo flight. Therefore, cross-country procedures would be an extraneous block detracting from the completion of this objective.
    Answer (A) is incorrect. The competent instructor will examine the appropriate blocks of learning and identify those blocks integral to the training objective. **Answer (C) is incorrect.** A block of learning containing cross-country procedures would be extraneous and would detract from, rather than assist in, this training objective.

4. Blocks of learning should represent units of learning that can

    A. Be taught on the ground.

    B. Be measured and evaluated.

    C. Follow a study guide.

Answer (B) is correct. (FAA-H-8083-9B Chap 7)
    DISCUSSION: The blocks of learning are designed to measure and evaluate the learning taking place.
    Answer (A) is incorrect. Blocks of learning should be present in ground and flight lessons. **Answer (C) is incorrect.** Blocks of learning may not always follow a study guide. The order may not be suitable for the lessons, and the units of learning should be measured and evaluated.

5. When a dual cross-country flight cannot be conducted as planned due to weather, an instructor should

    A. consider the current block of learning and select an appropriate alternate lesson.

    B. begin the next lesson in the training syllabus.

    C. cancel the lesson to prevent the learner from becoming frustrated.

Answer (A) is correct. (FAA-H-8083-9B Chap 7)
    DISCUSSION: It is the instructor's responsibility to consider how the relationships of the blocks of learning and the order of training can and should be altered to suit the progress of the learner and the demands of special circumstances.
    Answer (B) is incorrect. The instructor is responsible for considering how the relationships of the blocks of learning are affected, and the subsequent lesson content may be contingent on the canceled lesson. **Answer (C) is incorrect.** Even if the cross-country event cannot be conducted, the syllabus should be flexible enough to be adapted to weather variations, aircraft availability, and scheduling changes without disrupting the teaching process or completely suspending training.

6. When it is impossible to conduct a scheduled lesson, it is preferable for the instructor to

A. review and possibly revise the training syllabus.

B. proceed to the next scheduled lesson, or if this is not practical, cancel the lesson.

C. conduct a lesson that is not predicated completely on skills to be developed during the lesson which was postponed.

Answer (C) is correct. (FAA-H-8083-9B Chap 7)
DISCUSSION: It is preferable for the instructor to skip to a completely different part of the syllabus when it is impossible to conduct a scheduled lesson, rather than proceeding to the next lesson, which may be predicated completely on skills to be developed during the lesson that was postponed.
Answer (A) is incorrect. An instructor should review and possibly revise the training syllabus when there is an applicable change to the Federal Aviation Regulations or PTSs/ACSs, not because a lesson had to be postponed. **Answer (B) is incorrect.** The next lesson may need skills that were to be learned in the postponed lesson.

7. Performance-based objectives consist of which three elements?

A. Flight training scenarios, judgment assessment, and maneuver assessment.

B. Cognitive skills, affective skills, and psychomotor skills.

C. Description of the skill or behavior, conditions, and criteria.

Answer (C) is correct. (FAA-H-8083-9B Chap 5)
DISCUSSION: Performance-based objectives are used to set measurable, reasonable standards that describe the desired performance of the learner. Performance-based objectives consist of three elements: description of the skill or behavior, conditions, and criteria.
Answer (A) is incorrect. This answer choice describes elements of decision-based, not performance-based, objectives. **Answer (B) is incorrect.** This answer choice describes the three domains of learning, not the elements of performance-based objectives.

8. Development and assembly of blocks of learning in their proper relationship will provide a means for

A. both the instructor and learner to easily correct faulty habit patterns.

B. challenging the learner by progressively increasing the units of learning.

C. allowing the learner to master the segments of the overall pilot performance requirements individually and combining these with other related segments.

Answer (C) is correct. (FAA-H-8083-9B Chap 7)
DISCUSSION: Training for a skill as complicated and involved as piloting an aircraft requires the development and assembly, in their appropriate sequence, of many segments or blocks of learning. In this way, a learner can master the segments of the overall pilot performance requirements individually and can progressively combine these with other related segments until (s)he learns to fly, which is the final objective.
Answer (A) is incorrect. Organizing the appropriate blocks of learning in their proper relationship should prevent the formation of bad habits. This is the basic reason for the building block technique of instruction. **Answer (B) is incorrect.** The challenge presented to the learner is one way to test for a useful size of a minimum block of learning, but progressively increasing the blocks of learning may deter the learner's progress.

9. As an instructor you should write performance-based objectives that

A. fit the desired outcome of a particular lesson.

B. do not require the consideration of conditions.

C. must be open to interpretation by knowledgeable readers.

Answer (A) is correct. (FAA-H-8083-9B Chap 5)
DISCUSSION: An instructor should write performance-based objectives to fit the desired outcome of the lesson.
Answer (B) is incorrect. Conditions are necessary to specifically explain the rules under which the skill or behavior is demonstrated. If a desired capability is to navigate from point A to point B, the objective as stated is not specific enough for all learners to do it in the same way. Information such as equipment, tools, reference material, and limiting parameters should be included. **Answer (C) is incorrect.** Performance-based objectives must be clear, measurable, and repeatable. In other words, they must mean the same thing to any knowledgeable reader.

10. A series of studies leading to an attainment of a goal is

A. a determination of objective.

B. a course of training.

C. a decision based objective.

Answer (B) is correct. (FAA-H-8083-9B Chap 5)
DISCUSSION: A course of training is a complete series of studies leading to attainment of a goal, such as a certificate of completion, graduation, etc.
Answer (A) is incorrect. A determination of objectives and standards is necessary before any important instruction can be presented. **Answer (C) is incorrect.** Decision-based objectives are a type of objective designed to develop pilot judgment and ADM skills.

11. What is the overall objective of any pilot training?

    A. To make sure all objectives are clear, measurable, and repeatable.

    B. To facilitate a higher level of learning and application.

    C. To qualify the learner to be a competent, efficient, safe pilot.

Answer (C) is correct. (FAA-H-8083-9B Chap 5)
    DISCUSSION: The broad overall objective of any pilot training is to qualify the learner to be a competent, efficient, safe pilot.
    Answer (A) is incorrect. Making sure written objectives are clear, measurable, and repeatable is an element of a performance-based objective. **Answer (B) is incorrect.** Decision-based objectives facilitate a higher level of learning and application and thus reduce improper pilot decision making and increase overall flight safety.

12. Which is not a type of objective used in aviation training?

    A. Performance-based objectives.

    B. Decision-based objectives.

    C. Description-based objectives.

Answer (C) is correct. (FAA-H-8083-9B Chap 5)
    DISCUSSION: A description-based objective is not a type of objective in aviation training.
    Answer (A) is incorrect. There are two types of objectives in aviation: performance-based objectives and decision-based objectives. Performance-based objectives are used to set measurable, reasonable standards that describe the required learner performance. **Answer (B) is incorrect.** There are two types of objectives in aviation: performance-based objectives and decision-based objectives. Decision-based objectives allow for a more dynamic training environment and are designed to develop pilot judgment and ADM skills.

13. Which element of a performance-based objective explains the standards used to measure the accomplishment of the objective?

    A. Description of the skill or behavior.

    B. Conditions.

    C. Criteria.

Answer (C) is correct. (FAA-H-8083-9B Chap 5)
    DISCUSSION: Criteria are the standards used to measure the accomplishment of the objective.
    Answer (A) is incorrect. The description of the skill or behavior is the desired outcome of training stated in concrete terms that can be measured. **Answer (B) is incorrect.** Conditions are used to explain the rules under which the skill or behavior is to be demonstrated.

14. After the instructor establishes the overall training objectives, his or her next step is

    A. the identification of the blocks of learning which constitute the necessary parts of the total objective.

    B. create a lesson plan for the unit of instruction.

    C. create a syllabus for the training objective.

Answer (A) is correct. (FAA-H-8083-9B Chap 7)
    DISCUSSION: After the overall training objectives have been established, the next step is the identification of the blocks of learning which constitute the necessary parts of the total objective.
    Answer (B) is incorrect. A lesson plan cannot be developed until the appropriate blocks of learning have been identified. **Answer (C) is incorrect.** A syllabus cannot be developed until the appropriate blocks of learning have been identified.

15. What is true of all syllabi?

    A. The order of training should not be altered as this will detract from the completion of the final objective.

    B. All syllabi should stress well-defined objectives and standards for each lesson.

    C. Common ground between the learner and instructor will be established by using a syllabus.

Answer (B) is correct. (FAA-H-8083-9B Chap 7)
    DISCUSSION: All syllabi should stress well-defined objectives and standards for each lesson.
    Answer (A) is incorrect. The order of training can and should be altered when necessary to suit the progress of the learner and the demands of special circumstances, such as weather conditions. **Answer (C) is incorrect.** Establishing a common ground between the instructor and learner is the purpose of a lesson introduction and is not dependent on a syllabus.

5.2 Organization of Training Material

16. The method of arranging lesson material from the simple to complex, past to present, and known to unknown, is one that

    A. creates learner thought pattern departures.

    B. shows the relationships of the main points of the lesson.

    C. requires learners to actively participate in the lesson.

Answer (B) is correct. (FAA-H-8083-9B Chap 5)
    DISCUSSION: An instructor must logically organize the lesson material to show the relationships of the main points. This can be done by arranging the material from the simple to the complex, past to present, known to unknown, and from the most frequently used to the least frequently used.
    Answer (A) is incorrect. By arranging lesson material from the simple to complex, past to present, and known to unknown, the instructor will make meaningful transitions from one point to another and thus keep the learners oriented, not create thought pattern departures. **Answer (C) is incorrect.** The objective of each lesson, not the method of arranging material, should require learners to actively participate (either directly or indirectly) in the lesson in order to achieve the desired learning outcomes.

17. In organizing lesson material, which step sets the stage for everything to come?

    A. Overview.

    B. Conclusion.

    C. Introduction.

Answer (C) is correct. (FAA-H-8083-9B Chap 5)
    DISCUSSION: The introduction to a lesson should set the stage for everything to come. The introduction is made up of three elements: attention, motivation, and overview.
    Answer (A) is incorrect. The overview is included in the introduction and tells the group what is to be covered during the period of instruction, not how it relates to the entire course. **Answer (B) is incorrect.** The conclusion retraces the important elements of the lesson and relates them to the lesson objective. It does not set the stage for everything to come because it is at the end of a lesson.

18. In developing a lesson, the instructor should organize explanations and demonstrations to help the learner

    A. achieve the desired learning outcome.

    B. acquire a thorough understanding of the material presented.

    C. acquire new concepts, generally progressing from the known to the unknown.

Answer (A) is correct. (FAA-H-8083-9B Chap 5)
    DISCUSSION: In developing a lesson, the instructor should organize the subject matter (explanations and demonstrations) in a manner that helps the learner achieve the desired learning outcome.
    Answer (B) is incorrect. The learner's ability to acquire a thorough understanding of the material is dependent on more than an instructor's organized presentation, e.g., motivation, needs, etc. **Answer (C) is incorrect.** Progressing from the known to the unknown is a way of logically organizing the lesson material to show the relationships of the main points, not the intent of developing a lesson, which is to help the learner achieve the desired learning outcome.

19. When teaching from the known to the unknown, an instructor is using the learner's

    A. current knowledge of the subject.

    B. previous experiences and knowledge.

    C. previously held opinions, both valid and invalid.

Answer (B) is correct. (FAA-H-8083-9B Chap 5)
    DISCUSSION: Teaching from the known to the unknown allows the instructor to use the learner's previous experience and knowledge as the point of departure from which to lead into new ideas and concepts.
    Answer (A) is incorrect. When teaching from the known to the unknown, an instructor is using a learner's knowledge of related subjects, not the subject at hand. **Answer (C) is incorrect.** Organizing lessons using the known to the unknown pattern requires learners' previous knowledge, not their previously held opinions.

20. The proper sequence for the subparts of an introduction is

   A. attention, motivation, and overview.

   B. attention, development, and overview.

   C. overview, motivation, and conclusion.

Answer (A) is correct. (FAA-H-8083-9B Chap 5)
    DISCUSSION: The proper sequence for the subparts of an introduction is attention, motivation, and overview. First, the instructor must gain the learner's attention and focus it on the subject at hand. Second, the introduction should offer the learners specific reasons for needing to be familiar with, to know, to understand, to apply, or to be able to perform whatever they are about to learn. This motivation should appeal to each learner personally and accentuate the desire to learn. Third, every lesson introduction should contain an overview that tells the group what is to be covered during the period.
    Answer (B) is incorrect. Development is the main part of the lesson, not a subpart of the introduction. **Answer (C) is incorrect.** Conclusion is the review portion of the lesson, not a subpart of the introduction.

21. Instructors should utilize the proper sequence for the subparts of an introduction. These are

   A. attention, motivation, and overview.

   B. application, correlation, and understanding.

   C. anecdote or story, motivation, and overview.

Answer (A) is correct. (FAA-H-8083-9B Chap 5)
    DISCUSSION: The basic introduction to a period of instruction consists of three elements: attention, motivation, and overview. By organizing the content in this manner, the instructor helps the learner obtain a firm grasp of the subject matter while minimizing the possibility of a rambling discussion.
    Answer (B) is incorrect. Application, correlation, and understanding are levels of learning, not the elements of an introduction to instruction. **Answer (C) is incorrect.** The introduction should be free of stories, jokes, or incidents that do not help the learners focus their attention on the lesson objective.

22. The known to unknown pattern helps the instructor lead the learner into new ideas and concepts by

   A. anxieties and insecurities.

   B. using something the learner already knows.

   C. previously held opinions, both valid and invalid.

Answer (B) is correct. (FAA-H-8083-9B Chap 5)
    DISCUSSION: By using something the learner already knows as the point of departure, the instructor can lead into new ideas and concepts. For example, in developing a lesson on heading indicators, the instructor could begin with a discussion of the vacuum-driven heading indicator before proceeding to a description of the radio magnetic indicator (RMI).
    Answer (A) is incorrect. The known to unknown pattern helps the instructor lead the learner into new ideas and concepts by using something the learner already knows, not through anxieties and insecurities. **Answer (C) is incorrect.** By using something the learner already knows as the point of departure, the instructor can lead into new ideas and concepts, not through previously held opinions.

23. Examples of methods to gain learner attention include

   A. Jokes, video clips, questions.

   B. Lectures, guided discussions, demonstrations.

   C. Review problems, case studies, explanations.

Answer (A) is correct. (FAA-H-8083-9B Chap 5)
    DISCUSSION: Stories, video clips, questions, or jokes can all be used to gain learner attention.
    Answer (B) is incorrect. Lectures do not prompt learner attention. Stories, video clips, questions, or jokes are all methods to gain learner attention. **Answer (C) is incorrect.** While case studies are a type of story, they are a type of problem-based learning and are used in the development stage of a lesson, not in the introduction.

24. Reinforcement of learner learning occurs primarily during which state of lesson organization?

   A. Introduction.

   B. Development.

   C. Conclusion.

Answer (C) is correct. (FAA-H-8083-9B Chap 5)
    DISCUSSION: Conclusions retrace important elements of the lesson and relate them to the objective. This reinforces learning and improves retention.
    Answer (A) is incorrect. The introduction sets the stage for everything to come. **Answer (B) is incorrect.** The development is the main part of the lesson during which the instructor organizes the explanations and demonstrations in a manner that helps the learners achieve the desired learning outcomes.

5.3 Lesson Plan

25. Which statement is true regarding lesson plans?

A. Lesson plans should not be directed toward the course objective; only to the lesson objective.

B. A well-thought-out mental outline of a lesson may be used any time as long as the instructor is well prepared.

C. Lesson plans help instructors keep a constant check on their own activity as well as that of their learners.

Answer (C) is correct. (FAA-H-8083-9B Chap 7)
DISCUSSION: Lesson plans help instructors keep a constant check on their own activity, as well as that of learners. The development of lesson plans by instructors signifies, in effect, that they have taught the lesson to themselves prior to attempting to teach the lesson to learners.
Answer (A) is incorrect. A lesson plan should serve as a means of relating the lesson to the objectives of the course, as well as the lesson. **Answer (B) is incorrect.** A mental outline of a lesson is not a lesson plan. A lesson plan should be in written form regardless of an instructor's preparation.

26. When the instructor keeps the learner informed of lesson objectives and completion standards, it minimizes the learner's feelings of

A. insecurity.

B. resignation.

C. aggressiveness.

Answer (A) is correct. (FAA-H-8083-9B Chap 8)
DISCUSSION: Learners feel insecure when they do not know the lesson objectives and the completion standards to which they will be held. Instructors can minimize such feelings of insecurity by telling learners what is expected of them and what to anticipate.
Answer (B) is incorrect. Resignation occurs when a learner completes the early phase of training without understanding the fundamentals, not the objectives or completion standards, and becomes lost in the advanced phase. **Answer (C) is incorrect.** Aggression occurs when a learner becomes angry at something or someone. Aggression (or any other defense mechanism) may be used to defend a feeling of insecurity when a learner is not kept informed.

27. Which statement is true about lesson plans?

A. Lesson plans should follow a prescribed format.

B. Standard prepared lesson plans are effective for teaching all learners.

C. The use of standard lesson plans may not be effective for learners requiring a different approach.

Answer (C) is correct. (FAA-H-8083-9B Chap 7)
DISCUSSION: A lesson plan for an instructional period should be appropriate to the background, experience, and ability of the particular learner(s). If the procedures outlined in the lesson plan are not leading to the desired results, the instructor should change the approach. Thus, the use of standard lesson plans may not be effective for learners requiring a different approach.
Answer (A) is incorrect. Although lesson plans should all contain certain items, the format to be followed should be tailored to the particular learner(s). **Answer (B) is incorrect.** Lesson plans are only an outline of the lesson. An instructor may have to adapt the procedures in a standard prepared lesson plan so it will be effective with different learners.

28. A well-developed lesson plan should

A. promote uniformity of instruction regardless of the instructor teaching it.

B. be a sketch of a program or teaching lecture.

C. be a document that will not require changes or alterations.

Answer (A) is correct. (FAA-H-8083-9B Chap 7)
DISCUSSION: A well-developed lesson plan should

- Ensure the proper material is included and eliminate unimportant details.
- Make certain that due consideration is given to each part of the lesson.
- Aid the instructor in presenting the material in a suitable sequence for efficient learning.
- Provide an outline of the teaching procedure to be used.
- Serve as a means of relating the lesson to the objectives of the course of training.
- Give the inexperienced instructor confidence.
- Promote uniformity of instruction regardless of the instructor or the date on which the lesson is given.

Answer (B) is incorrect. A well-developed lesson plan should be a well-written outline, not a vague sketch. **Answer (C) is incorrect.** A well-developed lesson plan should be a working document that can and should be revised as changes occur or are needed.

29. (Refer to Figure 1 on page 141.) Section A is titled:

    A. Overview.

    B. Objective.

    C. Introduction.

Answer (B) is correct. (FAA-H-8083-9B Chap 7)
    DISCUSSION: Section A of Fig. 1 is titled "Objective." The objective of the lesson is the reason for the lesson and should clearly state what the instructor expects the learner to know or do at the completion of the lesson.
    Answer (A) is incorrect. An overview is a subpart of an introduction to a lesson, not a titled section of a lesson plan.
    Answer (C) is incorrect. An introduction is part of an effective way to organize a lesson, not a titled section of a lesson plan.

30. (Refer to Figure 1 on page 141.) Section B is titled:

    A. Content.

    B. Elements.

    C. Course of Training.

Answer (A) is correct. (FAA-H-8083-9B Chap 7)
    DISCUSSION: Section B of Fig. 1 is titled "Content." This is a statement of the knowledge and skill necessary for the fulfillment of the lesson objective. This may include both elements previously learned and those to be introduced during this lesson.
    Answer (B) is incorrect. "Elements" is not a titled section of a lesson plan. **Answer (C) is incorrect.** The course of training is the overall objective of the instruction and is comprised of many different lesson plans, not a titled section of a lesson plan.

31. (Refer to Figure 1 on page 141.) Section C is titled:

    A. Schedule.

    B. Overview.

    C. Training Schedule.

Answer (A) is correct. (FAA-H-8083-9B Chap 7)
    DISCUSSION: Section C of Fig. 1 is titled "Schedule." The instructor should estimate the amount of time to be devoted to the presentation of the elements of that lesson.
    Answer (B) is incorrect. An overview is a subpart of an introduction to a lesson, not a titled section of a lesson plan.
    Answer (C) is incorrect. The correct title is "Schedule," not "Training Schedule."

32. (Refer to Figure 1 on page 141.) Section D is titled:

    A. Instructor's Actions.

    B. Equipment.

    C. Content.

Answer (B) is correct. (FAA-H-8083-9B Chap 7)
    DISCUSSION: Section D of Fig. 1 is titled "Equipment." This includes all instructional materials and training aids required to teach the lesson.
    Answer (A) is incorrect. "Instructor's Actions" is the title of the section of a lesson plan that contains a statement of the instructor's proposed procedures for presenting the elements of knowledge and performance involved in the lesson (Section E). **Answer (C) is incorrect.** "Content" is a statement of the knowledge and skill necessary for fulfillment of the lesson objective, not a list of instructional materials to be used in the lesson.

33. (Refer to Figure 1 on page 141.) Section E is titled:

    A. Content.

    B. Discussion.

    C. Instructor's Actions.

Answer (C) is correct. (FAA-H-8083-9B Chap 7)
    DISCUSSION: Section E of Fig. 1 is titled "Instructor's Actions." This is a statement of the instructor's proposed procedures for presenting the elements of knowledge and performance involved in the lesson.
    Answer (A) is incorrect. "Content" is a statement of the knowledge and skill necessary for fulfillment of the lesson objective, not a list of the instructor's actions. **Answer (B) is incorrect.** While this section states that a discussion will take place, it is specifically those actions taken by the instructor and not the learner.

34. (Refer to Figure 1 on page 141.) Section F is titled:

    A. Application.

    B. Understanding.

    C. Learner's Actions.

Answer (C) is correct. (FAA-H-8083-9B Chap 7)
    DISCUSSION: Section F of Fig. 1 is titled "Learner's Actions." This is a statement of desired learner responses to instruction.
    Answer (A) is incorrect. While this involves application of what the instructor has presented to the learner, this section is the instructor's desired learner's action during the lesson. **Answer (B) is incorrect.** Understanding is a level of learning, not a titled section of a lesson plan.

35. (Refer to Figure 1 below.) Section G is titled:

A. Summary.

B. Evaluation.

C. Completion Standards.

Answer (C) is correct. *(FAA-H-8083-9B Chap 7)*
  DISCUSSION: Section G of Fig. 1 is titled "Completion Standards." This is the evaluation basis for determining how well the learner has met the objective of the lesson in terms of knowledge and skill.
  Answer (A) is incorrect. A summary of a lesson would take place during the postflight discussion. **Answer (B) is incorrect.** Evaluation is part of the teaching process and would be used by the instructor to compare the learner's performance to the completion standards.

LESSON	Ground reference maneuvers	STUDENT		DATE	/ /

A Objective — To develop the student's skill in planning and following a pattern over the ground compensating for wind drift at varying angles.

B Content —
Use of ground references to control path
Observation and control of wind effect
Control of airplane attitude, altitude, and heading

C Schedule —
Preflight discussion	:10
Instructor demonstrations	:25
Learner practice	:45
Postflight critique	:10

D Equipment —
Chalkboard for preflight discussion
IFR visor for maneuvers reviewed

E Instructor's Actions —
Preflight—discuss lesson objective. Diagram "S" turns, eight along a road, and rectangular course on a chalkboard.

Inflight—demonstrate elements.
Demonstrate following a road, "S" turns, eights along a road, and rectangular course, coach student practice.

Postflight—critique learner performance and make study assignment.

F Learner's Actions —
Preflight—discuss lesson objective and resolve questions.

Inflight—review previous maneuvers including power-off stalls and flight at minimum controllable airspeed. Perform each new maneuver as directed.

Postflight—ask pertinent questions.

G Completion Standards —
Student should demonstrate competency in maintaining orientation, airspeed within 10 knots, altitude within 100 feet, and headings within 10 degrees, and in making proper correction for wind drift.

Figure 1. Lesson Plan.

36. The main concern in developing a lesson plan is the

   A. format.

   B. content.

   C. learner.

Answer (C) is correct. (FAA-H-8083-9B Chap 7)
   DISCUSSION: The lesson plan must be appropriate for the particular learner. Because standard lesson plans may not be effective for learners who require a different approach, the main concern in developing a lesson plan is the learner.
   Answer (A) is incorrect. The format of the lesson plan will be developed based on the needs of the learner and the subject being taught. One lesson plan format does not work well for all learners; therefore, the format of a lesson plan is an ending point, not a starting point, in lesson plan development. **Answer (B) is incorrect.** While the content of a lesson plan is a concern in its development (e.g., how much time should be devoted to which subjects), the main concern in developing a lesson plan is the learner.

37. With regard to the characteristics of a well-planned lesson, each lesson should contain

   A. new material that is related to the lesson previously presented.

   B. one basic element of the principle, procedure, or skill appropriate to that lesson.

   C. every bit of information needed to reach the objective of the training syllabus.

Answer (A) is correct. (FAA-H-8083-9B Chap 7)
   DISCUSSION: One characteristic of a well-planned lesson is content, which means each lesson should contain new material. However, the new facts, principles, or skills should be related to the lesson previously presented. A short review of earlier lessons is usually necessary, especially in flight training.
   Answer (B) is incorrect. All of the elements, not only one, necessary to learn a simple procedure, principle, or skill should be presented. **Answer (C) is incorrect.** Each lesson should include all of the information needed to reach the objective of a particular lesson but not everything needed for the entire syllabus.

38. A primary consideration in planning for learner performance is the

   A. learner's motivational level.

   B. learner's intellectual level.

   C. length of the practice session.

Answer (C) is correct. (FAA-H-8083-9B Chap 3)
   DISCUSSION: In planning for learner performance, a primary consideration is the length of time devoted to practice. A beginning learner reaches a point where additional practice is not only unproductive but may even be harmful. When that point is reached, errors increase and motivation declines. As a learner gains experience, longer periods of practice are profitable.
   Answer (A) is incorrect. A learner's motivational level is important to an instructor since it directly relates to the learner's progress and ability to learn, not as a primary consideration in planning for learner performance. **Answer (B) is incorrect.** A primary consideration in learner performance is the length of time devoted to practice, not the learner's intellectual level.

39. A lesson plan, if constructed properly, will provide an outline for

   A. proceeding from the unknown to the known.

   B. the teaching procedure to be used in a single instructional period.

   C. establishing blocks of learning that become progressively larger in scope.

Answer (B) is correct. (FAA-H-8083-9B Chap 7)
   DISCUSSION: A properly constructed lesson plan is an organized outline or blueprint for a single instructional period. It is a necessary guide for the instructor in that it tells what to do, in what order to do it, and what procedure to use in teaching the material of the lesson.
   Answer (A) is incorrect. The lesson plan will usually proceed from the known to the unknown, not unknown to known. **Answer (C) is incorrect.** A syllabus, not a lesson plan, will provide an outline for establishing blocks of learning that become progressively larger in scope.

40. Each lesson of a training syllabus includes

   A. attention, motivation, and overview.

   B. introduction, development, and conclusion.

   C. objective, content, and completion standards.

Answer (C) is correct. (FAA-H-8083-9B Chap 7)
   DISCUSSION: Each lesson of a written training syllabus includes an objective, content, and completion standards.
   Answer (A) is incorrect. Attention, motivation, and overview are the parts of an introduction to a lesson. **Answer (B) is incorrect.** The structure of every lesson as it is being presented to a learner, not as found in a written syllabus, should be based on an introduction, a development, and a conclusion.

41. A primary consideration in planning for learner performance is the

- A. length of time devoted to practice.
- B. length of time devoted to evaluation.
- C. segmentation of the practice session.

Answer (A) is correct. (FAA-H-8083-9B Chap 3)
    DISCUSSION: In planning for learner performance, a primary consideration is the length of time devoted to practice. A beginning learner reaches a point where additional practice is not only unproductive, but may even be harmful. When this point is reached, errors increase, and motivation declines. As a learner gains experience, longer periods of practice are profitable.
    Answer (B) is incorrect. In the initial stages of learning, practical suggestions are more valuable to the learner than a grade. Early evaluation is usually teacher-oriented. It provides a check on teaching effectiveness; thus, it is not a primary consideration in learner performance planning. **Answer (C) is incorrect.** While the consideration of how to properly divide or segment a practice session is important, it is futile without first determining the appropriate length of the practice session itself.

42. Which of the following statements is true in regards to the properties of overlearning?

- A. Overlearning allows the learner to bypass the learning plateau phenomenon.
- B. Overlearning is the continued study of a skill after initial proficiency has been achieved.
- C. Targets the learner's deep memory.

Answer (B) is correct. (FAA-H-8083-9B Chap 3)
    DISCUSSION: Overlearning is the continued study of a skill after initial proficiency has been achieved. Practice proceeds beyond the point at which the act can be performed with the required degree of excellence. The phenomenon of overlearning sometimes occurs when knowledge used frequently begins to take on the properties of a skill.
    Answer (A) is incorrect. The learning plateau phenomenon can be present whether overlearning takes place or not. **Answer (C) is incorrect.** Overlearning does not pertain to the concept of deep memory.

43. Which is true regarding the overlearning of knowledge?

- A. Overlearning can result in automatic responses that are undesirable.
- B. Overlearning is helpful in increasing learner proficiency of a topic.
- C. Overlearning develops higher-order thinking skills.

Answer (A) is correct. (FAA-H-8083-9B Chap 3)
    DISCUSSION: Overlearning is the continued study of a skill after initial proficiency has been achieved. Practice proceeds beyond the point at which the act can be performed with the required degree of excellence. One common effect of overlearning is the development of automated routines rather than development of concept application skills.
    Answer (B) is incorrect. Overlearning generally degrades learner proficiency by creating automatic responses on the part of the learner, which limit the learner's understanding of a given topic. **Answer (C) is incorrect.** On the contrary, overlearning creates a barrier to the development of higher-order thinking skills by creating automated responses from the learner rather than actual concept mastery.

44. When teaching new material, the traditional teaching process can be divided into which steps?

- A. Preparation, presentation, application, and review/evaluation.
- B. Preparation, demonstration, practice, and review.
- C. Explanation, demonstration, practice, and evaluation.

Answer (A) is correct. (FAA-H-8083-9B Chap 5)
    DISCUSSION: The four basic steps in the teaching process are preparation, presentation, application, and review/evaluation.
    Answer (B) is incorrect. Demonstration and practice are examples of teaching methods, not basic steps in the teaching process. **Answer (C) is incorrect.** Explanation, demonstration, and practice are examples of teaching methods, not basic steps in the teaching process.

45. Every lesson, when adequately developed, falls logically into the four steps of the traditional teaching process, which are

- A. preparation, introduction, presentation, and review/evaluation.
- B. preparation, introduction, presentation, and review/application.
- C. preparation, presentation, application, and review/evaluation.

Answer (C) is correct. (FAA-H-8083-9B Chap 7)
    DISCUSSION: Every lesson, when developed adequately, falls logically into the four steps of the teaching process: preparation, presentation, application, and review/evaluation.
    Answer (A) is incorrect. The second basic step in the teaching process is presentation, not introduction, and the third basic step is application, not presentation. **Answer (B) is incorrect.** The second basic step in the teaching process is presentation, not introduction, the third basic step is application, not presentation, and the fourth basic step is review/evaluation, not review/application.

46. What are the four steps in the teaching process?

   A. Research, presentation, grading, and review.

   B. Preparation, presentation, application, and assessment.

   C. Presentation, explanation, review, and critique.

Answer (B) is correct. (FAA-H-8083-9B Chap 7)
   DISCUSSION: The teaching process organizes the material in a way the learner can understand. Regardless of the teaching or training method used, the overall sequence of the process remains the same: preparation, presentation, application, and assessment.
   Answer (A) is incorrect. Research is a step in the planning phase of preparation. The four steps of the teaching process are preparation, presentation, application, and assessment. **Answer (C) is incorrect.** The four steps of the teaching process will always involve preparation. The steps are preparation, presentation, application, and assessment.

47. Which is not a step to ensuring a quality lesson?

   A. Instructor research.

   B. Assembling training aids.

   C. Determining the length of the practice session.

Answer (C) is correct. (FAA-H-8083-9B Chap 7)
   DISCUSSION: While a primary consideration in planning for learner performance, determining the length of the practice session is not a step to ensuring a quality lesson.
   Answer (A) is incorrect. Instructor research is a step to ensuring a quality lesson is provided to the learner. **Answer (B) is incorrect.** Assembling training aids is a step to ensuring a quality lesson is provided to the learner.

48. What are lesson plans designed to ensure?

   A. That each learner receive the best possible instruction under existing circumstances.

   B. To reinforce learning and retention of the stated objective.

   C. To provide a boost of self-confidence to each learner.

Answer (A) is correct. (FAA-H-8083-9B Chap 7)
   DISCUSSION: Lesson plans are designed to ensure that each learner receives the best possible instruction under existing circumstances.
   Answer (B) is incorrect. Conclusions reinforce learning and improve retention of what has been learned previously. **Answer (C) is incorrect.** Upon successful completion of a given block of learning, a learner's self-confidence should be boosted. Lesson plans are not designed to accomplish this.

49. How long should a flight lesson be?

   A. Shorter lessons for new learners.

   B. Longer lessons for new learners.

   C. Shorter lessons as learners gain experience.

Answer (A) is correct. (FAA-H-8083-9B Chap 3)
   DISCUSSION: In planning for learner skill acquisition, a primary consideration is the length of time devoted to practice. A beginning learner reaches a point where additional practice is not only unproductive but may even be harmful. As a learner gains experience, longer periods of practice become profitable.
   Answer (B) is incorrect. Lessons for new learners should be shorter, not longer, in length. **Answer (C) is incorrect.** As learners gain experience, the lesson length can be increased.

50. How might understanding learning styles help in the design of lesson plans?

   A. It may predict the learner's performance during training.

   B. It can help instructors make adjustments in how material is presented.

   C. It may identify ways to motivate groups of learners to work as a unit.

Answer (B) is correct. (FAA-H-8083-9B Chap 3)
   DISCUSSION: Understanding of learning styles truly helps an instructor in making adjustments in how material is presented even when their personal learning style differs from the way an individual learns. This is especially useful in designing effective lesson plans.
   Answer (A) is incorrect. Early evaluation in the initial stages of skill acquisition can be used to predict learner outcomes, ergo learner performance, and locate problem areas. **Answer (C) is incorrect.** Knowledge of learning styles and approaches can help an instructor make adjustments in how material is presented if their personal learning/teaching style differs from the way an individual learns.

5.4 Scenario-Based Training Lesson Planning

51. How does scenario-based training (SBT) differ from traditional knowledge-based learning?

A. SBT teaches recollection from lectures and learning materials.

B. SBT teaches learners to assess situations and react appropriately.

C. SBT involves rote memorization.

Answer (B) is correct. (FAA-H-8083-9B Chap 7)
DISCUSSION: A goal of SBT is to challenge the learner to improve decision-making skills. Assessing the situations given and reacting properly is part of SBT. SBT relies on knowledge and proper assessment of the situation so the learner can act appropriately.
Answer (A) is incorrect. Recollection from lectures and learning materials is traditional knowledge-based learning.
Answer (C) is incorrect. Both SBT and traditional knowledge-based learning involve rote memorization.

52. When planning a scenario-based training (SBT) lesson, a goal should be to

A. Use a previously created ground lesson plan.

B. Teach the learner to rely on study materials.

C. Help the learner become a confident planner.

Answer (C) is correct. (FAA-H-8083-9B Chap 7)
DISCUSSION: A goal of SBT is to help the learner become a confident planner. The SBT method helps learners gather all information and assess their current situation to react appropriately.
Answer (A) is incorrect. Using a previously created lesson may not fit the current lesson. **Answer (B) is incorrect.** Teaching the learner to rely on study materials is rote memorization.

5.5 Instructional Aids and Training Technology

53. The use of instructional aids should be based on their ability to support a specific point in the lesson. What is the first step in determining if and where instructional aids are necessary?

A. Organize subject material into an outline or a lesson plan.

B. Determine what ideas should be supported with instructional aids.

C. Clearly establish the lesson objective, being certain what must be communicated.

Answer (C) is correct. (FAA-H-8083-9B Chap 5)
DISCUSSION: The first step in developing a lesson plan using instructional aids is, as in any lesson plan, to establish the lesson objective. Visual or other aids must help achieve the overall lesson objective. They should be strategically placed to recapture interest, shift to a new topic, or provide emphasis.
Answer (A) is incorrect. Organizing the outline or lesson plan is the third, not first, step in the process. **Answer (B) is incorrect.** The final, not first, step in determining if and where instructional aids are necessary is to determine what ideas in the lesson should be supported with instructional aids.

54. Instructional aids may be used

A. to clarify the relationships between material objects and concepts.

B. to cover broad subject areas.

C. to add to the time it takes instructors to teach learners.

Answer (A) is correct. (FAA-H-8083-9B Chap 5)
DISCUSSION: One use for instructional aids is to clarify the relationships between material objects and concepts. When relationships are presented visually, they often are much easier to understand.
Answer (B) is incorrect. Ideally, instructional aids should be designed to cover the key points and concepts rather than broad subject areas or abstractions. **Answer (C) is incorrect.** Instructors are frequently asked to teach more and more in a smaller time frame. Instructional aids can help them do this. For example, instead of using many words to describe a sound, object, or function, the instructor plays a recording of the sound, shows a picture of the object, or presents a diagram of the function. Consequently, the learner learns faster and more accurately, and the instructor saves time in the process.

55. What kind of software responds quickly to a learner's choices and commands?

A. Interactive video.

B. Projected material.

C. Programmed text.

Answer (A) is correct. (FAA-H-8083-9B Chap 5)
DISCUSSION: Interactive video is a type of computer software that responds quickly to certain choices and commands by the user. The questions or directions are programmed using a branching technique, which provides several possible courses of action for the user to choose in order to move from one sequence to another.
Answer (B) is incorrect. Projected learning involves lessons projected on a screen that are presented and paced by an instructor. This instructional aid is not a form of software that responds to a learner's choices and commands. **Answer (C) is incorrect.** Programmed text involves learning and assessment in small steps. The content is predetermined and does not give the learner the ability to make choices or commands.

56. Which is a true statement concerning the use of instructional aids?

- A. Instructional aids ensure getting and holding the learner's attention.
- B. Instructional aids should be designed to cover the key points in a lesson.
- C. Instructional aids should not be used simply to cover a subject in less time.

Answer (B) is correct. (FAA-H-8083-9B Chap 5)
   DISCUSSION: Instructional aids are a good way to improve communication between the instructor and the learners. Instructional aids should be designed to cover the key points in a lesson.
   Answer (A) is incorrect. Appropriate instructional aids will help get the learner's attention, but they cannot ensure that it will hold the learner's attention. **Answer (C) is incorrect.** Instructional aids can help get a point across quickly and clearly, thus reducing the time spent on some subjects.

57. Instructional aids used in the teaching/learning process should be

- A. self-supporting and require no explanation.
- B. compatible with the learning outcomes to be achieved.
- C. selected prior to developing and organizing the lesson plan.

Answer (B) is correct. (FAA-H-8083-9B Chap 5)
   DISCUSSION: After establishing lesson objectives, researching the subject, and organizing the material into a lesson plan, the instructor should determine what needs to be supported by visual or other instructional aids. The aids should be compatible with the learning outcomes to be achieved.
   Answer (A) is incorrect. Instructional aids are not self-supporting and will require explanation. **Answer (C) is incorrect.** Instructional aids should be compatible with the desired learning outcomes, which can best be done after, not prior to, developing and organizing the lesson plan.

58. Instructional aids used in the teaching/learning process should not be used

- A. as a crutch by the instructor.
- B. for teaching more in less time.
- C. to visualize relationships between abstracts.

Answer (A) is correct. (FAA-H-8083-9B Chap 5)
   DISCUSSION: Aids used in conjunction with oral presentation should emphasize, not distract from, the oral message. Also, the instructor should realize that such aids do not take the place of a sound lesson plan or instructor's input.
   Answer (B) is incorrect. Aids do help teach more in less time because they clarify and emphasize the lecture. The class can move to new material sooner. **Answer (C) is incorrect.** Instructional aids should be used to help learners to visualize relationships between abstracts.

59. What is one reason an instructor would use an instructional aid?

- A. To describe a desired outcome of training.
- B. To gain and hold learner attention.
- C. To describe the standards used to measure the objective.

Answer (B) is correct. (FAA-H-8083-9B Chap 5)
   DISCUSSION: A reason to use instructional aids in the teaching/learning process is that they will gain and hold the attention of learners.
   Answer (A) is incorrect. An element of a performance-based objective, the description of the skill or behavior describes a desired outcome of training in concrete terms that can be measured. **Answer (C) is incorrect.** Criteria describe the standards used to measure the accomplishment of the objective.

60. What is a use of instructional aids?

- A. Using instructional aids as a substitute for verbal instruction.
- B. Demonstrating simple concepts, but not complicated ideas.
- C. Clarifying relationships between material objects and concepts.

Answer (C) is correct. (FAA-H-8083-9B Chap 5)
   DISCUSSION: Instructional aids are used to clarify the relationships between material objects and concepts in addition to helping an instructor gain and hold the attention of learners.
   Answer (A) is incorrect. Instructional aids should not be used as a substitute for verbal instruction. These aids are normally used in conjunction with a verbal presentation, while words on the aid should be kept to a minimum. **Answer (B) is incorrect.** Instructional aids cover key concepts and points especially those that may be difficult to put into words.

61. When using instructional aids, they should be

- A. Visible throughout the lesson.
- B. Created for all lessons.
- C. Used as the main component of the lesson.

Answer (A) is correct. (FAA-H-8083-9B Chap 5)
   DISCUSSION: Making instructional aids visible throughout the lesson allows the learner to access the visual tool and stay engaged in the lesson.
   Answer (B) is incorrect. Not every lesson needs an instructional aid. Using aids for all lessons can be overwhelming for the learner. **Answer (C) is incorrect.** Instructional aids supplement the main component in the lesson.

STUDY UNIT SIX

CRITIQUE AND EVALUATION

(12 pages of outline)

6.1 THE INSTRUCTOR'S ASSESSMENT

1. No instructor skill is more important than the ability to analyze, appraise, and judge learner performance. Assessment is an essential and continuous component of the teaching and learning process.

   a. **Assessment** is the process of gathering measurable information to meet evaluation needs. It involves judgment by the instructor and collaboration with the learner during the evaluation stage.

   b. Instructors continuously evaluate learner performance in order to provide guidance, suggestions for improvement, and positive reinforcement.

   c. To enhance a learner's acceptance of further instruction, the instructor should keep the learner informed of the progress made.

      1) This will help minimize learner frustrations, which will keep the learner motivated to learn.

   d. Assessment helps the instructor see where more emphasis is needed and determine the readiness of the learner to move forward.

2. In order to provide direction and increase learner performance, assessments must be factual and must be aligned with the completion standards of the lesson.

3. An assessment should be **objective**.

   a. The effective assessment is focused on learner performance and should not reflect the personal opinions, likes, dislikes, and biases of the instructor.

   b. The assessment must be honest and based on the performance as it was, not as it could have been.

4. An assessment should be **flexible**.

   a. The instructor must fit the tone, technique, and content of the critique to the occasion and the learner.

   b. The instructor must evaluate the entire performance in the context it was accomplished and allow for variables, whether they occur on the part of the learner or from factors outside the learner's control.

   c. It should satisfy the requirements for the moment.

5.   An assessment should be **acceptable**.

   a.   Before learners willingly accept their instructor's assessment, they must first willingly accept the instructor.

   b.   The learners must have confidence in the instructor's qualifications, teaching ability, sincerity, competence, and authority.

      1)   An instructor's manner, attitude, and familiarity with the subject at hand does much to serve this purpose.

   c.   Instructors cannot rely solely on their position to make an assessment acceptable to their learners.

6.   An assessment should be **comprehensive**.

   a.   A comprehensive assessment is not necessarily long, nor must it treat every aspect of the performance in detail.

   b.   The instructor must decide whether the greater benefit will come from a discussion of a few major points or a number of minor points.

   c.   An effective assessment covers strengths as well as weaknesses.

7.   An assessment should be **constructive**.

   a.   An assessment is meaningless unless a learner profits from it.

   b.   Praise for praise's sake is of no value if a learner is not taught how to capitalize on things that are done well and to improve in areas of lesser accomplishment.

   c.   An instructor must give positive guidance when identifying a mistake or weakness.

      1)   Negative comments that discourage should be omitted altogether.

8.   An assessment must be **organized**.

   a.   Almost any pattern is acceptable as long as it is logical and makes sense to the learner.
   b.   An organizational pattern might be the sequence of the performance itself.

      1)   EXAMPLE: A flight instructor may explain the sequence of events that lead to an undesirable performance on a given flight maneuver.

9.   An assessment should be **thoughtful**.

   a.   An effective assessment reflects an instructor's thoughtfulness toward the learner's need for self-esteem, recognition, and approval from others.

      1)   The assessment must not minimize the inherent dignity and importance of the individual.

   b.   Ridicule, anger, or fun at the expense of the learner has no place in the assessment.

      1)   EXAMPLE: An instructor should try to deliver the assessment in private rather than in a group setting.

10. An assessment should be **specific**.

    a. The instructor's comments and recommendations should be specific, not so general that the learner can find nothing to hold onto.

        1) Learners cannot act on recommendations and strive to improve unless they know specifically what the recommendations are.

    b. Instructors should express ideas with firmness and authority in terms that cannot be misunderstood.

        1) Learners should have no doubt what they did well, what they did poorly, and specifically how they can improve.

6.2 TYPES OF ASSESSMENT

1. There are two categories of assessment: traditional assessment and authentic assessment.

    a. Assessments can be either formal or informal.

        1) Formal assessments usually involve documentation, e.g., quizzes or written exams.
        2) Informal assessments can include verbal critique and generally occur as needed.

2. **Traditional assessment** often involves written testing and is more likely to be used to evaluate a learner's progress at the rote level of learning.

    a. In a traditional assessment, one single answer will be correct (i.e., multiple choice, true/false, etc.).

        1) EXAMPLE: The FAA knowledge test for a given certificate or rating is a traditional assessment.

    b. Traditional assessments are formal in nature.

3. **Authentic assessment** requires the learner to demonstrate not only the rote and understanding levels, but also the application and correlation levels of learning. Authentic assessment generally requires the learner to perform real-world tasks.

    a. In an authentic assessment, specific standards are used to define acceptable performance on a task.

        1) EXAMPLE: The practical, or flight, portion of the FAA test is an authentic assessment.

    b. Learners must generate responses from skills and concepts previously learned.

    c. Authentic assessment focuses on the learning process, enhances the development of real-world skills, encourages higher order thinking skills (HOTS), and teaches learners to assess their own work and performance.

    d. Authentic assessment may not be as useful as traditional assessment in the early phases of training because the learner may not have enough information or knowledge about the concepts to participate fully.

4. Learner-centered assessment, an aspect of authentic assessment, is a form of learner-centered grading that uses open-ended questions to guide the learner through a self-assessment. The purpose of self-assessment is to stimulate growth in the learner's thought process and, in turn, behaviors. The four steps in this process include the following:

    a. **Replay** – Asking the learner to verbally replay the flight or procedure.

        1) This step gives the learner a chance to validate his or her own perceptions. It also gives the instructor critical insight into the learner's judgment abilities.

    b. **Reconstruct** – Having the learner identify key things that (s)he should or could have done differently during the flight or maneuver.

    c. **Reflect** – Asking questions that require reflection on the event, often leading to insight.

        1) EXAMPLES

            a) What was the most important thing you learned today?
            b) What part of the session was easiest for you? What part was hardest?
            c) Did anything make you uncomfortable? If so, when did it occur?
            d) How would you assess your performance and your decisions?
            e) How did your performance compare to the standards in the ACS?

    d. **Redirect** – Helping the learner relate the lessons learned to other experiences and consider how they might help in future sessions.

        1) EXAMPLE: "Which aspects of this flight might apply to future situations, and how?"

5. Learner-centered assessment uses two broad grading rubrics:

    a. One rubric that assesses proficiency in skill-focused maneuvers or procedures.

    b. Another rubric that focuses on the decision-making aspect of flight training (referred to as Single-Pilot Resource Management, or SRM).

    c. Advantages of these forms of assessment include the following:

        1) It actively involves the learner.

        2) It establishes the habit of reflection and self-assessment.

        3) The grades are not self-esteem related because they describe a level of performance. A learner cannot flunk a lesson.

        4) This assessment is conducted jointly between the instructor and the learner.

6. The grading dimensions of maneuvers or procedures include the following:

    a. **Describe** – Learner is able to describe the elements of the scenario but needs assistance to execute the maneuver properly.

    b. **Explain** – Learner is able to describe the elements of the scenario and understands the concepts and principles that comprise the activity but needs assistance to execute the maneuver properly.

    c. **Practice** – Learner is able to plan and execute the scenario with some coaching.

    d. **Perform** – Learner is able to perform the activity without instructor assistance and identifies and makes corrections in a timely manner. Indicates satisfactory demonstration.

    e. **Not observed** – Any event not accomplished or required.

7. The grading dimensions of SRM include the following:

    a. **Explain** – Learner can verbally identify, describe, and understand risks but needs to be prompted to make decisions.

    b. **Practice** – Learner properly identifies, understands, and applies SRM principles and corrects minor deviations identified by the instructor.

    c. **Manage-Decide** – Learner correctly gathers information, identifies proper courses of action, evaluates risks for each course of action, and makes the appropriate decision without instructor input.

8. To choose an effective assessment method, flight instructors can use a four-step process.

    a. Determine Level-of-Learning Objectives

        1) The individual objectives are stated as general level-of-learning objectives.

        2) Because it defines the scope of the learning task, this is a good starting point for developing a test.

    b. List Indicators/Samples of Desired Behaviors

        1) List the indicators of behavior that give the best indication of the achievement of the objective.

        2) By carefully choosing these indicators of behavior, an instructor can obtain adequate evidence of learning.

    c. Establish Criterion Objectives

        1) Define criterion (performance-based) objectives that state the conditions under which the behavior is to be performed and the criteria that must be met.

        2) Criterion objectives provide the framework for developing test items that will measure the level of learning objectives.

            a) EXAMPLE: "The learner will demonstrate understanding of navigational charts and their symbols by completing a quiz with a minimum passing score of 70%."

    d. Develop Criterion-Referenced Assessment Items

        1) Criterion-referenced testing measures a learner's performance against a carefully written, measurable standard or criterion.

            a) Practical tests for pilot certification are an example of criterion-referenced testing because they are based on the predetermined Practical Test Standards (PTS)/Airman Certification Standards (ACS) as set forth by the FAA.

            b) The objective of the PTS/ACS is to ensure the certification of pilots at a high level of performance and proficiency, consistent with safety.

            c) The PTS/ACS should not be used merely to "teach the test;" rather, the document should be used as both a training tool and an assessment tool during flight training to ensure learners are adequately prepared for the practical test.

            d) The PTS/ACS is not a teaching tool. It is a testing tool. The overall focus of flight training should be on education, learning, and understanding why the standards are there and how they were set.

                i) Instructors should not introduce the PTS/ACS until the last 3 hours of training prior to the practical test.

    2)   Criterion-referenced tests feature performance-based objectives that can be reliably, rather than subjectively, measured. Performance testing is desirable for evaluating training that involves an operation, a procedure, or a process.

        a)   EXAMPLE: A pretest constructed to measure knowledge and skills necessary to begin a course is a criterion-referenced test, as is a pre-solo aeronautical knowledge test.

    3)   The test results (questions missed) identify areas that were not adequately covered.

9.   Airman Certification Standards (ACS) for Remote Pilot – General (UAG), Private Pilot – Airplane (PAR), Commercial Pilot – Airplane (CAX), and Instrument Rating – Airplane (IRA) are currently effective. So too are the Practical Test Standards (PTS) for Sport Pilot – Airplane (SPA), Flight Instructor Sport – Airplane (SIA), and Flight Instructor – Airplane (FIA).

    a.   The FAA has worked closely with a diverse group of aviation community stakeholders to help the agency improve the testing and training standards, guidance, and test development and management components of the airman certification process.

        1)   The industry participants in this effort developed the ACS framework to improve airman training and testing by providing an integrated, holistic system that clearly aligns airman testing with certification standards and guidance.

    b.   The PTS documents explicitly define the performance metrics and tolerances for each flight proficiency element listed in the Federal Aviation Regulations. The ACS enhances the PTS by defining the specific task elements for aeronautical knowledge, risk management, and skills needed to support each Area of Operation and Task.

        1)   Simply, the ACS describes what an applicant must know, consider, and do to pass the knowledge and practical tests for a given airman certificate or rating. It is thus the single-source set of standards for both the knowledge test and practical test for a certificate or rating. It contains tasks in addition to those presented in 14 CFR Part 61.

        2)   By presenting the elements of knowledge, risk management, and skill in the integrated ACS format, the ACS approach better serves the applicant, the instructor, and the evaluator. In addition, the ACS approach enables the FAA to create and maintain a clear link among the regulations, knowledge and skill performance standards, guidance, and test materials.

NOTE: Most of the study questions for this subunit are based on known questions relevant to the PTS only and specific guidance from the FAA's *Aviation Instructor's Handbook*. If more questions specific to the ACS become available, an update will be published.

6.3 CRITIQUES AND ORAL ASSESSMENTS

1. A critique is an instructor-to-learner assessment.

    a. A critique is not necessarily negative in content. It considers the good along with the bad, the individual parts, the parts in relation to each other, and overall performance.

    b. It may be written, oral, or both.

    c. A critique should always be conducted immediately after the learner's performance while the details are easy to recall.

    d. The instructor may critique any activity that a learner performs or practices to improve skill, proficiency, and learning.

    e. A critique can and usually should be as varied in content as the performance being evaluated.

    f. Its purpose should be to provide guidance and direction to raise the level of the learner's performance.

2. Types of Critiques

    a. **Instructor/Learner Critique**

        1) Group discussion in which members of the class are invited to offer criticism of a performance

        2) Should be carefully controlled and organized by the instructor

    b. **Learner-Led Critique**

        1) Learner-led assessment that, while generating learner interest, may not be effective because of learner inexperience

    c. **Small Group Critique**

        1) Small groups are assigned to analyze a specific area of performance.
        2) Once combined, a comprehensive assessment results.

    d. **Individual Learner Critique by Another Learner**

        1) This type of critique often allows the group to accept more ownership of the ideas expressed.

        2) Careful oversight should be maintained by the instructor to control the process.

    e. **Self-Critique**

        1) This type of critique still requires oversight from the instructor.

    f. **Written Critique**

        1) Instructors can devote more time and thought to it than an oral assessment.
        2) Learners can refer to them as needed.
        3) Learner has a permanent record of suggestions, recommendations, and opinions.

3.   The most common means of assessment is direct or indirect oral questioning of learners by the instructor. Questions may be loosely classified as fact questions and HOTS questions.

    a.   The answer to a fact question is based on memory or recall (i.e., who, what, where, when, why).

    b.   HOTS questions require the learner to combine a knowledge of facts with an ability to analyze situations, solve problems, and arrive at conclusions.

4.   Proper quizzing by the instructor can have a number of desirable results. It can

    a.   Reveal the effectiveness of the instructor's training methods,

    b.   Check learner retention and comprehension of what has been learned,

    c.   Review material already presented to the learner,

    d.   Help retain learner interest and stimulate thinking,

    e.   Emphasize the important points of training,

    f.   Identify points that need more emphasis, and

    g.   Promote active learner participation.

5.   Characteristics of effective questions:

    a.   Objective, or fact, questions have only one correct answer, while the answer to open-ended HOTS (higher order thinking skills) questions can be expressed in a variety of possible situations. Each question should call for a specific answer that can be readily evaluated by the instructor.

    b.   Effective questions must

        1)   Apply to the subject being taught

        2)   Be brief and concise, but also clear and definite

        3)   Be adapted to the ability, experience, and stage of training of the learner

        4)   Center on only one idea (who, what, when, where, how, or why; not a combination)

        5)   Present a challenge to the learner

            a)   A question must be of suitable difficulty for the learners at that particular stage of training.

6.   The following types of questions should be **avoided**:

    a.   Yes/no questions. For example: "Do you understand?"

    b.   Puzzling questions – ones that do not provide a clear, definite objective. For example: "Which of the airplane systems is the most responsive to pilot inputs?"

    c.   Oversize questions – ones that are too broad in scope and could have multiple correct/incorrect responses. Again, no definite objective is stated. For example: "What is required before going flying?"

    d.   Toss-up questions – more than one correct response is possible. For example: "In an emergency, should you squawk 7700 or pick a landing spot?"

    e.   Bewilderment questions – questions that mentally confuse. For example: "In reading the altimeter, if you take temperature into account, as when flying from a cold air mass through a warm front, what precaution should you take when in mountainous areas?"

    f.   Trick questions – questions that cause the learner to feel (s)he is engaged in a battle of wits with the instructor, thus changing learner focus from the message to the messenger. For example: Using double negatives. "What is not a characteristic of not relying solely on flight instruments during flight in IMC?"

    g.   Irrelevant questions – diversions that introduce unrelated facts and thoughts and slow learner progress. For example: "How would the wing produce lift in outer space?"

7. When answering learner questions, the instructor needs to clearly understand the question before attempting an answer.

    a. The instructor should display interest in the learner's questions and give as direct and accurate an answer as possible.

    b. If a learner's question is too advanced for the particular lesson and confusion may result from a complete answer, the instructor may

        1) Carefully explain that the question was good and pertinent;

        2) Explain that to answer would unnecessarily complicate the learning task at hand; and

        3) Advise the learner to reintroduce the question later at the appropriate point in training or meet outside class for a more complete discussion.

8. Occasionally, a learner will ask a question the instructor cannot answer. The best course is to freely admit not knowing the answer.

    a. The instructor should then promise to find out or offer to help the learner look it up in appropriate references.

6.4 TYPES OF WRITTEN TEST QUESTIONS

1. Written test questions fall into two general categories:

    a. Supply-type and
    b. Selection-type.

2. Supply-type questions require the learner to furnish a response in the form of a word, sentence, or paragraph.

    a. Supply-type test items

        1) Require learners to organize their thoughts and ideas

        2) Demand the ability to express ideas

            a) This makes them valuable in measuring the learner's generalized understanding of a subject.

        3) Are subjective

            a) Thus, their main disadvantage is that they cannot be graded uniformly. The same test graded by different instructors probably would be assigned different scores.

        4) Take longer for learners to answer and for instructors to grade, which is a disadvantage

3. Selection-type questions include items for which two or more alternative responses are provided and there is only one single correct response.

    a. Selection-type test items

        1) Are highly objective.

            a) Thus, they are graded uniformly regardless of the learner or grader.

        2) Allow direct comparison of learners' accomplishments. For example, it is possible to compare learner performance

            a) Within the same class,
            b) Between classes, and
            c) Under different instructors.

    b. True/false, multiple-choice, and matching type questions are prime examples.

4. The **true/false** test item is well adapted to the testing of knowledge of facts and detail, especially when there are only two possible answers.

    a. The chief disadvantage of the true/false test item is it creates the greatest probability of guessing because the learner always has a 50% chance of guessing correctly.

    b. Guidelines for effective use of true/false questions

        1) Include only one idea in each statement
        2) Make the statement either entirely true or entirely false
        3) Avoid the unnecessary use of negatives
        4) Avoid absolutes such as "all," "every," "only," "never," etc.

5. **Multiple-choice** test items may be used to determine learner achievement, ranging from acquisition of facts to understanding, reasoning, and ability to apply what has been learned.

    a. Multiple-choice test items consist of two parts: the stem and a list of possible responses.

        1) The **stem** includes the question, statement, or problem.
        2) Incorrect responses are called distractors.

    b. When multiple-choice items are intended to measure achievement at a higher level of learning, some or all of the alternatives should be acceptable, but one should be clearly better than the others.

    c. Multiple-choice test items should have all alternatives of approximately equal length.

        1) A common error made by instructors is to make the correct alternative longer than the incorrect ones.

    d. Three major challenges are common in the construction of multiple-choice test items.

        1) Developing a question or item stem that must be expressed clearly and without ambiguity
        2) Developing a statement or correct answer choice that cannot be refuted
        3) Writing distractors that are attractive to learners who do not possess the knowledge or understanding necessary to recognize the correct response

    e. The following are popular distractors:

        1) An incorrect response related to the situation that sounds convincing
        2) A common misconception
        3) A true statement that does not satisfy the requirements of the problem
        4) A statement that is too broad or too narrow for the requirements of the problem

6. **Matching-type** test items are particularly good for measuring the learner's ability to recognize relationships and to make associations between terms, parts, words, phrases, or symbols listed in one column with related items in another column.

    a. Matching reduces the probability of guessing correct responses compared to a series of multiple-choice items covering the same material.

6.5 CHARACTERISTICS OF A GOOD TEST

1. **Reliability**

   a. The degree to which test results are consistent with repeated measurements.

   b. The reliability of a written test is determined by whether it gives consistent measurement to a particular individual or group.

   c. EXAMPLE: A written test that has reliability yields consistent results.

2. **Validity**

   a. The extent to which a test measures what it is supposed to measure.

   b. This is the most important consideration in test evaluation.

   c. EXAMPLE: A written test has validity when it measures what it is supposed to measure and nothing else.

3. **Usability**

   a. The functionality of a test.

   b. EXAMPLE: A written test is usable when it is easy to give, easy to read, the wording is clear and concise, figures are appropriate to the test items and clearly drawn, and it is easily graded.

4. **Objectivity**

   a. Describes singleness of scoring a test.

   b. Selection-type test items (true/false, multiple-choice) are much easier to grade with objectivity.

   c. EXAMPLE: In essay questions, it is nearly impossible to prevent an instructor's own biases from affecting the grade subject.

5. **Comprehensiveness**

   a. The degree to which a test measures the overall objectives.

   b. A written test must sample an appropriate cross-section of the objectives of instruction.

   c. EXAMPLE: A written test is said to be comprehensive when it liberally samples whatever is being measured.

6. **Discrimination**

   a. The degree to which a test distinguishes the differences between learners.

   b. Three features of a test constructed to identify the difference in achievement of learners are

      1) A wide range of scores,

      2) All levels of difficulty, and

      3) Items that distinguish between learners with differing levels of achievement of the course objectives.

   c. EXAMPLE: A written test having the characteristic of discrimination will measure small differences in achievement between learners.

6.6 REVIEW AND EVALUATION

1.   Review and evaluation of the learner's learning should be an integral part of each lesson.

   a.   Evaluation of learner performance and accomplishment should be based on the objectives and goals established in the lesson plan.

2.   Performance testing is desirable for evaluating training that involves an operation, procedure, or process.

   a.   This method of evaluation is particularly suited to the measurement of a learner's ability in performing a task, either mental or physical.

3.   Learners may perform a procedure or maneuver correctly but not fully understand the principles and objectives involved. If the instructor suspects this, learners should be required to vary the performance of the maneuver or procedure slightly.

   a.   Learners who do not understand the principles involved will probably not be able to successfully complete the revised maneuver or procedure.

QUESTIONS AND ANSWER EXPLANATIONS: All of the Fundamentals of Instructing knowledge test questions chosen by the FAA for release as well as additional questions selected by Gleim relating to the material in the previous outlines are provided on the following pages. These questions have been organized into the same subunits as the outlines. To the immediate right of each question are the correct answer and answer explanations. You should cover these answers and answer explanations while responding to the questions. Refer to the general discussion in the Introduction on how to take the FAA knowledge test.

Remember that the questions from the FAA knowledge test bank have been reordered by topic and organized into a meaningful sequence. Also, the first line of the answer explanation gives the citation of the authoritative source for the answer.

QUESTIONS

6.1 The Instructor's Assessment

1. To be effective, an assessment should

    A. not contain negative remarks.

    B. treat every aspect of the performance in detail.

    C. be flexible enough to satisfy the requirements of the moment.

Answer (C) is correct. *(FAA-H-8083-9B Chap 7)*
    DISCUSSION: An effective assessment is one that is flexible enough to satisfy the requirements of the moment. The instructor must fit the tone, technique, and content of the assessment to the occasion and the learner. Thus, the instructor is faced with the problem of what to say, what to omit, and what to minimize. The challenge of the assessment is that the instructor must determine what to say at the proper moment.
    Answer (A) is incorrect. An assessment may contain negative remarks as long as they point toward improvement or a higher level of performance. **Answer (B) is incorrect.** A comprehensive assessment is not necessarily a long one, nor must it treat every aspect of the performance in detail. The instructor must decide whether the greater benefit will come from discussing a few major points or a number of minor points.

2. An instructor's assessment of a learner's performance should

    A. treat every aspect of the performance in detail.

    B. be conducted in private so that the learner is not embarrassed.

    C. provide direction and guidance to improve performance.

Answer (C) is correct. *(FAA-H-8083-9B Chap 9)*
    DISCUSSION: An assessment should improve a learner's performance and provide something constructive with which (s)he can work and advance. It should provide direction and guidance to improve performance.
    Answer (A) is incorrect. A comprehensive assessment is not necessarily a long one, nor must it treat every aspect of the performance in detail. The instructor must decide whether the greater benefit will come from discussing a few major points or a number of minor points. **Answer (B) is incorrect.** An assessment may be conducted in private or before the entire class. An assessment presented before the entire class can be beneficial to every learner in the classroom as well as to the learner who performed the exercise.

3. Which is true about an instructor's assessment of a learner's performance?

    A. Praise for praise's sake is of value.

    B. It should be constructive and objective.

    C. It should treat every aspect of the performance in detail.

Answer (B) is correct. *(FAA-H-8083-9B Chap 6)*
    DISCUSSION: An assessment must be constructive by explaining to the learner how to capitalize on things that are done well and to use them to compensate for lesser accomplishments. An assessment must also be objective by basing it on the performance as it was, not as it could have been.
    Answer (A) is incorrect. Praise for praise's sake is of no value if a learner is not taught how to capitalize on things that are done well and to use them to compensate for lesser accomplishments. **Answer (C) is incorrect.** A comprehensive assessment is not necessarily a long one, nor must it treat every aspect of the performance in detail. The instructor must decide whether the greater benefit will come from discussing a few major points or a number of minor points.

4. Which statement is true about instructors' assessment?

    A. Instructors should rely on their personality to make an assessment more acceptable.

    B. A comprehensive assessment should emphasize the positive aspects of learner performance.

    C. Before learners willingly accept their instructor's assessment, they must first accept the instructor.

Answer (C) is correct. *(FAA-H-8083-9B Chap 6)*
    DISCUSSION: Learners must have confidence in the instructor's qualifications, teaching ability, sincerity, competence, and authority before they will willingly accept their instructor's assessment. An assessment holds little weight if the learner has no respect for the instructor.
    Answer (A) is incorrect. The effective assessment is focused on learner performance and should not reflect the personal opinions, likes, dislikes, and biases (i.e., personality) of the instructor. **Answer (B) is incorrect.** A comprehensive assessment means that good and bad points are covered adequately but not necessarily in exhaustive detail.

5. Which statement is true regarding an assessment that is constructive?

A. An instructor's manner and attitude make an assessment constructive.

B. Constructive assessments can inspire a learner to improve in areas of lesser accomplishment.

C. A constructive assessment should express ideas with authority in terms that cannot be misunderstood.

Answer (B) is correct. (FAA-H-8083-9B Chap 6)
DISCUSSION: Constructive assessments, including praise, can inspire a learner to improve in areas of lesser accomplishment.
Answer (A) is incorrect. An instructor's manner and attitude make an assessment acceptable to the learner. **Answer (C) is incorrect.** For an assessment to be specific, ideas should be expressed with firmness and in terms the learner cannot misunderstand.

6. What must an instructor do to ensure an assessment is thoughtful?

A. The instructor must not minimize the importance and dignity of the individual.

B. The instructor must give positive guidance when identifying a learner's mistakes.

C. The instructor must limit negative comments that discourage.

Answer (A) is correct. (FAA-H-8083-9B Chap 6)
DISCUSSION: The assessment given by the instructor must not minimize the inherent dignity and importance of the individual.
Answer (B) is incorrect. Instructor guidance should be constructive, which will not necessarily contain only positive comments. **Answer (C) is incorrect.** Negative comments that discourage should be omitted altogether, not simply limited.

7. Which of the following statements is true?

A. Instructor critiques should focus on only positive areas of the learner's performance.

B. Instructor critiques should only focus on areas where the learner needs to improve.

C. For an instructor's critique to be effective, the learner must first accept the instructor.

Answer (C) is correct. (FAA-H-8083-9B Chap 6)
DISCUSSION: The learner must accept the instructor in order to accept his or her assessment willingly. Learners must have confidence in the instructor's qualifications, teaching ability, sincerity, competence, and authority.
Answer (A) is incorrect. A proper critique should focus on both positive and negative aspects of the learner's performance. **Answer (B) is incorrect.** A proper critique should focus on both positive and negative aspects of the learner's performance.

8. The process of gathering measurable information to meet evaluation needs of a learner is known as what?

A. Critique.

B. Assessment.

C. Appraisal.

Answer (B) is correct. (FAA-H-8083-9B Chap 6)
DISCUSSION: Assessment is the process of gathering measurable information to meet evaluation needs.
Answer (A) is incorrect. The critique is an instructor-to-learner assessment used in conjunction with either a traditional or an authentic assessment. **Answer (C) is incorrect.** While an assessment includes a combination of the ability to analyze, appraise, and judge learner performance, appraisal is not as all-encompassing a term as an assessment.

6.2   Types of Assessment

9. FAA Airman Certification Standards are

A.   criterion-referenced.

B.   diagnostic-assessed.

C.   formative-assessed.

Answer (A) is correct. *(FAA-H-8083-9B Chap 6)*
DISCUSSION: Practical tests for maintenance technicians and pilots are criterion-referenced tests because the objective is for all successful applicants to meet the high standards of knowledge, skill, and safety required by one core standards document (the ACS) rather than other applicants seeking certification.
Answer (B) is incorrect. Diagnostic assessments are used to assess learner knowledge or skills prior to a course of instruction. **Answer (C) is incorrect.** Formative assessments, which are not graded, are used as a wrap-up of the lesson and to set the stage for the next lesson. This type of assessment, which is limited to what transpired during that lesson, informs and guides the instructor on which areas to reinforce.

10. The Airman Certification Standards should be used in

A.   flight training and testing.

B.   flight training only.

C.   testing only.

Answer (A) is correct. *(FAA-H-8083-9B Chap 6)*
DISCUSSION: Because the Airman Certification Standards (ACS) documents are the primary evaluation tool of the FAA for the issuance of a pilot certificate, they obviously are testing documents. Because this information is publicly accessible, these documents absolutely should be used to train pilot applicants to ensure they meet the ACS requirements. This training should not be merely to "teach the test," but the ACS is a very valuable resource in evaluating a pilot applicant's eligibility to take the practical test.
Answer (B) is incorrect. The ACS documents are the primary evaluation tool of the FAA for the issuance of a pilot certificate; therefore, they are to be used as testing documents in addition to their use as flight training skill standards. **Answer (C) is incorrect.** While the ACS documents are the primary evaluation tool of the FAA for the issuance of a pilot certificate, they are also a very valuable resource in evaluating a pilot applicant's eligibility to take the practical test.

11. The FAA Airman Certification Standards

A.   should be used as a primary training tool.

B.   contain tasks in addition to those presented in 14 CFR Part 61.

C.   contain testing standards only.

Answer (B) is correct. *(FAA-H-8083-9B Chap 6)*
DISCUSSION: The ACS Areas of Operation for each pilot certificate and rating are listed in 14 CFR Part 61. The ACS documents list specific tasks that must be performed for each Area of Operation during an FAA Airman Certification for a given certificate or rating.
Answer (A) is incorrect. Instructors should avoid merely teaching from the ACS as this encourages learner pilots to aim for the minimum passing standard. While the ACS should obviously be a measuring standard, it should not be the primary teaching tool for a course of training. Instead, CFIs should use a training syllabus appropriate to the training that addresses the ACS tasks in a logical, productive way. **Answer (C) is incorrect.** In addition to testing standards, the ACS documents also contain important information on the conduct of the test, special emphasis items, pilot/instructor/ examiner considerations, and test checklists.

12. To evaluate a learner's ability to use critical thinking skills in performing real-world tasks, which assessment method is most appropriate?

A.   Authentic.

B.   Supply-type.

C.   Learner-centered.

Answer (A) is correct. *(FAA-H-8083-9B Chap 6)*
DISCUSSION: Authentic assessment is a type of assessment in which the learner is asked to perform real-world tasks and demonstrate a meaningful application of skills and competencies. Authentic assessment lies at the heart of training today's aviation learners to use critical thinking skills.
Answer (B) is incorrect. A supply-type test can be very helpful, for example, on a pre-solo knowledge test in determining whether the pilot in training has adequate knowledge of procedures, but it would not offer insight into a learner's critical thinking skills in performing real-world tasks. **Answer (C) is incorrect.** Learner-centered assessment is a component of authentic assessment, but it is not the same thing.

13. Practical tests for pilot certification are

    A. evaluation-referenced.

    B. selection type tests.

    C. criterion-referenced.

Answer (C) is correct. (FAA-H-8083-9B Chap 6)
    DISCUSSION: Criterion-referenced tests measure an applicant's performance against carefully written, measurable standards or criteria. Practical tests for pilot certification are criterion-referenced. The ACS are the criteria.
    Answer (A) is incorrect. Practical tests are a form of evaluation, not evaluation-referenced. Evaluation-referenced is not a type of testing. **Answer (B) is incorrect.** Selection type tests require the learner to select an answer from two or more alternatives.

14. The objective of the Airman Certification Standards (ACS) is to ensure the certification of pilots at a high level of performance and proficiency, consistent with

    A. the time available.

    B. safety.

    C. their abilities.

Answer (B) is correct. (FAA-H-8083-9B Chap 6)
    DISCUSSION: The objective of the ACS is to ensure the certification of pilots at a high level of performance and proficiency, consistent with safety.
    Answer (A) is incorrect. The objective of the ACS is to ensure the certification of pilots at a high level of performance and proficiency, consistent with safety, not the time available. **Answer (C) is incorrect.** The objective of the ACS is to ensure the certification of pilots at a high level of performance and proficiency, consistent with safety, not their abilities.

15. Instructors must be aware of the fact that

    A. FAA Airman Certification Standards (ACS) books are testing documents only.

    B. FAA Airman Certification Standards (ACS) books should be introduced early in training and used as a measuring stick for learner performance and progress.

    C. FAA Airman Certification Standards (ACS) books should be introduced 6 hours prior to the practical test.

Answer (A) is correct. (FAA-H-8083-9B Chap 6)
    DISCUSSION: The ACS is a testing tool, not a teaching tool. The overall focus of flight training should be on education, learning, and understanding why the standards are there and how they were set. The minimum standards to pass the checkride should not be introduced until the 3 hours of preparation for the checkride. To accommodate this, the FAA requires 3 hours of training in the 60 days preceding the practical test.
    Answer (B) is incorrect. The ACS should only be introduced in the last 3 hours of flight training prior to the checkride. **Answer (C) is incorrect.** The ACS should be introduced 3 hours, not 6 hours, prior to the checkride.

16. A pretest constructed to measure knowledge and skills necessary to begin a course is referred to as a

    A. virtual-reality test.

    B. evaluation-referenced.

    C. criterion-referenced test.

Answer (C) is correct. (FAA-H-8083-9B Chap 6)
    DISCUSSION: A pretest is a criterion-referenced test constructed to measure the knowledge and skills that are necessary to begin a course. Criterion-referenced tests measure a learner's performance against carefully written, measurable standards or criteria.
    Answer (A) is incorrect. Virtual reality is a potential future method of computer-based training (CBT) that can simulate environments very realistically. It is not a type of test. **Answer (B) is incorrect.** Practical tests are a form of evaluation, not evaluation-referenced. Evaluation-referenced is not a type of testing.

17. Which of the following assessment types focuses on real-world tasks?

    A. Traditional.

    B. Formal.

    C. Authentic.

Answer (C) is correct. (FAA-H-8083-9B Chap 6)
    DISCUSSION: Authentic assessment requires the learner to demonstrate not just the rote and understanding levels, but also the application and correlation levels of learning. Authentic assessment generally requires the learner to perform real-world tasks.
    Answer (A) is incorrect. During traditional assessment, the learner usually has a set amount of time to recognize or reproduce memorized terms, formulas, or data. There is a single answer that is correct. Consequently, the traditional assessment is more likely to be used to judge or evaluate the learner's progress at the rote and understanding levels of learning. **Answer (B) is incorrect.** Whether traditional or authentic, an assessment can be either formal or informal. Formal assessments usually involve documentation, such as a quiz or written examination. They are used periodically throughout a course, as well as at the end of a course, to measure and document whether or not the course objectives have been met.

18. Criterion-based assessment items would most likely be part of

  A. performance-based tests.

  B. multiple choice tests.

  C. oral quizzing.

Answer (A) is correct. (FAA-H-8083-9B Chap 6)

DISCUSSION: Criterion-based tests are performance-based tests. In addition to the behavior expected, criterion objectives state the conditions under which the behavior is to be performed and the criteria that must be met. If the instructor developed performance-based objectives during the creation of lesson plans, criterion objectives have already been formulated. The criterion objective provides the framework for developing the test items used to measure the level of learning objectives.

    Answer (B) is incorrect. Criterion-based assessments are performance-based tests that may be administered through multiple formats. **Answer (C) is incorrect.** Criterion-based assessments are performance-based tests that may be administered through multiple formats.

19. Performance-based objectives are a distinguishable characteristic of

  A. formative assessments.

  B. subjective grading.

  C. criterion-referenced testing.

Answer (C) is correct. (FAA-H-8083-9B Chap 6)

DISCUSSION: Performance-based objectives serve as a reference for the development of test items in criterion-referenced testing. Criterion-referenced tests evaluate based on carefully written, measurable standards or criteria.

    Answer (A) is incorrect. Formative assessments, which are not graded, are used as a wrap-up of the lesson and to set the stage for the next lesson. This type of assessment, which is limited to what transpired during that lesson, informs and guides the instructor on which areas to reinforce. **Answer (B) is incorrect.** Performance-based objectives provide carefully written, measurable standards or criteria for testing. They do not allow for subjective grading.

20. What is true of traditional assessments?

  A. They require the learner to demonstrate meaningful application of skills.

  B. They evaluate a learner's progress at a rote level of learning.

  C. There are multiple correct responses in traditional assessments.

Answer (B) is correct. (FAA-H-8083-9B Chap 6)

DISCUSSION: Traditional assessments often involve written tests and are more likely to be used to evaluate a learner's progress at the rote level of learning.

    Answer (A) is incorrect. Authentic assessment, not traditional assessment, requires the learner to demonstrate meaningful application of skills and competencies. **Answer (C) is incorrect.** In a traditional assessment, only one single answer will be correct.

21. Which type of assessment is more beneficial during the early stages of training?

  A. Learner-centered assessments.

  B. Traditional assessments.

  C. Authentic assessments.

Answer (B) is correct. (FAA-H-8083-9B Chap 6)

DISCUSSION: Traditional assessments are generally more useful in the early phases of training, as the learner may not have enough information or knowledge about the concepts to participate fully.

    Answer (A) is incorrect. A learner-centered assessment, an aspect assessment, is a form of learner-centered grading that uses open-ended questions to guide the learner through a self-assessment. **Answer (C) is incorrect.** Authentic assessments may not be as useful as traditional assessments in the early phases of training, as the learner may not have enough information or knowledge about the concepts to participate fully.

22. What is a characteristic of a learner-centered assessment?

  A. It is conducted jointly between the learner and the instructor.

  B. The learner is not directly involved in the assessment until reaching a specific level.

  C. The instructor provides the assessment directly to the learner.

Answer (A) is correct. (FAA-H-8083-9B Chap 6)

DISCUSSION: A learner-centered assessment is a collaborative process conducted between the learner and instructor and often culminates with the instructor and learner jointly determining the learner's progress.

    Answer (B) is incorrect. The learner is directly involved in learner-centered assessment as this is a collaborative assessment process. **Answer (C) is incorrect.** The instructor providing assessment directly to the learner would be a form of traditional assessment, which is more of an instructor-centered style.

23. What are the four steps in the learner-centered assessment process?

    A. Replay, reconstruct, redesign, redirect.

    B. Replay, reconstruct, reflect, redirect.

    C. Replay, repeat, reflect, redirect.

Answer (B) is correct. (FAA-H-8083-9B Chap 6)
    DISCUSSION: The four steps in the learner-centered assessment process are replay, reconstruct, reflect, redirect.
    Answer (A) is incorrect. Redesign is not a step in the learner-centered assessment process. The four steps in the learner-centered assessment process are replay, reconstruct, reflect, redirect. **Answer (C) is incorrect.** Repeat is not a step in the learner-centered assessment process and is the same as replay. The four steps in the learner-centered assessment process are replay, reconstruct, reflect, redirect.

24. What step in the learner-centered assessment process helps the learner relate the lessons learned to other experiences?

    A. Redirect.

    B. Replay.

    C. Reconstruct.

Answer (A) is correct. (FAA-H-8083-9B Chap 6)
    DISCUSSION: The last step, that of redirecting, helps the learner relate the lessons learned to other experiences and consider how they might help in future sessions.
    Answer (B) is incorrect. Replay occurs when a learner is asked to verbally replay or repeat the flight or procedure. **Answer (C) is incorrect.** Reconstruction occurs when the learner identifies key things that (s)he should or could have done differently during the flight or maneuver.

25. What grading dimension or level has a learner reached when they correctly gather information, identify proper courses of action, evaluate risk, and make an appropriate decision without instructor input?

    A. Explain.

    B. Practice.

    C. Manage-Decide.

Answer (C) is correct. (FAA-H-8083-9B Chap 6)
    DISCUSSION: A learner who correctly gathers information, identifies proper courses of action, evaluates risks for each course of action, and makes the appropriate decision without instructor input is at the "Manage-Decide" grading dimension of Single-Pilot Management.
    Answer (A) is incorrect. The grading dimension "Explain" describes when a learner can verbally identify, describe, and understand risks but needs to be prompted to make decisions. **Answer (B) is incorrect.** The grading dimension "Practice" describes a learner who properly identifies, understands, and applies SRM principles and corrects minor deviations identified by the instructor.

6.3   Critiques and Oral Assessments

26. Which is a valid reason for the use of proper oral quizzing during a lesson?

    A. Promotes active learner participation.

    B. Identifies points that need less emphasis.

    C. Helps the instructor determine the general intelligence level of the learners.

Answer (A) is correct. (FAA-H-8083-9B Chap 6)
    DISCUSSION: A valid reason for the use of proper oral quizzing during a lesson is to promote active learner participation, which is important to effective teaching.
    Answer (B) is incorrect. A valid reason for the use of proper oral quizzing during a lesson is that it identifies points that need more, not less, emphasis. **Answer (C) is incorrect.** A valid reason for the use of proper oral quizzing during a lesson is to check the learners' comprehension of what has been learned, not their general intelligence level.

27. Proper oral quizzing by the instructor during a lesson can have which result?

    A. Alerts the instructor to the level of learner motivation.

    B. Identifies points which need more emphasis.

    C. Can serve as a lead-in to introduce new material.

Answer (B) is correct. (FAA-H-8083-9B Chap 6)
    DISCUSSION: One desirable result of oral quizzing is that it helps the instructor identify points that need more emphasis. By noting learners' answers, the instructor can quickly spot weak points in understanding and give these extra attention.
    Answer (A) is incorrect. Learner performance on oral quizzes can indicate weak points in understanding but will not help the instructor gauge learner motivation. **Answer (C) is incorrect.** The introduction of new material is accomplished during the presentation, not evaluation, step of the teaching process.

28. One desirable result of proper oral quizzing by the instructor is to

A. reveal the effectiveness of the instructor's training procedures.

B. fulfill the requirements set forth in the overall objectives of the course.

C. reveal the essential information from which the learner can determine progress.

Answer (A) is correct. (FAA-H-8083-9B Chap 6)
DISCUSSION: One desirable result of proper oral quizzing by the instructor is that it reveals the effectiveness of the instructor's training procedures.
Answer (B) is incorrect. Quizzing can only measure achievement, not fulfill the requirements, of the overall objectives of the course. **Answer (C) is incorrect.** An instructor should use the critique, not a quiz, to reveal the essential information from which the learner can determine progress.

29. When conducting an oral assessment, which of the following is an example of a type of question to avoid?

A. What is the first step in conducting a preflight?

B. What do you do before beginning a flight?

C. How do you check for correct tire pressure?

Answer (B) is correct. (FAA-H-8083-9B Chap 6)
DISCUSSION: Effective oral assessment will avoid this type of question, as the scope of the potential answer is out of scale with a specific topic being evaluated. This is considered an over-sized question.
Answer (A) is incorrect. This is an effective question that emphasizes the important points of training. **Answer (C) is incorrect.** This is an effective question that checks comprehension of what has been learned while promoting active learner participation.

30. During oral quizzing, which type of questions should an instructor expect a learner to answer based on memory or recall?

A. Trick questions.

B. Fact questions.

C. HOTS (higher order thinking skills) questions.

Answer (B) is correct. (FAA-H-8083-9B Chap 6)
DISCUSSION: The most common means of assessment is direct or indirect oral questioning of learners by the instructor. Questions may be loosely classified as fact questions and HOTS questions. The answer to a fact question is based on memory or recall. This type of question usually concerns who, what, when, and where. HOTS questions involve why or how, and they require the learner to combine knowledge of facts with an ability to analyze situations, solve problems, and arrive at conclusions.
Answer (A) is incorrect. Trick questions should be avoided because they are a detriment to the learning process, but they can exist as either fact questions or HOTS questions. **Answer (C) is incorrect.** A HOTS question involves why or how, and it requires the learner to combine knowledge of facts with an ability to analyze situations, solve problems, and arrive at conclusions.

31. To be effective in oral quizzing during the conduct of a lesson, a question should

A. be of suitable difficulty for that stage of training.

B. include a combination of where, how, and why.

C. divert the learner's thoughts to subjects covered in other lessons.

Answer (A) is correct. (FAA-H-8083-9B Chap 6)
DISCUSSION: During oral quizzing, an effective question must present a challenge to the learner. A question must be of suitable difficulty for the learner at that particular stage of training. These types of questions stimulate learning.
Answer (B) is incorrect. An effective question should be limited to who, what, when, where, how, or why, not a combination. **Answer (C) is incorrect.** An effective question must apply to the subject of instruction, not divert the learner's thoughts to subjects covered in other lessons.

32. During oral quizzing in a given lesson, effective questions should

A. be brief and concise.

B. provide answers that can be expressed in a variety of ways.

C. divert the learner's thoughts to subjects covered in previous lessons.

Answer (A) is correct. (FAA-H-8083-9B Chap 6)
DISCUSSION: During oral quizzing, an effective question should be brief and concise but should also be clear and definite. Enough words must be used to establish the conditions or situations exactly so that instructor and learners will have the same mental picture.
Answer (B) is incorrect. All effective questions will have only one correct answer. **Answer (C) is incorrect.** An effective question must apply to the subject of instruction, not divert the learner's thoughts to subjects covered in previous lessons.

33. In all quizzing as a portion of the instruction process, the questions should

    A. include catch questions to develop the learner's perceptive power.

    B. call for specific answers and be readily evaluated by the instructor.

    C. include questions with more than one central idea to evaluate how completely a learner understands the subject.

Answer (B) is correct. (FAA-H-8083-9B Chap 6)
    DISCUSSION: In any kind of testing, questions should have one specific answer so that the instructor can readily evaluate the learner's response. General questions tend to confuse rather than help, and unanswered questions serve no useful purpose at all.
    Answer (A) is incorrect. Catch questions should be avoided at all times. The learners will feel they are engaged in a battle of wits with the instructor, and the whole significance of the subject of instruction will be lost. **Answer (C) is incorrect.** Effective questions used in quizzing should center on only one central idea.

34. To answer a learner's question, it is most important that the instructor

    A. clearly understand the question.

    B. have complete knowledge of the subject.

    C. introduce more complicated information to partially answer the question, if necessary.

Answer (A) is correct. (FAA-H-8083-9B Chap 6)
    DISCUSSION: The answering of learners' questions can be an effective teaching method. To answer a learner's question, it is most important that the instructor clearly understands the question.
    Answer (B) is incorrect. While an instructor may have knowledge of a subject, occasionally a learner will ask a question the instructor cannot answer. The instructor should admit not knowing the answer and should promise to get the answer or help the learner to find it. **Answer (C) is incorrect.** Introducing more complicated information to partially answer the question is normally unwise. Doing so would confuse the learner and complicate the learning task at hand.

35. With regards to oral quizzing, which type of question requires the learner to combine knowledge with the ability to analyze, solve problems, and arrive at conclusions?

    A. Fact questions.

    B. HOTS questions.

    C. Provocative questions.

Answer (B) is correct. (FAA-H-8083-9B Chap 6)
    DISCUSSION: HOTS, or higher order thinking skills, questions usually involve why or how and require the learner to combine knowledge of facts with the ability to analyze situations, solve problems, and arrive at conclusions.
    Answer (A) is incorrect. Fact questions involve answers that are based on memory or recall. This type of question usually concerns who, what, when, and where. **Answer (C) is incorrect.** Provocative, or controversial, questions are a type that should be avoided in oral quizzing.

36. For oral quizzing to be effective during a lesson, a question should

    A. be limited to who, what, when, where, why, or how, not a combination.

    B. include a combination of where, how, and why.

    C. be easy for the learner at that particular stage of training.

Answer (A) is correct. (FAA-H-8083-9B Chap 6)
    DISCUSSION: To be effective in oral quizzing, each question should center on only one idea, which is limited to who, what, where, when, how, or why, not a combination.
    Answer (B) is incorrect. A single question should be limited to who, what, when, where, how, or why, not a combination. **Answer (C) is incorrect.** Questions of suitable difficulty serve to stimulate learning. To be effective, questions must be adapted to the ability, experience, and stage of training of the learners and be of suitable difficulty.

37. When an instructor critiques a learner, it should always be

    A. done in private.

    B. subjective rather than objective.

    C. conducted immediately after the learner's performance.

Answer (C) is correct. (FAA-H-8083-9B Chap 6)
    DISCUSSION: The critique should always be conducted immediately after the learner's performance while the performance is still fresh in the learner's mind. Specific comments on "your third turn," for instance, would have little value a week after the maneuver was performed.
    Answer (A) is incorrect. A critique may be conducted in private or before the entire class. A critique presented before the entire class can be beneficial to every learner in the classroom as well as to the learner who performed the exercise. **Answer (B) is incorrect.** The critique should be objective rather than subjective.

38. Using double negatives is an example of which type of question that should be avoided?

A. Irrelevant questions.

B. Oversize questions.

C. Trick questions.

Answer (C) is correct. (FAA-H-8083-9B Chap 6)
DISCUSSION: Trick questions, such as double negatives, cause a learner to feel (s)he is engaged in a battle of wits with the instructor, thus changing learner focus from the message to the messenger.
Answer (A) is incorrect. Irrelevant questions are diversions that introduce unrelated facts and thoughts and slow learner progress. **Answer (B) is incorrect.** Oversize questions are too broad in scope and could have multiple correct/incorrect responses. An example might be: "What is required before going flying?"

39. Which of the following is not a type of critique?

A. Written critique.

B. Instructor-absence critique.

C. Individual learner critique by another learner.

Answer (B) is correct. (FAA-H-8083-9B Chap 6)
DISCUSSION: Instructor-absence is not a type of critique. During all types of critiques, the instructor should be present to carefully control the process.
Answer (A) is incorrect. The written critique is a type of critique. **Answer (C) is incorrect.** Individual learner critique by another learner is a type of critique.

40. What is a benefit of a written critique?

A. The learner will have a permanent record of suggestions.

B. Learners get to work together, thus sharing ideas.

C. The written critique is always positive.

Answer (A) is correct. (FAA-H-8083-9B Chap 6)
DISCUSSION: Learners will have a permanent record of suggestions, recommendations, and opinions to reference at a later date if needed.
Answer (B) is incorrect. The sharing of ideas is a characteristic of the small group critique, not the written critique. **Answer (C) is incorrect.** All critiques, no matter what the format, can include both positive and negative comments.

41. What is true of irrelevant questions?

A. They are too broad in scope and could have multiple correct responses.

B. They change the learner's focus from the message to the messenger.

C. They introduce unrelated facts and slow learner progress.

Answer (C) is correct. (FAA-H-8083-9B Chap 6)
DISCUSSION: Irrelevant questions are diversions that introduce unrelated facts and thoughts and slow learner progress.
Answer (A) is incorrect. Oversize questions, not irrelevant questions, are too broad in scope and could have multiple correct/incorrect responses. **Answer (B) is incorrect.** Trick questions are questions that cause the learner to feel (s)he is engaged in a battle of wits with the instructor, thus changing learner focus from the message to the messenger.

42. How should an instructor critique a learner?

A. The critique should be conducted in public to promote peer feedback and a group learning experience.

B. The critique should vary in content as necessary to accommodate the performance being evaluated.

C. The critique should be delivered verbally with a focus on exemplary performance.

Answer (B) is correct. (FAA-H-8083-9B Chap 6)
DISCUSSION: An effective critique accounts for the overall performance and should be as varied in content as the performance itself.
Answer (A) is incorrect. An effective critique may be conducted in private or in public depending on many variables and the aptitude of the instructor. **Answer (C) is incorrect.** An effective critique considers all aspects of performance, both negative and positive, and may be delivered in oral or written format.

43. The purpose of a critique is to

A. identify only the learner's faults and weaknesses.

B. give a delayed evaluation of the learner's performance.

C. provide direction and guidance to raise the level of the learner's performance.

Answer (C) is correct. (FAA-H-8083-9B Chap 6)
DISCUSSION: A critique provides the learner with constructive feedback (s)he can build upon. It should provide direction and guidance to raise the learner's level of performance.
Answer (A) is incorrect. An effective critique considers good as well as bad performance. It is not necessarily negative in content. **Answer (B) is incorrect.** A critique is not the same thing as an evaluation, as it does not determine a learner's progress in a course. Even as part of an evaluation, a critique (guidance) should not be delayed.

44. An instructor's critique of a learner's performance should be

    A. as varied in content as the performance being evaluated.

    B. an opportunity for an instructor to be critical of a learner's performance.

    C. always conducted in private.

Answer (A) is correct. (FAA-H-8083-9B Chap 6)
    DISCUSSION: An effective critique considers good as well as bad performance, the individual parts, relationships of the individual parts, and the overall performance. A critique can and usually should be as varied in content as the performance being evaluated.
    Answer (B) is incorrect. The word "critique" sometimes has a negative connotation, and the instructor needs to avoid using this method as an opportunity to be overly critical of learner performance. **Answer (C) is incorrect.** A critique may be conducted privately or before the entire class. A critique presented before the entire class can be beneficial to every learner in the classroom, as well as to the learner who performed the exercise or assignment. In this case, however, the instructor should avoid embarrassing the learner in front of the class.

6.4 Types of Written Test Questions

45. What is a characteristic of supply-type test items?

    A. They are easily adapted to testing knowledge of facts and details.

    B. Test results would be graded the same regardless of the learner or the grader.

    C. The same test graded by different instructors would probably be given different scores.

Answer (C) is correct. (FAA-H-8083-9B Chap 6)
    DISCUSSION: A characteristic of supply-type test items is that they cannot be graded with uniformity. The same test graded by different instructors would probably be assigned different scores. The same test graded by the same instructor on consecutive days might be assigned two different scores. There is no assurance that the grade assigned is the grade deserved.
    Answer (A) is incorrect. True/false, not supply-type, test items are easily adapted to testing knowledge of facts and details. **Answer (B) is incorrect.** Selection-type, not supply-type, test items would be graded the same regardless of the learner or the grader.

46. Which is the main disadvantage of supply-type test items?

    A. They cannot be graded with uniformity.

    B. They are readily answered by guessing.

    C. They are easily adapted to statistical analysis.

Answer (A) is correct. (FAA-H-8083-9B Chap 6)
    DISCUSSION: The main disadvantage of supply-type test items is that they cannot be graded with uniformity. The same test graded by different instructors would probably be assigned different scores. The same test graded by the same instructor on consecutive days might be assigned two different scores. There is no assurance that the grade assigned is the grade deserved.
    Answer (B) is incorrect. The main disadvantage of true/false, not supply-type, test items is they are readily answered by guessing. **Answer (C) is incorrect.** An advantage, not disadvantage, of selection-type, not supply-type, test items is that they are easily adapted to statistical analysis.

47. The primary advantage of supply-type testing is that

    A. it can be graded quickly.

    B. the learner is required to organize knowledge.

    C. it can be graded with an answer key.

Answer (B) is correct. (FAA-H-8083-9B Appendix B)
    DISCUSSION: Supply-type test items require the learner to furnish a response in the form of a word, sentence, or paragraph. The supply-type item requires the learner to organize knowledge. It demands an ability to express ideas and is thus valuable in measuring the learner's generalized understanding of a subject. For example, the supply-type item on a pre-solo knowledge test can be very helpful in determining whether the pilot in training has adequate knowledge of procedures.
    Answer (A) is incorrect. Supply-type tests require more time for the learner to complete and more time for the instructor to grade. **Answer (C) is incorrect.** Supply-type tests cannot be effectively graded with an answer key. The same test graded by different instructors could be assigned different scores. Even the same test graded by the same instructor on consecutive days might be assigned altogether different scores.

48. Which statement is true relative to effective multiple-choice test items?

A. Negative words or phrases need not be emphasized.

B. Items should call for abstract background knowledge.

C. Keep all alternatives of approximately equal length.

Answer (C) is correct. (FAA-H-8083-9B Chap 6)
    DISCUSSION: In preparing and reviewing the alternatives to a multiple-choice item, it is advisable to keep all alternatives approximately the same length. Research of instructor-made tests reveals that, in general, correct alternatives are longer than incorrect ones.
    Answer (A) is incorrect. When negative words or phrases are used, they should be emphasized in order to be effective.
Answer (B) is incorrect. Items should call for essential knowledge rather than for abstract background knowledge or unimportant facts.

49. Which type of test item creates the greatest probability of guessing?

A. True/false.

B. Supply-type.

C. Multiple-choice.

Answer (A) is correct. (FAA-H-8083-9B Chap 6)
    DISCUSSION: The true/false test item creates the greatest probability of guessing because the learner always has a 50% chance of guessing correctly.
    Answer (B) is incorrect. The true/false, not the supply-type, test item creates the greatest probability of guessing.
Answer (C) is incorrect. The true/false, not the multiple-choice, test item creates the greatest probability of guessing.

50. One of the main advantages of selection-type test items over supply-type test items is that the selection-type

A. decreases discrimination between responses.

B. would be graded objectively regardless of the learner or the grader.

C. precludes comparison of learners under one instructor with those under another instructor.

Answer (B) is correct. (FAA-H-8083-9B Chap 6)
    DISCUSSION: One of the main advantages of selection-type test items over supply-type test items is that the selection-type are graded objectively regardless of the learner or grader.
    Answer (A) is incorrect. An advantage of the selection-type test item over the supply-type test item is that more areas of knowledge can be tested in a given time, thus increasing, not decreasing, comprehensiveness, validity, and discrimination. **Answer (C) is incorrect.** An advantage of the selection-type test item over supply-type test item is the ability to compare, not to preclude comparison of, learner performance under one instructor with those of another instructor.

51. Which statement is true about multiple-choice test items that are intended to measure achievement at a higher level of learning?

A. It is unethical to mislead learners into selecting an incorrect alternative.

B. Some or all of the alternatives should be acceptable, but only one should be clearly better than the others.

C. The use of common errors as distracting alternatives to divert the learner from the correct response is ineffective and invalid.

Answer (B) is correct. (FAA-H-8083-9B Chap 6)
    DISCUSSION: When multiple-choice test items are intended to measure achievement at a higher level of learning, some or all of the alternatives should be acceptable, but only one should be clearly better than the others. The instructions given should direct the learner to select the best alternative.
    Answer (A) is incorrect. When using multiple-choice test items, the learners are not supposed to guess the correct answer; they should select it only if they know it is correct. Thus, it is ethical, not unethical, to mislead learners into selecting an incorrect alternative. **Answer (C) is incorrect.** When using multiple-choice test items, the use of common errors as distracting alternatives to divert the learner from the correct response is effective, not ineffective, and valid, not invalid.

52. Which is one of the major difficulties encountered in the construction of multiple-choice test items?

A. Adapting the items to statistical item analysis.

B. Keeping all responses approximately equal in length.

C. Inventing distractors which will be attractive to learners lacking knowledge or understanding.

Answer (C) is correct. (FAA-H-8083-9B Chap 6)
    DISCUSSION: Three major difficulties are encountered in the construction of multiple-choice test items:

1. Development of a question or an item stem that can be expressed clearly without ambiguity.
2. Statement of an answer that cannot be refuted.
3. The invention of lures or distractors attractive to those learners who do not possess the knowledge or understanding necessary to recognize the correct answer.

    Answer (A) is incorrect. It is a major advantage, not difficulty, for a multiple-choice test item to be well adapted to statistical item analysis. **Answer (B) is incorrect.** A principle, not difficulty, of constructing a multiple-choice test item is to keep all responses approximately equal in length.

53. In a written test, which type of selection-type test items reduces the probability of guessing correct responses?

    A. Essay.

    B. Matching.

    C. Multiple-choice.

Answer (B) is correct. (FAA-H-8083-9B Chap 6)
    DISCUSSION: In a written test, matching-type test items reduce the probability of guessing correct responses compared to a series of multiple-choice items covering the same material, especially if alternatives are used more than once.
    Answer (A) is incorrect. An essay question is a supply-type, not selection-type, test item. **Answer (C) is incorrect.** Matching, not multiple-choice, test items reduce the probability of guessing correct responses.

54. Which part of a multiple-choice test includes the question, statement, or problem?

    A. The response.

    B. The root.

    C. The stem.

Answer (C) is correct. (FAA-H-8083-9B Chap 6)
    DISCUSSION: The stem includes the question, statement, or problem.
    Answer (A) is incorrect. The responses in a multiple-choice test are the combination of both the distractors and the one correct answer. **Answer (B) is incorrect.** The stem, not the root, of a question includes the question, statement, or problem.

55. When taking a written test, what selection-type test items reduce the probability of guessing correct responses?

    A. Multiple choice.

    B. Matching.

    C. True-false.

Answer (B) is correct. (FAA-H-8083-9B Chap 6)
    DISCUSSION: In a written test, matching-type test items reduce the probability of guessing correct responses compared to a series of multiple-choice items covering the same material, especially if alternatives are used more than once.
    Answer (A) is incorrect. Matching, not multiple-choice, test items reduce the probability of guessing correct responses. **Answer (C) is incorrect.** True-false items create the greatest probability of guessing and are more likely to utilize rote memory than subject knowledge.

6.5 Characteristics of a Good Test

56. A written test that has reliability

    A. yields consistent results.

    B. measures small differences in the achievement of learners.

    C. actually measures what it is supposed to measure and nothing else.

Answer (A) is correct. (FAA-H-8083-9B Chap 6)
    DISCUSSION: A written test that has reliability is one that yields consistent results.
    Answer (B) is incorrect. A written test that shows discrimination, not reliability, measures small differences in the achievement of learners. **Answer (C) is incorrect.** A written test that has validity, not reliability, actually measures what it is supposed to measure and nothing else.

57. A written test has validity when it

    A. yields consistent results.

    B. samples liberally whatever is being measured.

    C. measures what it is supposed to measure.

Answer (C) is correct. (FAA-H-8083-9B Chap 6)
    DISCUSSION: A written test has validity when it measures what it is supposed to measure.
    Answer (A) is incorrect. A written test has reliability, not validity, when it yields consistent results. **Answer (B) is incorrect.** A written test has comprehensiveness, not validity, when it samples liberally whatever is being measured.

58. Comprehensiveness is the degree to which a test

    A. measures the overall objectives.

    B. consists of an appropriate mix of easy, medium, and difficult questions.

    C. includes multiple-choice, essay, and true/false questions.

Answer (A) is correct. (FAA-H-8083-9B Chap 6)
    DISCUSSION: Comprehensiveness is the degree to which a test measures the overall objectives. A written test must sample an appropriate cross-section of the objectives of instruction. The instructor has to make certain the evaluation includes a representative and comprehensive sampling of the objectives of the course.
    Answer (B) is incorrect. Determining an "appropriate" mix of the difficulty level of questions is not necessary for a test to be comprehensive. **Answer (C) is incorrect.** The degree to which a test measures the overall objectives is not determined by the question type, but instead by the question content.

59. A written test is said to be comprehensive when it

   A. includes all levels of difficulty.

   B. samples liberally whatever is being measured.

   C. measures knowledge of the same topic in many different ways.

Answer (B) is correct. (FAA-H-8083-9B Chap 6)
   DISCUSSION: A written test is said to be comprehensive when it samples liberally whatever is being measured.
   Answer (A) is incorrect. A written test shows discrimination, not comprehensiveness, when it includes all levels of difficulty. **Answer (C) is incorrect.** A written test shows discrimination, not comprehensiveness, when it measures knowledge of the same topic in many different ways.

60. The characteristic of a written test, which measures small differences in achievement between learners, is its

   A. validity.

   B. reliability.

   C. discrimination.

Answer (C) is correct. (FAA-H-8083-9B Chap 6)
   DISCUSSION: The characteristic of a written test that measures small differences in achievement between learners is its discrimination.
   Answer (A) is incorrect. A written test has validity when it measures what it is supposed to and nothing else, not when it measures small differences in achievement between learners. **Answer (B) is incorrect.** A written test that has reliability is one that yields consistent results, not which measures small differences in achievement between learners.

61. A written test having the characteristic of discrimination will

   A. be easy to give and be easily graded.

   B. distinguish between learners both low and high in achievement.

   C. include a representative and comprehensive sampling of the course objectives.

Answer (B) is correct. (FAA-H-8083-9B Chap 6)
   DISCUSSION: When a written test has the characteristic of discrimination, each item will distinguish between learners who are low and learners who are high in achievement of the course objectives.
   Answer (A) is incorrect. A written test having the characteristic of usability, not discrimination, will be easy to give and be easily graded. **Answer (C) is incorrect.** A written test having the characteristic of comprehensiveness, not discrimination, will include a representative and comprehensive sampling of the course objectives.

62. A written test that is objective

   A. distinguishes the differences between learners.

   B. measures what is supposed to be measured.

   C. describes the singleness of scoring a test.

Answer (C) is correct. (FAA-H-8083-9B Chap 6)
   DISCUSSION: Objectivity describes singleness of scoring a test.
   Answer (A) is incorrect. Discrimination, not objectivity, distinguishes the differences between learners. **Answer (B) is incorrect.** Validity, not objectivity, measures what is supposed to be measured.

63. The most important consideration in test evaluation is what?

   A. Usability.

   B. Validity.

   C. Comprehensiveness.

Answer (B) is correct. (FAA-H-8083-9B Chap 6)
   DISCUSSION: Validity is the most important consideration in test evaluation.
   Answer (A) is incorrect. Validity, not usability, is the most important consideration in test evaluation. **Answer (C) is incorrect.** Validity, not comprehensiveness, is the most important consideration in test evaluation.

6.6   Review and Evaluation

64. Evaluation of learner performance and accomplishment during a lesson should be based on

A. objectives and goals established in the lesson plan.

B. performance of each learner compared to an objective standard.

C. each learner's ability to make an objective evaluation of their own progress.

Answer (A) is correct. (FAA-H-8083-9B Chap 5)
DISCUSSION: The evaluation of learner performance and accomplishment during a lesson should be based on the objectives and goals that were established in the instructor's lesson plan.
   Answer (B) is incorrect. A critique, not an evaluation, is based on comparing a learner's performance to an objective standard. **Answer (C) is incorrect.** A learner's own evaluation can only be subjective, not objective. Only the instructor can provide a realistic evaluation of performance and progress.

65. Which statement is true regarding learner evaluation?

A. The learner's own evaluations can only be objective.

B. Evaluation of the learner's learning should be an integral part of each lesson.

C. If deficiencies or faults not associated with the present lesson are revealed, they should be corrected immediately.

Answer (B) is correct. (FAA-H-8083-9B Chap 5)
DISCUSSION: Review and evaluation should be an integral part of each classroom or flight lesson. At the end of each class period, the instructor should review what has been covered during the lesson and require the learners to demonstrate the extent to which the lesson objectives have been met. Evaluation can be formal (performance, written tests) or informal (oral quiz or guided discussion).
   Answer (A) is incorrect. The learner's own evaluations can only be subjective, not objective. **Answer (C) is incorrect.** If deficiencies or faults not associated with the present lesson are revealed, they should be noted and pointed out. Corrective measures that are practicable at the time should be taken immediately, but more thorough remedial actions must be included in future lesson plans.

66. Which type test is desirable for evaluating training that involves an operation, procedure, or process?

A. Oral.

B. Performance.

C. Proficiency.

Answer (B) is correct. (FAA-H-8083-9B Chap 6)
DISCUSSION: Performance testing is desirable for evaluating training that involves an operation, procedure, or process. This method of evaluation is particularly suited to the measurement of a learner's ability in performing a task, either mental or physical.
   Answer (A) is incorrect. Performance, not oral, testing is desirable for evaluating training that involves an operation, procedure, or process. **Answer (C) is incorrect.** There is no proficiency-type test in evaluation, only oral, written, or performance.

67. When a learner performs a maneuver correctly but the instructor suspects the learner does not fully understand the principles and objectives involved, the instructor should

A. defer on the matter to avoid lowering learner confidence.

B. point out the suspected flaw to the learner.

C. vary the performance of the maneuver slightly.

Answer (C) is correct. (FAA-H-8083-9B Chap 9)
DISCUSSION: Learners may perform a procedure or maneuver correctly but not fully understand the principles and objectives involved. If the instructor suspects this, learners should be required to vary the performance of the maneuver or procedure slightly. Learners who do not understand the principles involved will probably not be able to successfully complete the revised maneuver or procedure.
   Answer (A) is incorrect. While it is important to prevent learner discouragement, it is more important to ensure that the learner possesses the required level of skill in each phase of training. Rather than ignoring the situation, an instructor can require that the learner repeat the maneuver in a slightly different way, thus evaluating the depth of the learner's mastery of the maneuver. **Answer (B) is incorrect.** Rather than projecting negativity onto the learner in a situation where the instructor could well be mistaken, it is best to have the learner perform the maneuver in a slightly different way, thus evaluating the depth of the learner's mastery of the maneuver.

APPENDIX A
FUNDAMENTALS OF INSTRUCTING PRACTICE TEST

The following 50 questions have been randomly selected from the fundamentals of instructing questions in our flight and ground instructor test bank. Topical coverage in this practice test is similar to that of the FAA pilot knowledge test. Use the correct answer listing on page 178 to grade your practice test.

1. To communicate effectively, instructors must

A — recognize the level of comprehension.
B — provide an atmosphere which encourages questioning.
C — reveal a positive attitude while delivering their message.

2. A communicator's words cannot communicate the desired meaning to another person unless the

A — words have meaningful referents.
B — words give the meaning that is in the mind of the receiver.
C — listener or reader has had some experience with the objects or concepts to which these words refer.

3. During integrated flight instruction, the instructor must be sure the learner

A — develops the habit of looking for other traffic.
B — is able to control the aircraft for extended periods under IMC.
C — can depend on the flight instruments when maneuvering by outside references.

4. Which statement is true regarding lesson plans?

A — Lesson plans should not be directed toward the course objective; only to the lesson objective.
B — A well-thought-out mental outline of a lesson may be used any time as long as the instructor is well prepared.
C — Lesson plans help instructors keep a constant check on their own activity as well as that of their learners.

5. (Refer to Figure 1 on page 141.) Section A is titled:

A — Overview.
B — Objective.
C — Introduction.

6. (Refer to Figure 1 on page 141.) Section C is titled:

A — Schedule.
B — Overview.
C — Training Schedule.

7. Which statement is true regarding true professionalism as an instructor?

A — Anything less than sincere performance destroys the effectiveness of the professional instructor.
B — To achieve professionalism, actions and decisions must be limited to standard patterns and practices.
C — A single definition of professionalism would encompass all of the qualifications and considerations which must be present.

8. Learner confidence tends to be destroyed if instructors

A — bluff whenever in doubt about some point.
B — continually identify learner errors and failures.
C — direct and control the learner's actions and behavior.

9. Learners quickly become apathetic when they

A — realize material is being withheld by the instructor.
B — understand the objectives toward which they are working.
C — recognize that the instructor is not adequately prepared.

10. In the learning process, fear or the element of threat will

A — narrow the learner's perceptual field.
B — decrease the rate of associative reactions.
C — cause a learner to focus on several areas of perception.

11. When under stress, normal individuals usually react

A — by showing excellent morale followed by deep depression.

B — by responding rapidly and exactly, often automatically, within the limits of their experience and training.

C — inappropriately such as extreme overcooperation, painstaking self-control, and inappropriate laughing or singing.

12. When learners display the defense mechanism called repression, they

A — refuse to accept reality.

B — place uncomfortable thoughts into inaccessible areas of the unconscious mind.

C — attempt to justify actions by asking numerous questions.

13. When a learner presents a belief opposite to what (s)he truly believes, it usually is an indication of the defense mechanism known as

A — fantasy.

B — reaction formation.

C — displacement.

14. Which of the learner's human needs offer the greatest challenge to an instructor?

A — Physiological.

B — Psychological.

C — Self-Actualization.

15. What should an instructor do with a learner who assumes that correction of errors is not important?

A — Divide complex flight maneuvers into elements.

B — Try to reduce the learner's overconfidence to reduce the chance of an accident.

C — Raise the standard of performance for each lesson, demanding greater effort.

16. By using abstractions in the communication process, the communicator will

A — bring forth specific items of experience in the minds of the receivers.

B — be using words which refer to objects or ideas that human beings can experience directly.

C — not evoke in the listener's or reader's mind the specific items of experience the communicator intends.

17. To ensure proper habits and correct techniques during training, an instructor should

A — use the building block technique of instruction.

B — repeat subject matter the learner has already learned.

C — introduce challenging material to continually motivate the learner.

18. During the flight portion of a practical test, the examiner simulates complete loss of engine power by closing the throttle and announcing "simulated engine failure." What level of learning is being tested?

A — Application.

B — Correlation.

C — Understanding.

19. According to one theory, some forgetting is due to the unconscious practice of submerging an unpleasant experience into the subconscious. This is called

A — suppression.

B — immersion.

C — repression.

20. Responses that produce a pleasurable return are called

A — reward.

B — praise.

C — positive feedback.

21. A change in behavior as a result of experience can be defined as

A — learning.

B — knowledge.

C — understanding.

22. Individuals make more progress learning if they have a clear objective. This is one feature of the principle of

A — primacy.

B — readiness.

C — willingness.

23. Things most often repeated are best remembered because of which principle of learning?

A — Principle of effect.

B — Principle of recency.

C — Principle of exercise.

24. Which principle of learning often creates a strong impression?

A — Principle of primacy.

B — Principle of intensity.

C — Principle of readiness.

25. The factor which contributes most to a learner's failure to remain receptive to new experiences and which creates a tendency to reject additional training is

A — basic needs.

B — element of threat.

C — negative self-concept.

26. Instruction, as opposed to the trial and error method of learning, is desirable because competent instruction speeds the learning process by

A — motivating the learner to a better performance.
B — emphasizing only the important points of training.
C — teaching the relationship of perceptions as they occur.

27. The best way to prepare a learner to perform a task is to

A — explain the purpose of the task.
B — provide a clear, step-by-step example.
C — give the learner an outline of the task.

28. To be effective, an assessment should

A — not contain negative remarks.
B — treat every aspect of the performance in detail.
C — be flexible enough to satisfy the requirements of the moment.

29. Which statement is true regarding an assessment that is constructive?

A — An instructor's manner and attitude make an assessment constructive.
B — Constructive assessments can inspire a learner to improve in areas of lesser accomplishment.
C — A constructive assessment should express ideas with authority in terms that cannot be misunderstood.

30. One desirable result of proper oral quizzing by the instructor is to

A — reveal the effectiveness of the instructor's training procedures.
B — fulfill the requirements set forth in the overall objectives of the course.
C — reveal the essential information from which the learner can determine progress.

31. To be effective in oral quizzing during the conduct of a lesson, a question should

A — be of suitable difficulty for that stage of training.
B — include a combination of where, how, and why.
C — divert the learner's thoughts to subjects covered in other lessons.

32. One of the main advantages of selection-type test items over supply-type test items is that the selection-type

A — decreases discrimination between responses.
B — would be graded objectively regardless of the learner or the grader.
C — precludes comparison of learners under one instructor with those under another instructor.

33. In a written test, which type of selection-type test items reduces the probability of guessing correct responses?

A — Essay.
B — Matching.
C — Multiple-choice.

34. A written test that has reliability

A — yields consistent results.
B — measures small differences in the achievement of learners.
C — actually measures what it is supposed to measure and nothing else.

35. A written test is said to be comprehensive when it

A — includes all levels of difficulty.
B — samples liberally whatever is being measured.
C — measures knowledge of the same topic in many different ways.

36. Which statement is true regarding learner evaluation?

A — The learner's own evaluations can only be objective.
B — Evaluation of the learner's learning should be an integral part of each lesson.
C — If deficiencies or faults not associated with the present lesson are revealed, they should be corrected immediately.

37. What is the last step in the demonstration/performance method?

A — Summary.
B — Evaluation.
C — Learner performance.

38. The basic demonstration/performance method of instruction consists of several steps in proper order. They are

A — instructor tells--learner does; learner tells--learner does; learner does--instructor evaluates.
B — instructor tells--instructor does; learner tells--instructor does; learner does--instructor evaluates.
C — instructor tells--instructor does; learner tells--instructor does; learner tells--learner does; learner does--instructor evaluates.

39. What is one advantage of a lecture?

A — A lecture is effective in showing relationships between theory and practice.
B — Excellent when additional research is required.
C — Allows for maximum attainment of certain types of learning outcomes.

40. Which teaching method is most economical in terms of the time required to present a given amount of material?

A — Briefing.
B — Teaching lecture.
C — Demonstration/performance.

41. The first step in preparing a lecture is to

A — research the subject.
B — develop the main ideas or key points.
C — establish the objective and desired outcome.

42. In a guided discussion, learning is achieved through the

A — skillful use of questions.
B — use of questions, each of which contains several ideas.
C — use of reverse questions directed to the class as a whole.

43. When it appears learners have adequately discussed the ideas presented during a guided discussion, one of the most valuable tools an instructor can use is

A — a session of verbal testing.
B — a written test on the subject discussed.
C — an interim summary of what the learners accomplished.

44. Which is generally the more effective way for an instructor to properly motivate learners?

A — Maintain pleasant personal relationships with learners.
B — Provide positive motivations by the promise or achievement of rewards.
C — Reinforce their self-confidence by requiring no tasks beyond their ability to perform.

45. Which statement is true concerning motivations?

A — Motivations must be tangible to be effective.
B — Motivations may be very subtle and difficult to identify.
C — Negative motivations often are as effective as positive motivations.

46. The overall learning objective of scenario-based training (SBT) is

A — that learners will improve their ability to recall previously learned information.
B — for the learner to be more prepared to make good decisions based on a variety of real world situations.
C — to promote situational awareness and opportunities for decision making.

47. What is a characteristic of an effective scenario?

A — It should not promote errors.
B — It should be in the form of a test.
C — It should include an account of a real world situation that contains an educational message.

48. Development and assembly of blocks of learning in their proper relationship will provide a means for

A — both the instructor and learner to easily correct faulty habit patterns.
B — challenging the learner by progressively increasing the units of learning.
C — allowing the learner to master the segments of the overall pilot performance requirements individually and combining these with other related segments.

49. The method of arranging lesson material from the simple to complex, past to present, and known to unknown, is one that

A — creates learner thought pattern departures.
B — shows the relationships of the main points of the lesson.
C — requires learners to actively participate in the lesson.

50. Instructional aids used in the teaching/learning process should not be used

A — as a crutch by the instructor.
B — for teaching more in less time.
C — to visualize relationships between abstracts.

Page
Intentionally
Left Blank

PRACTICE TEST LIST OF ANSWERS

The listing below gives the correct answers for your fundamentals of instructing practice knowledge test and the page number in this book on which you will find each question with the complete Gleim answer explanation.

Q. #	Answer	Page	Q. #	Answer	Page	Q. #	Answer	Page	Q. #	Answer	Page
1.	C	91	14.	C	82	27.	B	45	40.	B	112
2.	C	93	15.	C	62	28.	C	159	41.	C	113
3.	A	122	16.	C	93	29.	B	160	42.	A	115
4.	C	139	17.	A	38	30.	A	165	43.	C	116
5.	B	140	18.	B	39	31.	A	165	44.	B	83
6.	A	140	19.	C	37	32.	B	169	45.	B	84
7.	A	99	20.	B	37	33.	B	170	46.	B	119
8.	A	100	21.	A	31	34.	A	170	47.	A	119
9.	C	100	22.	B	31	35.	B	171	48.	C	135
10.	A	34	23.	C	31	36.	B	172	49.	B	137
11.	B	58	24.	A	32	37.	B	118	50.	A	146
12.	B	57	25.	C	55	38.	C	118			
13.	B	57	26.	C	34	39.	A	111			

Appendix B
The FAA's
Aviation Instructor's Handbook

(FAA-H-8083-9B)

Scan the QR code below or visit
GleimAviation.com/AIH
to review the entirety of the FAA's
Aviation Instructor's Handbook online.

Gleim® AVIATION
Excellence in Aviation Training

APPENDIX C
GROUND SCHOOL COURSE SUGGESTIONS

The purpose of this appendix is to suggest ideas concerning marketing, organization, and presentation of ground schools for pilot knowledge tests. We would appreciate any comments or suggestions you may have after reading this material, as will other aviation professionals when we incorporate this information into subsequent editions. Please send feedback to us at your convenience at www.GleimAviation.com/questions. Thank you.

RATIONALE FOR CONDUCTING A GROUND SCHOOL

1. **Aid to the industry.** General aviation (including flight instruction), while more financially sound than it has been in years past, is still not normally a high-profit enterprise.

   a. A ground school is the first step into aviation for many learners who will one day become aircraft renters and owners--the people who sustain GA. While it will not generate large profits for a business on its own, a ground school sets the stage for a lasting relationship between a flight school/FBO and its learners.

2. **Maintaining a professional level of currency and familiarity with aviation subjects.** Obtaining your flight and/or ground instructor certificate will keep you up to date on the Federal Aviation Regulations and all other academic areas of flight. Additionally, teaching will challenge you to learn and understand a wide variety of material.

3. **Finding new customers.** Many flight instructors use ground schools as a source of new pilots.

4. **Public service.** Many flight and/or ground instructors provide ground schools to Civil Air Patrol (CAP) chapters, high school classes, etc., as a public service to young people.

5. **Personal employment.** Obtaining your flight and/or ground instructor certificate can lead to opportunities for part-time work at FBOs, community colleges, and adult education programs.

6. **STEM education** is a growing sector of aviation critical in equipping learners to succeed in an information-based, high-tech society. Teaching aviation helps learners understand the science, technology, and applications of flight.

   a. Visit the Gleim Aviation STEM Resource Hub (www.GleimAviation.com/STEM) for more information.

POTENTIAL SPONSORS OF GROUND SCHOOLS

1. **Community colleges.** Call your local junior college and ask if a ground school is offered. Ask what division it is in and call the dean or director to indicate your interest in teaching the ground school. While talking to the dean or director, you should obtain a course outline, as well as information on the cost and class schedule. The college may already have an instructor, but you should make known your interest in teaching in case there should be an opening.

    a. Send us the dean or director's name and address and your own name and address. We will send him or her a complimentary copy of ***Private Pilot FAA Knowledge Test Prep*** or ***Sport Pilot FAA Knowledge Test Prep*** and explain that it was at your suggestion. We will reiterate your interest in presenting a ground school.

2. **Local high school adult education centers.** Call all local high schools for more information.

3. **FBOs.** Inquire at your local airport, or search on the Internet (e.g., www.airnav.com).

4. **Civil Air Patrol units.** Inquire at your local armed forces recruiting or training station for the name and telephone number of local CAP unit commanders (see the U.S. Government section of your telephone book).

    a. You can also find information about the CAP's aerospace education program at the Civil Air Patrol National Headquarters website (www.gocivilairpatrol.com).

MARKETING GROUND SCHOOLS

The objective of marketing a ground school is to contact interested learners if you are beginning a new ground school and to increase enrollment if you are associated with an existing ground school. The following are only a few suggestions.

1. **Internet.** Create a simple website or have one built for you to advertise your services, schedule, location, etc. Gleim can provide you with buttons leading directly to our products in our aviation store.

2. **Social media.** Advertise your services on various social media platforms, such as Facebook, Twitter, and Instagram. Participate in forums where you can connect with prospective learners and fellow instructors. Create videos introducing yourself and your services to share on hosts, such as YouTube, and share links to these videos on social media.

3. **Radio ads.** Call your local radio station and pay for an advertisement or, preferably, have it broadcast as a public service announcement.

4. **Posters.** Prepare posters and provide a telephone number. Post them at your local community college, university, airport, stores, etc.

GROUND SCHOOL COURSE ORGANIZATION

We hope you will use *Pilot Handbook*, as well as *Private Pilot FAA Knowledge Test Prep*, **FAA Test Prep Online**, and/or **Gleim Online Ground School** for your ground school. Based on that presumption, it is probably easiest to follow our study unit organization, which is the same in both *Pilot Handbook* and *Private Pilot FAA Knowledge Test Prep*.

We recommend that you incorporate a Sport Pilot ground school with your Private Pilot ground school to help you maximize the number of learners interested in the course. Sport pilots need to know approximately 70% of the required material for Private Pilot to pass their FAA knowledge test. It is beneficial for them to learn more than what is required for them to pass the FAA knowledge test; therefore, we include additional study units in *Sport Pilot FAA Knowledge Test Prep*.

Make sure that you are aware of the differences between Sport Pilot and Private Pilot and make it clear to your learners which information they may omit for Sport Pilot.

Private Pilot FAA Knowledge Test Prep

Study Unit 1 • Airplanes and Aerodynamics
Study Unit 2 • Airplane Instruments, Engines, and Systems
Study Unit 3 • Airports, Air Traffic Control, and Airspace
Study Unit 4 • Federal Aviation Regulations
Study Unit 5 • Airplane Performance and Weight and Balance
Study Unit 6 • Aeromedical Factors and Aeronautical Decision Making (ADM)
Study Unit 7 • Aviation Weather
Study Unit 8 • Aviation Weather Services
Study Unit 9 • Navigation: Charts and Publications
Study Unit 10 • Navigation Systems
Study Unit 11 • Cross-Country Flight Planning

Sport Pilot FAA Knowledge Test Prep

Study Unit 1 • Airports
Study Unit 2 • Airspace
Study Unit 3 • Federal Aviation Regulations – 14 CFR Parts 1 through 61
Study Unit 4 • Federal Aviation Regulations – 14 CFR Parts 91.3 through 91.123
Study Unit 5 • Federal Aviation Regulations – 14 CFR Parts 91.159 through 91.421 and
        NTSB Part 830
Study Unit 6 • Aeromedical Factors and Aeronautical Decision Making (ADM)
Study Unit 7 • Aviation Weather
Study Unit 8 • Weather Services
Study Unit 9 • Sectional Charts and Airspace
Study Unit 10 • Navigation and Preflight Preparation
Study Unit 11 • Airplanes and Aerodynamics
Study Unit 12 • Airplane Instruments
Study Unit 13 • Airplane Engines and Systems
Study Unit 14 • Airplane Performance and Weight and Balance

You will probably not have exactly 11 class sessions, which may necessitate combining study units for various classes. Approximately 12 sessions of 2 hours each should be adequate if your course objective is to get your learners ready for their pilot knowledge test. Even if you have 11 sessions, you may still want to combine certain study units and spend more time on other units. As an example of how study units might be combined for Private Pilot, if you have a 5-week program that meets for 10 sessions, you might want to combine Study Units 9, 10, and 11. You could easily cover the Introduction in Session 1 and still use a good part of the session to get into Study Unit 1. Then spend another entire meeting to finish Study Unit 1.

If your course objective is to cover all the subjects in the amount of detail needed by proficient pilots (rather than simply to "teach the test"), 16 to 18 2-hour sessions should be adequate. More time is needed for this comprehensive course because the FAA does not test every topic that your learners need to know in order to be safe, capable pilots. Having 16 to 18 sessions will allow you to spend more than one session on the largest and most important study units in *Pilot Handbook* (Study Units 1 through 4) and will allow you to spend extra time on challenging concepts like airspace and radio navigation. A comprehensive course outline for Private Pilot might entail two sessions for the Introduction and Study Unit 1, two sessions for Study Unit 2, two sessions for Study Unit 3, one to two sessions for Study Unit 4 (depending on how detailed you wish to get), one to two sessions for Study Unit 5, and one session each for Study Units 6 through 11. Any extra time left in the course can be spent reviewing difficult topics and engaging in test-specific preparation.

Regardless of your course objective, you may wish to reserve 5 or 10 minutes at the end of each session for an overview and introduction of the material to be covered in the next session. That will help your learners study for the next session and help them understand it. Remember to always assign additional study at home to keep your learners engaged and prepared.

COURSE SYLLABUS AND HANDOUTS

1. At the beginning of the course, you should distribute an outline of the material to be covered in the course. It should show the meeting times, quiz schedule, and reading assignments for each session.

2. A suggested syllabus for a 9-week class (whose objective is to prepare learners for the test) that meets for 3 hours one night per week is presented on the following page.

    a. Undoubtedly, you will have to change the scheduling of topics. The topics have been overlapped so that you can talk about the same topic during two periods; i.e., you can provide double exposure. Introducing the topic the week before provides 3 weeks' coverage, which may be useful to your learners.

3. Of course, the six study units in this book will be helpful to you as general background in preparing and presenting your ground school.

GLEIM PILOT KITS

The Gleim **Private Pilot Kit** and **Sport Pilot Kit** are designed to simplify and facilitate your learners' flight and ground training. There are different levels of each kit available. The Pilot Kits may include

*   *FAA Knowledge Test Prep*
*   *Flight Maneuvers and Practical Test Prep*
*   *Pilot Handbook*
*   *FAR/AIM*
*   *Syllabus*
*   *ACS and Oral Exam Guide* (Private Pilot only)
*   Logbook (hard cover)
*   Training Record
*   Online Ground School
*   FAA Test Prep Online
*   Audio Review (Private Pilot only)
*   Online Communication Course
*   Security-Related Airspace Course
*   Navigational plotter
*   Flight computer
*   Flight bag

For ground training, your learners will need to have at least a textbook *(Pilot Handbook)*, a **FAR/AIM**, a means of test preparation (**Private Pilot FAA Knowledge Test Prep** or **Sport Pilot FAA Knowledge Test Prep**, **FAA Test Prep Online**, and/or Gleim **Online Ground School**), a navigational plotter, and a flight computer. These items make up most of the Pilot Kits; the remaining items are primarily concerned with flight training. Because most people who take ground school courses intend to undertake flight training, it makes sense for your learners to go ahead and obtain everything they will need at one time (at substantial savings) by purchasing the Pilot Kit.

SAMPLE COURSE SYLLABUS

COURSE SYLLABUS

Jonesville Community College
Evening Education Course 1121

PRIVATE PILOT/SPORT PILOT GROUND SCHOOL
Summer Term A, 20XX
June 1 - July 27

Tuesday evenings, 7:00 - 10:00 p.m.
North Campus, Building C, Room 171

INSTRUCTOR: Mr. Harold Gray, AGI
Office: (111) 555-5252
Home: (111) 555-2525

COURSE OBJECTIVE: Learn the material required by the FAA for the private pilot knowledge test (airplane) and sport pilot knowledge test with the objective of each learner passing the test.

CLASSROOM PROCEDURE: Lecture and guided discussion.

1. Each class will begin with a review and questions from the last class (approximately 5-15 minutes).

2. Next, there will be a brief overview and core concepts for the current evening's assignment, followed by class discussion and questions.

3. When appropriate, after the class break, an in-class quiz will be administered, self-graded, and analyzed through class discussion.

4. The last 15-30 minutes of each class session will be directed toward an overview and discussion of the next class's assignment.

5. Visual aids and handouts will be used as appropriate.

REQUIRED TEXT: *Private Pilot FAA Knowledge Test Prep*, by Irvin N. Gleim and Garrett W. Gleim, or *Sport Pilot FAA Knowledge Test Prep*, by Irvin N. Gleim and Garrett W. Gleim

RECOMMENDED TEXT: *Pilot Handbook*, by Irvin N. Gleim and Garrett W. Gleim

These texts are available in the College Bookstore on the North Campus, which is open until 8:00 p.m. each Tuesday.

SCHEDULE

Class	Date	PPKT* Study Units	SPKT** Study Units	Topic
1	June 1	Introduction, 1	Introduction, 11	Introduction, Aerodynamic Theory
2	June 8	1, 2	11, 13	Aerodynamics and Airplane Systems
3	June 15	2, 3	1, 2, 13	Airplane Systems, Airports, ATC
4	June 22	3, 4	2-5	Airspace, 14 CFR
5	June 29	4, 5	3-5, 14	14 CFR, Airplane Performance
6	July 6	5, 6	6, 14	Weight and Balance, Aeromedical Factors
7	July 13	7, 8	7, 8	Aviation Weather and Weather Services
8	July 20	9, 10, 11	9, 10	Navigation, Cross-Country Flight
9	July 27			Review for pilot knowledge test

* PPKT = *Private Pilot FAA Knowledge Test Prep*
** SPKT = *Sport Pilot FAA Knowledge Test Prep*

You may photocopy this syllabus and change it in any way you like.

ENROLLMENT PROCEDURES

1. You should make a list of the learners and their contact information so you can contact them in the event the classes need to be changed, rescheduled, etc.

    a. Note the form and date of their payment.

2. As each learner enrolls, you can sell (or give, if the materials are included in the cost of the ground school course) him or her book(s), software, and/or online course access.

3. If you have a syllabus ready, distribute copies to your learners and encourage them to do some study in advance.

4. With respect to requiring or recommending **Pilot Handbook** and **Aviation Weather and Weather Services**, you may proceed as follows:

    a. For each learner, put one copy of each title on reserve in the bookstore of your choice.

    b. Get one copy of each book and pass them around to the class; indicate learners can purchase another one from you, a local FBO, or the bookstore you are using.

    c. Alternatively, have them order the materials by calling us at (800) 874-5346 or ordering online at www.GleimAviation.com.

5. Note that you may wish to encourage each person who enrolls or even inquires about the program to invite friends to take the course with him or her. The idea is to build enrollment through enthusiasm for and interest in aviation.

THE FIRST CLASS SESSION

1. Preliminaries

    a. Arrive early with a supply of books, handouts, and your lecture notes for the first lecture.

    b. Ensure that all digital presentation equipment is ready to begin and all instructional aids are organized for presentation.

    c. Begin by enrolling any learners who show up at the first class without having already enrolled.

    d. Go over the roll and pass out the syllabus.

    e. Introduce yourself.

2. Learner-Instructor Interaction

    a. Tell the learners about your background, the origin of the course, your reasons for teaching, and any other relevant personal things.

    b. Tell the class that you need to learn more about them in order to teach effectively.

        1) Ask people to introduce themselves.

        2) Unless the class is too large, make notes on your roster to individualize participants and help you learn their names.

        3) Ask them why they are taking the course, if they have any flying experience, if they know anyone else who flies, if they have ever flown before in a small aircraft, etc.

    c. Such interaction is an ice-breaker, allowing you to get to know your learners and allowing them to get to know you and one another.

3.   Discussion of Course Objective (FAA Pilot Knowledge Test)

   a.   Display *Private Pilot FAA Knowledge Test Prep* and *Sport Pilot FAA Knowledge Test Prep*.

   b.   Point out that the textbooks have sample FAA questions reorganized by topic with answer explanations next to them.

   c.   Indicate that the areas tested on the exams will be the topics specified on your syllabus (course outline), that the test will be only 60 questions for private and 40 questions for sport, and that the learners need to get at least 42 questions correct for private and 28 questions correct for sport in order to pass.

      1)   This will be very easy because they will have gone over many possible test questions during your course (all of which appear in *Private Pilot FAA Knowledge Test Prep* and *Sport Pilot FAA Knowledge Test Prep*), as well as additional material to help them learn how to fly safely.

   d.   Explain the content of *Private Pilot FAA Knowledge Test Prep* and/or *Sport Pilot FAA Knowledge Test Prep*.

      1)   Explain that the Introduction is the current topic of discussion.

      2)   Show them the organization of Study Units 1 through 11 for Private Pilot and Study Units 1 through 14 for Sport Pilot.

         a)   Each study unit begins with an outline, subunit by subunit (topic by topic).

         b)   Following the outlines are questions and answer explanations organized in the same subunits and presented in the same order.

         c)   Thus, the learners are able to study and try to learn the material before they answer the questions. This format provides an extra level of reinforcement as they study the material.

4.   Discussion of Course Objective (Comprehensive Coverage)

   a.   Display *Pilot Handbook* and *Private Pilot FAA Knowledge Test Prep* or *Sport Pilot FAA Knowledge Test Prep*.

   b.   Explain that both *Pilot Handbook* and *Private Pilot FAA Knowledge Test Prep* have the same study unit numbers and titles, which means that the content of each study unit number in both books will correspond (for *Sport Pilot FAA Knowledge Test Prep*, they will need to refer to the index).

      1)   Explain that, because the study units of these books are complementary, Study Units 1 through 4 of *Pilot Handbook* are disproportionately larger than their counterparts in *Private Pilot FAA Knowledge Test Prep* and *Sport Pilot FAA Knowledge Test Prep*. Explain that this is because there is a lot of material that the FAA does not test, but with which a pilot must be familiar in order to fly safely (much of this untested material happens to fit into the first four study units).

      2)   Explain that more time will therefore be spent on Study Units 1 through 4 of *Pilot Handbook*.

   c.   Explain that, while your learners will be well prepared for their pilot knowledge test at the completion of this course, it is not your goal to simply "teach the test" and that you plan to give them a solid background in aviation topics.

      1)   Explain that they will be expected to follow the progress of the course in *Private Pilot FAA Knowledge Test Prep* or *Sport Pilot FAA Knowledge Test Prep* on their own and that you will primarily be teaching out of *Pilot Handbook*.

      2)   Provide additional background about how to use *Private Pilot FAA Knowledge Test Prep* or *Sport Pilot FAA Knowledge Test Prep* based on item 3. above.

LECTURE PRESENTATION

1. There are many ways to present a lecture, and you should use the method with which you feel most comfortable. The best method for you will be the best method for your learners because you will perform better.

2. One approach to keep in mind is the idea of hitting the high points or key concepts.

    a. What are the basic or major concepts within any topic? These are generally outlined at the opening of each study unit in *Private Pilot FAA Knowledge Test Prep* and *Sport Pilot FAA Knowledge Test Prep*.

    b. To amplify these concepts and provide additional discussion, consult *Pilot Handbook*, after which you can use additional examples from other textbooks, including the FAA/government textbooks.

3. A major objective of your lecture presentation is to make it interactive: The learners must respond to you and participate.

    a. Learning is **not** a one-way communication from you to your learners.

    b. You need to ask questions of individual learners and of the class as a whole so that they can react and commit to an answer (silently or orally) and then get immediate feedback about the accuracy of their responses.

4. Have them work examples, e.g., provide them with a calculation and ask them to determine the answer.

    a. You could present a series of sample questions, take away the alternative answers, and have them work through a couple of exercises.

    b. You might also put these on overhead projectors.

5. Your preparation before class is very important. You should consult the lesson plan discussed in Study Unit 5, Subunit 3, "Lesson Plan," beginning on page 128 and review Study Unit 4, "Teaching Methods," beginning on page 101.

VISUAL AIDS

1. Visual aids include small model airplanes, videos, slides, blackboard presentations, overhead projector pictures, etc.

2. Visual aids are most helpful in explaining ideas that are abstract when presented verbally (e.g., airspace).

3. You can bring items to class and pass them around, such as navigation tools/charts and operating manuals from airplanes.

4. Experiment with visual aids. Use them as attention-getters or to break the pace of the normal presentation.

5. If using presentation software (such as Microsoft PowerPoint), avoid reading from slides. Use this tool to present important (i.e., tested) concepts as well as images, animations, and/or video.

COURSE EVALUATIONS

1. At the end of the course, but before the session set aside for the FAA knowledge test, you should administer a course evaluation.

    a. Your objective is to obtain feedback from your learners about how the course can be improved in several aspects, including

        1) Course organization
        2) Textbook(s)
        3) Lecture presentation
        4) Physical facilities

    b. Let the learners know that you are seeking constructive criticism across many areas.

    c. Tell them that you do not want to make them ill at ease, so you are going to ask one member (tell them who) to hold the evaluations until the course is over.

    d. If the course is for grade credit, the evaluations should be held until after you have turned in the grades.

2. Please feel free to photocopy and modify the course evaluation illustrated below. Note that you should leave the back blank for additional written comments.

3. Remember that, at the conclusion of the last class session prior to your learners taking the FAA pilot knowledge test, you need to complete the Instructor Certification Form at the back of *Private Pilot FAA Knowledge Test Prep* or *Sport Pilot FAA Knowledge Test Prep* for each learner.

Date _____

(NAME OF COURSE)
GROUND SCHOOL EVALUATION FORM

This Ground School is being presented to aid you in your preparation for the FAA knowledge test. Please help us by answering the following questions, keeping in mind our objective: to help you prepare for the FAA knowledge test. Please check one response for each line. Return the completed form to the person designated to hold the evaluations until the completion of the last class (or after grades have been turned in).

	Excellent	Good	Adequate	Poor
Instructor				
1. Instructor presentation of material	—	—	—	—
2. Instructor knowledge of subject	—	—	—	—
3. Allocation of time to topics	—	—	—	—
4. Use of slides, boards, visual aids, etc.	—	—	—	—
5. Use of handouts, problems, etc.	—	—	—	—
Other questions				
6. Overall rating of instructor	—	—	—	—
7. Classroom comfort	—	—	—	—
8. Progress of class as a whole	—	—	—	—
9. Outlines in *FAA Knowledge Test Prep*	—	—	—	—
10. Answer explanations in *FAA Knowledge Test Prep*	—	—	—	—
11. Overall rating of *FAA Knowledge Test Prep*	—	—	—	—

12. **Other comments.** Please explain poor responses and make any other suggestions you feel may be relevant in the space provided below and on the back of this sheet. **Thank you.**

HELPING YOUR LEARNERS SELECT A COMPUTER TESTING CENTER

1.   Since most computer testing centers have limited seating, it is unlikely that you will be able to have all of your learners take the test at the same time and place.

   a.   Thus, you will need to help your learners in the selection of a computer testing center.

2.   Call each testing service to determine if any discounts are being offered and the payment policy. Explain your class situation (number of learners, etc.).

   a.   Some learners may not have a credit card, so they need to select a computer testing center that will accept a check or cash at the time of the test.

   1)   Some computer testing services may require that a check or money order be sent before the learner can take the test.

   b.   Make yourself available to assist your learners as necessary.

3.   Provide your learners with the contact information for the following PSI computer testing service and the results of your inquiries.

   PSI   (800) 211-2754 or www.psiexams.com

4.   Discuss the examination process and demonstrate testing procedures by using Gleim **FAA Test Prep Online**.

5.   You, as a flight instructor, are required to maintain a record of each person for whom you sign a certification for a pilot knowledge test, including the kind of test, date of test, and the test result (14 CFR 61.189).

   a.   An efficient way of obtaining test results is to pre-address and stamp one postcard for each learner (include the learner's name on the card) and explain why you need these returned.

   1)   Hand them out on the exam day.
   2)   Ask learners to mail their numerical scores to you.
   3)   List the learner scores on your roster as they come in the mail.
   4)   Call any individuals who have not submitted cards.

   b.   Email is another simple method for obtaining this information.

   c.   You can use these pass rates in future advertising.

AN ALTERNATIVE APPROACH: EXPANDING YOUR MARKET

1. You may wish to broaden your ground school course so that it appeals to aviation enthusiasts interested in doing more than passing the FAA private pilot (airplane) or sport pilot knowledge test. If so, you need to

    a. Diversify your marketing plan and advertisements.
    b. Edit the suggested syllabus (make it more general).
    c. Prepare fewer class assignments focused on the FAA pilot knowledge test.

2. Can you prepare learner pilots for the FAA pilot knowledge test **and** provide a general-interest aviation course?

    a. Many ground schools are so directed, especially at community colleges where a considerable number of enrollees do not take the FAA pilot knowledge test.

    b. One approach is to emphasize discussion of sample FAA test questions at the end (optional part) of each class, e.g., in a 100-minute class.

        1) The last 30 minutes might be restricted to discussion of sample FAA questions in *Private Pilot FAA Knowledge Test Prep* and/or *Sport Pilot FAA Knowledge Test Prep*.

        2) The first 70 minutes would involve lecture discussion.

    c. Occasional questions might be discussed, but the emphasis would be on learning about airplanes, weather, and navigation rather than passing the FAA pilot knowledge test.

    d. In such a course, *Pilot Handbook* would be the required text instead of *Private Pilot FAA Knowledge Test Prep* or *Sport Pilot FAA Knowledge Test Prep*, which can be optional.

3. With these general guidelines, we trust you will take the plunge and **start your class** (or at least begin to prepare for it) **right now**! It is fun, and it provides a valuable service -- teaching new aviation enthusiasts to **ENJOY FLYING -- SAFELY!**

CROSS-REFERENCES TO
THE FAA LEARNING STATEMENT CODES

Pages 193 through 196 contain a listing of all of the questions from our fundamentals of instructing knowledge test bank. The questions are in FAA learning statement code (LSC) sequence. (Refer to page 14 in the Introduction for a complete listing and description of each.) To the right of each LSC, we present our study unit/question number and our answer. For example, note below that PLT022 is cross-referenced to 3-19, which represents our Study Unit 3, question 19; the correct answer is B.

The first line of each of our answer explanations in Study Units 1 through 6 contains

1. The correct answer and
2. A reference for the answer explanation, e.g., *FAA-H-8083-9B Chap 1*. If this reference is not useful, use the following chart to identify the learning statement code to determine the specific reference appropriate for the question.

FAA Learning Code	Gleim SU/ Q. No.	Gleim Answer	FAA Learning Code	Gleim SU/ Q. No.	Gleim Answer	FAA Learning Code	Gleim SU/ Q. No.	Gleim Answer
PLT022	3-19	B	PLT204	3-64	B	PLT228	5-47	C
PLT022	3-23	C	PLT204	3-65	B	PLT228	5-48	A
PLT022	3-26	A	PLT204	3-66	A	PLT228	5-55	A
PLT022	3-39	C	PLT211	6-10	A	PLT229	3-83	A
PLT022	3-41	C	PLT211	6-11	B	PLT229	3-84	B
PLT103	3-20	B	PLT211	6-19	C	PLT229	3-85	B
PLT103	3-25	A	PLT211	6-62	C	PLT229	3-86	B
PLT103	3-31	A	PLT211	6-63	B	PLT229	3-87	A
PLT103	3-35	B	PLT218	2-45	A	PLT229	3-88	C
PLT104	3-40	B	PLT227	4-50	A	PLT229	3-89	A
PLT204	3-42	B	PLT227	4-51	A	PLT229	3-90	C
PLT204	3-43	C	PLT227	4-52	C	PLT229	3-91	B
PLT204	3-44	B	PLT227	4-53	B	PLT229	6-7	C
PLT204	3-45	A	PLT227	4-54	A	PLT230	2-41	A
PLT204	3-46	C	PLT227	4-55	B	PLT230	3-16	A
PLT204	3-47	C	PLT227	4-56	A	PLT230	3-21	B
PLT204	3-48	B	PLT228	5-5	A	PLT230	3-74	C
PLT204	3-49	A	PLT228	5-25	C	PLT230	3-75	B
PLT204	3-50	B	PLT228	5-27	C	PLT230	3-76	B
PLT204	3-51	C	PLT228	5-29	B	PLT230	3-77	A
PLT204	3-52	C	PLT228	5-30	A	PLT230	3-78	B
PLT204	3-53	C	PLT228	5-31	A	PLT230	3-79	B
PLT204	3-57	C	PLT228	5-32	B	PLT230	3-80	C
PLT204	3-58	B	PLT228	5-33	C	PLT230	3-81	B
PLT204	3-59	B	PLT228	5-34	C	PLT230	4-58	B
PLT204	3-60	C	PLT228	5-35	C	PLT231	1-16	A
PLT204	3-61	A	PLT228	5-36	C	PLT231	1-17	A
PLT204	3-62	C	PLT228	5-39	B	PLT231	1-22	A
PLT204	3-63	A	PLT228	5-40	C	PLT231	2-19	B

FAA Learning Code	Gleim SU/ Q. No.	Gleim Answer	FAA Learning Code	Gleim SU/ Q. No.	Gleim Answer	FAA Learning Code	Gleim SU/ Q. No.	Gleim Answer
PLT231	2–20	C	PLT271	3–22	C	PLT306	1–59	A
PLT231	2–21	B	PLT271	3–28	C	PLT306	1–69	A
PLT231	2–22	B	PLT271	3–29	A	PLT306	1–71	C
PLT231	2–23	A	PLT271	3–30	A	PLT306	1–77	A
PLT231	2–24	A	PLT271	3–32	C	PLT306	1–78	B
PLT231	2–25	C	PLT272	2–26	A	PLT306	5–50	B
PLT231	2–27	A	PLT272	3–27	C	PLT306	5–51	B
PLT231	2–29	A	PLT272	3–36	C	PLT307	1–2	C
PLT231	2–31	C	PLT272	3–37	C	PLT307	1–23	B
PLT231	2–32	A	PLT295	1–70	B	PLT307	1–24	C
PLT231	2–33	C	PLT295	1–72	A	PLT307	1–26	A
PLT231	2–35	C	PLT295	1–74	C	PLT307	1–27	A
PLT231	3–7	A	PLT295	1–81	B	PLT307	1–30	C
PLT232	2–28	C	PLT295	2–34	B	PLT307	1–31	C
PLT232	2–30	B	PLT295	2–36	B	PLT307	1–33	A
PLT232	2–37	B	PLT295	2–39	C	PLT307	1–34	B
PLT232	2–38	B	PLT295	3–55	C	PLT307	1–35	C
PLT232	2–40	B	PLT295	3–56	C	PLT307	1–36	C
PLT232	3–33	B	PLT295	3–67	C	PLT307	1–37	B
PLT232	3–34	A	PLT295	4–59	B	PLT307	1–38	B
PLT232	3–38	A	PLT295	5–1	A	PLT307	1–39	C
PLT233	2–5	C	PLT295	5–3	B	PLT307	2–14	C
PLT233	2–6	C	PLT295	5–9	A	PLT307	5–42	B
PLT233	2–7	B	PLT295	5–14	A	PLT307	5–43	A
PLT233	2–8	C	PLT295	5–28	A	PLT308	1–1	A
PLT233	2–9	A	PLT295	5–38	C	PLT308	1–4	B
PLT233	2–10	B	PLT295	5–41	A	PLT308	1–5	C
PLT233	2–11	B	PLT295	5–49	A	PLT308	1–6	A
PLT233	2–12	B	PLT306	1–3	C	PLT308	1–7	B
PLT233	2–13	B	PLT306	1–20	B	PLT308	1–8	A
PLT233	2–15	B	PLT306	1–28	B	PLT308	1–9	A
PLT233	2–16	B	PLT306	1–32	B	PLT308	1–10	C
PLT233	2–17	C	PLT306	1–40	B	PLT308	1–11	B
PLT233	2–18	B	PLT306	1–41	C	PLT308	1–12	A
PLT270	1–54	B	PLT306	1–42	A	PLT308	1–13	A
PLT270	2–44	A	PLT306	1–43	A	PLT308	1–15	B
PLT270	3–1	B	PLT306	1–44	A	PLT308	1–19	A
PLT270	3–2	C	PLT306	1–46	B	PLT308	1–25	B
PLT270	3–3	C	PLT306	1–47	A	PLT308	1–29	A
PLT270	3–4	C	PLT306	1–50	C	PLT308	1–51	B
PLT270	3–24	B	PLT306	1–57	A	PLT308	1–52	C

FAA Learning Code	Gleim SU/ Q. No.	Gleim Answer	FAA Learning Code	Gleim SU/ Q. No.	Gleim Answer	FAA Learning Code	Gleim SU/ Q. No.	Gleim Answer
PLT308	1–53	C	PLT482	6–17	C	PLT482	6–60	C
PLT308	1–55	B	PLT482	6–18	A	PLT482	6–61	B
PLT308	1–56	A	PLT482	6–20	B	PLT482	6–64	A
PLT308	1–58	C	PLT482	6–21	B	PLT482	6–65	B
PLT308	1–60	A	PLT482	6–22	A	PLT482	6–66	B
PLT308	1–61	B	PLT482	6–23	B	PLT487	3–82	B
PLT308	1–62	C	PLT482	6–24	A	PLT487	4–26	C
PLT308	1–63	A	PLT482	6–25	C	PLT487	4–27	C
PLT308	1–64	C	PLT482	6–26	A	PLT487	4–28	C
PLT308	1–65	B	PLT482	6–27	B	PLT487	4–29	C
PLT308	1–66	A	PLT482	6–28	A	PLT487	4–30	B
PLT308	1–67	B	PLT482	6–29	B	PLT487	4–31	C
PLT308	1–76	B	PLT482	6–30	B	PLT487	4–32	B
PLT308	1–79	A	PLT482	6–31	A	PLT487	4–33	B
PLT308	2–1	C	PLT482	6–32	A	PLT487	4–34	B
PLT308	2–2	A	PLT482	6–33	B	PLT488	3–54	A
PLT481	1–21	C	PLT482	6–34	A	PLT488	4–1	A
PLT481	1–68	B	PLT482	6–35	B	PLT488	4–2	A
PLT481	1–73	B	PLT482	6–36	A	PLT488	4–3	B
PLT481	1–75	A	PLT482	6–37	C	PLT488	4–4	B
PLT481	1–80	B	PLT482	6–38	C	PLT488	4–5	B
PLT481	3–68	C	PLT482	6–39	B	PLT488	4–6	C
PLT481	3–69	C	PLT482	6–40	A	PLT488	4–7	A
PLT481	3–71	B	PLT482	6–41	C	PLT488	4–8	C
PLT481	3–73	A	PLT482	6–42	B	PLT488	4–9	B
PLT481	6–14	B	PLT482	6–44	A	PLT488	4–10	A
PLT481	6–43	C	PLT482	6–45	C	PLT488	4–11	C
PLT481	6–67	C	PLT482	6–46	A	PLT488	4–12	A
PLT482	1–48	C	PLT482	6–47	B	PLT488	4–13	B
PLT482	1–49	C	PLT482	6–48	C	PLT488	4–14	B
PLT482	4–60	C	PLT482	6–49	A	PLT488	4–15	B
PLT482	6–1	C	PLT482	6–50	B	PLT488	4–16	A
PLT482	6–2	C	PLT482	6–51	B	PLT488	4–17	A
PLT482	6–3	B	PLT482	6–52	C	PLT488	4–18	B
PLT482	6–4	C	PLT482	6–53	B	PLT488	4–19	A
PLT482	6–5	B	PLT482	6–54	C	PLT488	4–20	C
PLT482	6–6	A	PLT482	6–55	B	PLT488	4–21	B
PLT482	6–8	B	PLT482	6–56	A	PLT488	4–22	C
PLT482	6–12	A	PLT482	6–57	C	PLT488	4–23	C
PLT482	6–13	C	PLT482	6–58	A	PLT488	4–24	B
PLT482	6–16	C	PLT482	6–59	B	PLT489	5–19	B

FAA Learning Code	Gleim SU/ Q. No.	Gleim Answer	FAA Learning Code	Gleim SU/ Q. No.	Gleim Answer
PLT489	5–22	B	PLT491	5–11	C
PLT490	1–14	A	PLT491	5–12	C
PLT490	1–18	A	PLT491	5–13	C
PLT490	2–3	A	PLT491	5–15	B
PLT490	2–4	C	PLT491	5–16	B
PLT490	2–42	A	PLT491	5–17	C
PLT490	2–43	B	PLT491	5–18	A
PLT490	3–5	B	PLT491	5–20	A
PLT490	3–6	A	PLT491	5–21	A
PLT490	3–8	A	PLT491	5–23	A
PLT490	3–9	B	PLT491	5–24	C
PLT490	3–10	B	PLT491	5–37	A
PLT490	3–11	B	PLT491	5–44	A
PLT490	3–12	A	PLT491	5–45	C
PLT490	3–13	B	PLT491	5–46	B
PLT490	3–14	C	PLT491	5–52	C
PLT490	3–15	A	PLT504	5–56	B
PLT490	3–17	A	PLT504	5–58	A
PLT490	3–18	C	PLT504	5–59	B
PLT490	3–70	A	PLT504	5–60	C
PLT490	3–72	A	PLT504	5–61	A
PLT490	4–57	B	PLT504	6–9	A
PLT490	5–26	A	PLT504	6–15	A
PLT491	4–25	C	PLT505	1–45	A
PLT491	4–35	B	PLT505	4–44	A
PLT491	4–37	A	PLT505	4–45	C
PLT491	4–38	A	PLT505	4–46	C
PLT491	4–39	A	PLT505	5–53	C
PLT491	4–40	A	PLT505	5–54	A
PLT491	4–41	C	PLT505	5–57	B
PLT491	4–42	C	PLT545	4–36	B
PLT491	4–43	B			
PLT491	4–47	B			
PLT491	4–48	C			
PLT491	4–49	B			
PLT491	5–2	B			
PLT491	5–4	B			
PLT491	5–6	C			
PLT491	5–7	C			
PLT491	5–8	C			
PLT491	5–10	B			

LESSON:

LEARNER: _____ **DATE:** _____

OBJECTIVE

CONTENT

SCHEDULE

EQUIPMENT

INSTRUCTOR'S ACTIONS

LEARNER'S ACTIONS

COMPLETION STANDARDS

Gleim®
AVIATION

INDEX

AUTHORS' RECOMMENDATIONS

Gleim cooperates with and supports all aspects of the flight training industry, particularly organizations that focus on aviation recruitment and flight training. Below are some of the top organizations for anyone interested in aviation.

EXPERIMENTAL AIRCRAFT ASSOCIATION: YOUNG EAGLES PROGRAM

The Experimental Aircraft Association's (EAA) Young Eagles Program has provided free introductory flights to over 2 million young people ages 8 to 17. This program helps young people understand the important role aviation plays in our daily lives and provides insight into how an airplane flies, what it takes to become a pilot, and the high standards flying demands in terms of safety and quality.

NOTE: The Gleim *Learn to Fly* booklet (available for free at www.GleimAviation.com/learn-to-fly) is used within many Young Eagles programs and initiatives. For more information about the Young Eagles Program, visit www.youngeagles.org or call 1-800-564-6322.

AIRCRAFT OWNERS AND PILOTS ASSOCIATION

The Aircraft Owners and Pilots Association (AOPA) hosts an informational web page on getting started in aviation for those still dreaming about flying, those who are ready to begin, and those who are already making the journey. Interested individuals can order a FREE subscription to Flight Training Magazine, which explains how amazing it is to be a pilot. Other resources are available, such as a flight school finder, a guide on what to expect throughout training, an explanation of pilot certification options, a FREE flight training newsletter, and much more. To learn more, visit www.aopa.org.

CIVIL AIR PATROL: CADET ORIENTATION FLIGHT PROGRAM

The Civil Air Patrol (CAP) Cadet Orientation Flight Program is designed to introduce CAP cadets to flying. The program is voluntary and primarily motivational, and it is designed to stimulate cadets' interest in and knowledge of aviation.

Each orientation flight is approximately 1 hour, follows a prescribed syllabus, and is usually in the local area of the airport. Except for takeoff, landing, and a few other portions of the flight, cadets are encouraged to handle the controls. For information about the CAP cadet program nearest you, visit www.gocivilairpatrol.com.

WOMEN IN AVIATION INTERNATIONAL

Women in Aviation International (WAI) is a nonprofit organization dedicated to the encouragement and advancement of women in all aviation career fields and interests. Its diverse membership includes astronauts, corporate pilots, maintenance technicians, air traffic controllers, business owners, educators and learners, journalists, flight attendants, air show performers, airport managers, and many others.

WAI provides year-round resources to assist women in aviation and encourage young women to consider aviation as a career and offers educational outreach programs to educators, aviation industry members, and young people nationally and internationally. WAI also hosts an annual Girls in Aviation Day for girls ages 8 to 17. Learn more at www.wai.org.

NINETY-NINES

The Ninety-Nines (99s) is an international organization of women pilots with thousands of members from over 40 countries. Its goal is to promote advancement of aviation through education, scholarships, and mutual support. The 99s have co-sponsored over 75% of FAA pilot safety programs in the U.S. and annually sponsor hundreds of educational programs, such as aerospace workshops for teachers, airport tours for school children, fear-of-flying clinics for airline passengers, and flight instructor revalidation seminars. Learn more at www.ninety-nines.org.

GLEIM STEM RESOURCE HUB

STEM education is critical for learners to succeed in an information-based, high-tech society. Whether you are already teaching or making a case for a new STEM aviation program, Gleim can help. Visit www.GleimAviation.com/STEM today.